RATIONAL SUICIDE?

RATIONAL SUICIDE?
Implications for Mental Health Professionals

James L. Werth, Jr., Ph.D.
Counseling and Psychological Services
University of Arkansas

Taylor & Francis
Publishers since 1798

USA	Publishing Office:	Taylor & Francis 1101 Vermont Avenue, N.W., Suite 200 Washington, DC 20005-3521 Tel: (202) 289-2174 Fax: (202) 289-3665
	Distribution Center:	Taylor & Francis 1900 Frost Road, Suite 101 Bristol, PA 19007-1598 Tel: (215) 785-5800 Fax: (215) 785-5515
UK		Taylor & Francis Ltd. 1 Gunpowder Square London EC4A 3DE Tel: 071 583 0490 Fax: 071 583 0581

RATIONAL SUICIDE? Implications for Mental Health Professionals

1 2 3 4 5 6 7 8 9 0   B R B R   9 8 7 6

This book was set in Times Roman by Sandra F. Watts. The editors were Christine Williams and Megan Scheidt. Cover design by Michelle Fleitz. Printing and binding by Braun-Brumfield, Inc.

A CIP catalog record for this book is available from the British Library.
∞ The paper in this publication meets the requirements of the ANSI Standard Z39.48-1984 (Permanence of Paper)

Library of Congress Cataloging-in-Publication Data

Werth, James L.
    Rational suicide? : implications for mental health professionals / James L. Werth, Jr.
        p.   cm. — (Series in death education, aging, and health care, ISSN 0275-3510)
    Includes bibliographical references.

    1. Right to die.   2. Suicide—Moral and ethical aspects.   3. Mental health personnel—Attitudes.   4. Suicide—Public opinion.   I. Title.   II. Series.
R726.W466   1996
174'.24—dc20   95-38733
                                                                            CIP

ISBN 1-56032-424-4 (cloth)
ISBN 1-56032-450-3 (paper)
ISSN 0275-3510

Dedication

This book is respectfully dedicated to the following people associated with Lee County AIDS Outreach (located in Auburn, Alabama):

The untiring volunteers and staff: for inspiring me with their commitment and compassion;

The supportive significant others: for motivating me with their devotion and faithfulness;

The heroic clients themselves: for teaching me about life and living as well as about death and dying.

Contents

Acknowledgments

There are many people who deserve my thanks and praise for their support and inspiration. First and foremost I wish to thank the clients with HIV disease and their significant others with whom I had the opportunity to work as a volunteer. Being allowed to share in and witness their struggles provided the impetus for my thinking about the topic of rational suicide. These individuals truly taught me the meaning of the words courage, strength, and dignity and showed me how to live, and die, well. The unselfish and compassionate caring provided by the staff and volunteers of Lee County AIDS Outreach provided me with models of how to be truly present with people in crisis and embodied the characteristics of empathy, respect, and genuineness.

As I was beginning to think about the issue of rational suicide there were several professors at Auburn University who encouraged my continued examination of the topic. First and foremost was Randolph B. Pipes who spent countless hours editing my first paper on the topic and supervising my dissertation, which forms the foundation for this book. Also deserving of recognition are Becky Liddle and Debra Cobia, with whom I collaborated on studies about rational suicide. Becky Liddle also deserves thanks for being a member of my dissertation committee. Debra Cobia merits additional appreciation for teaching me about qualitative analysis, which is crucial to my ongoing investigation of this topic, and for her editorial assistance with parts of chapter 5. Jamie Carney helped foster my ongoing interest in research through our collaboration and also helped by serving on my dissertation committee. Tom Smith deserves credit for his willingness to join my committee at the last minute and for his constant support, while David Shannon warrants special recognition for his willingness to go above and beyond the call of duty as the statistical consultant and outside reader for my dissertation.

I would like to thank Bruce Bongar for being willing to cochair two symposia on rational suicide at American Psychological Association conventions, even though when I first called him he did not know anything about me or my work. Similarly, David Mayo warrants appreciation for his willingness to cochair a panel discussion at an American Association of Suicidology conference. I am indebted to both of these men for their counsel. In like fashion, Jerome Motto deserves my unqualified thanks for his willingness to write the foreword to this book and for his ongoing support.

Elaine Pirrone, Acquisitions Editor at Taylor & Francis, provided me with constant feedback and wise counsel when I was putting the book proposal together. Bernadette Capelle, the book's Development Editor, was wonderful at answering my (literally) hundreds of questions, providing me with encouraging feedback, and working hard to improve the book.

I wrote this book during my predoctoral internship at Arizona State University's Counseling and Consultation and would like to thank the staff (especially my sec-

ond semester supervisor, Stan Iwai), interns, and practicum students for their en-
couragement and support. Finally, sincere gratitude is expressed to Allyson K.
Hawkins, a fellow intern at ASU, who took the time and energy to review and edit
earlier versions of several chapters, which greatly enhanced the book's quality and
clarity.

Foreword

Any generalization founders in the arena of rational suicide. Nowhere is it more pertinent or better illustrated that every individual is unique. What may be an inconvenience, a source of discomfort, or an embarrassment to one person represents unbearable agony, excruciating pain, or intolerable humiliation to another. Uniqueness is also manifested on the side of the helping person, with a spectrum of views from considering rational suicide to be a contradiction in terms to regarding it as a logical and necessary aspect of autonomy and personal choice. And, as in any philosophical inquiry, one view is as defensible as the next.

Although it was not visible when he first looked for it, Werth probably has much more company in his views than he suggests. His discussion takes us on a fascinating journey of discovery and growth in his perception and appreciation of the concept of rational suicide, from a sound clinical background and familiarity with the literature on suicide, to the questions raised by working in an HIV/AIDS service organization, to a systematic exploration of those questions among clinical psychologists, and finally to an extended investigation of the concept among the varied disciplines in the mental health community.

The emphasis throughout is consistently on the effort to clarify, to define, to put in operational terms, and above all to encourage approaching the issue of rational suicide with an open mind. It is freely conceded that such an approach will add to the professional's burden, as it imposes the task of assessing whether the person is rational and managing the situation in a manner consistent with that assessment. Although a concerted effort is made to provide clear guidelines for this assessment, the uniqueness of each professional and the subjective judgments involved create inevitable room for controversy. Thus, a well-reasoned decision to one mental health worker may be considered hasty and ill-conceived to another.

Werth makes it amply clear that his goal is to allow at least the assessment process to take place, for only under such circumstances will suicidal persons receive the respectful care they deserve. The form of that care seems self-evident if the suicidal impulse is determined not to be rational. If found to be rational, the implications for society and the health-care community are not addressed, with the clear implication that whatever measures are taken will at least be based on the realities of the situation.

The effort to open the issue of rational suicide and to offer clarification of the concept could not be more timely. The pressures of a progressively aging population, life-prolonging technology, and as yet incurable and debilitating illnesses such as AIDS are forcing the health care community and society at large to cope with the issue with inadequate guidelines. Although clinicians respond covertly on a day-to-day basis, much unnecessary agony and legal liability is involved. Societal efforts to address rational suicide, such as legislation or initiatives to assure a humane and dignified death under specified conditions, founder in part because of a lack of objective information.

Patients, families, and health-care workers deserve a well-defined social policy to provide guidance in the increasingly frequent dilemmas they face. The discussion presented here, with its exhaustive documentation, focuses on operational clarity and presentation of pertinent empirical findings, providing a much-needed step in that direction.

Jerome A. Motto, M.D.
Professor of Psychiatry, Emeritus
University of California School of Medicine
San Francisco

Preface

Traditionally, mental health professionals have denied and denounced the idea of "rational suicide." The literature on suicide, for the most part, is replete with statements regarding the irrationality of anyone who might consider suicide. Since, it is argued, anyone considering suicide is irrational, the counselor has the responsibility to intervene—convince the client to abandon such thoughts, break confidentiality to notify others, or involuntarily hospitalize—and prevent the client from harming herself or himself.

The point of view taken in this book is that it is possible to make a rational decision to suicide (note: because I do not consider suicide a crime that is "committed" I will use suicide as a verb without the modifier "commit"). For anyone conversant with the literature on working with clients who are suicidal or familiar with mental health ethics, this position may appear ill-advised and potentially dangerous. Indeed, if one were to look only at the published literature, one would be bound to conclude that rational suicide exists only in the minds of a few extremists in the mental health field. However, if one actually asks practitioners about their beliefs regarding rational suicide, as I have done, a very different picture emerges.

This book is born out of two distinct, yet intertwined, areas. First is my involvement working with persons infected with the human immunodeficiency virus (HIV, the virus associated with acquired immunodeficiency syndrome [AIDS]) for several years. Through a community-based HIV/AIDS service organization I was given the opportunity to work with people infected with HIV and their significant others, supervise volunteers providing direct service to individuals infected and affected, and perform crisis intervention duties. As a result of these experiences I came to the conclusion that it is possible for *some* persons with AIDS to make rational decisions to suicide. However, I should note that even while I was developing this view in my mind and on paper, I was still performing suicide prevention activities with other persons with AIDS who did not appear to have made a rational choice to suicide.

Allow me to provide a brief example of what I would consider a rational and an irrational decision to suicide by two different persons with AIDS. Both of these are based on actual individuals with whom I worked. First will be Alan, who had been diagnosed with AIDS three years earlier. During these three years Alan became progressively weaker, suffered through innumerable opportunistic infections, and watched helplessly as he became more and more dependent on his wife to take care of him. Throughout these three years Alan found himself in the hospital more and more often, although his stays were usually limited to less than a week. However, when I met with him during his final hospitalization, he had been in the same hospital room for the past four weeks and over this time his pain had become progressively worse and more pervasive. The physicians had revealed to him that they did not know what was causing some of his symptoms and therefore could not treat them while also saying that they could not do anything to eliminate many of his other ailments. Furthermore, he was already on the maximum dosages of all the pain medications. His physicians had informed him and his wife there was nothing more they could do for him nor could they predict how much longer he would have to endure the pain. After discussing the prognosis with his wife and considering all available alternatives, Alan decided (and his wife agreed) that his best option was to kill himself and end the pain. I consider this an example of a suicide that would meet many of the criteria for rationality.

On the other hand, Pamela, a single mother of several young children, became suicidal after her youngest child died of AIDS-related complications. Pamela was very depressed after the child's death and she blamed herself since she had infected the child before or during birth. She also felt guilty because she had not been diagnosed with AIDS yet and was still in relatively good health but her child became sick quite quickly. Furthermore, even though Pamela did not know she was infected with HIV when the child was conceived and/or born, Pamela still could not get over the fact that she gave this deadly virus to her child. Her guilt was immense and no amount of reassurance that she had done all she could for the child was enough. For the two years after the child was diagnosed with AIDS Pamela's life revolved around the ill child. When the child died Pamela was unable to care for her other children and refused to move from her living room couch or to do anything besides sleep or stare at the television blankly. She stopped eating, stopped taking her medications, and she started drinking alcohol heavily. Eventually she began to openly talk about killing herself. It was at this point that pressure was exerted to have her hospitalized, voluntarily or involuntarily. I would, as would most people, consider this an irrationally based decision to suicide.

My experiences with individuals like Alan and Pamela helped me see that there were definitely at least two kinds of suicidal individuals—rational and irrational. As I became more interested in the idea of rational suicide I began searching the literature for evidence that others believed similarly. I found a few articles by mental health workers that paralleled my own thinking but I found many other references that disregarded the possibility of rational suicide. In reviewing works written by these traditionalists I noticed that they either did not talk about suicide precipitated by physical as opposed to emotional or mental circumstances or, if they did consider physical problems, they dismissed such instances as being too few in number to be of any consequence.

As I was reviewing the literature on acceptance of suicide I found that although some empirical studies examined the attitudes of college students toward suicide under varying circumstances, similar studies using mental health professionals were virtually nonexistent. This led to the second area that prompted the writing of this book: research on mental health workers' attitudes about rational suicide. In my early theoretical articles related to rational suicide I could not say much beyond what my own opinions were on the subject. However, once the data from the different studies in which I have been involved were analyzed, I realized that I was not alone in my beliefs on the subject; it was just that few people were putting their ideas in print.

Thus, this book is an attempt to set forth a point of view that is different from the traditional party line related to working with suicidal individuals. The intent is not to discount previous works that have guidelines for suicide prevention and intervention; rather, this book is intended to supplement these other works and expand the options available to counselors when working with suicidal individuals. In fact, this book will deal with the assessment of *rationality* with clients who are suicidal, not an appraisal of suicidality in and of itself, since it is assumed that if one is assessing for rational suicide, the assessor believes the client is suicidal. In addition, aside from suggesting the reader consider taking such action as she or he deems necessary with an *irrational* suicide, this book will not deal directly with issues of intervention or prevention. Finally, other than cursory mention, this book will not deal with either assisted suicide or euthanasia—aid-in-dying provided by a physician—since these are different, though related, matters with their own set of ethical and legal issues. One could view assisted suicide and euthanasia as forms of rational suicide so the issues discussed herein are relevant to the assisted suicide and euthanasia discussions.

As I mentioned previously, I do not believe that all suicidal individuals are rational. I do, however, believe that mental health professionals should have the option of listening to a rational-sounding client discuss her or his thoughts about suicide without the professional immediately considering breaking confidentiality or hospitalizing the person. In order to present my case that suicide can at times be rational and that a counselor should not be obligated to prevent a suicide by a rational individual, this book is divided into eight chapters and an appendix. Chapter 1 provides an introduction to rational suicide through examining the traditional and current beliefs about suicide held by mental health workers. In addition, the chapter includes information related to recent developments in the debate over therapists' roles when working with suicidal individuals. Finally, to set the stage for future chapters, there is brief mention of the data that will follow in chapters 4 and 5.

Chapter 2 presents a short history of how suicide has been viewed over the ages. Special attention is given to the fact that it was only in the Middle Ages that suicide came to be viewed negatively and that it was considered a sign of mental illness only near the end of the nineteenth century. Chapter 3 continues the examination of how suicide is viewed and focuses on arguments against rational suicide that are present in the mental health literature. Some responses to these arguments are also provided.

Chapter 4 deals with empirical research on mental health professionals' attitudes about suicide. The bulk of the chapter focuses on the results of two of the three national studies in which I have been involved. Briefly, in two surveys of psychologists, over 80% of the respondents stated that they believed in rational suicide; respondents were significantly more accepting of, and would take significantly less action to prevent, a suicide by a terminally ill individual than they would a person with endogenous depression. In the second survey 20% of the respondents reported having worked with a client they considered to be rational in her or his suicidality.

The question of which clients should be considered capable of rationally suiciding is the subject of chapter 5. The answer to this important question comes from a set of empirically based criteria that are based on the two studies introduced in chapter 4 and on a third national study of experts in mental health ethics, mental health law, or suicide. These criteria also provide a means for evaluating the rationality of a decision to suicide. According to the criteria outlined, in order for a decision to be considered rational, the person should have a hopeless condition, have made the choice to suicide free from external coercion, and have used a sound decision-making process. These criteria are described in more detail and case examples are presented.

Chapter 6 discusses some of the limitations with the research conducted thus far concerning rational suicide. A few of the important issues yet to be investigated relate to how certain characteristics of the suicidal person may impact the mental health professional who is attempting to assess for rationality. For example, the impact of the race, ethnicity, age, and disability characteristics of the suicidal person have not been investigated. Additional concerns revolve around cultural, spiritual, and family issues of both the client and the mental health professional. Consideration will be given to the issue of how the values, especially the spiritual or religious concerns, of the therapist and/or client must be taken into account.

Chapter 7 focuses on the topic of the ethical and legal standards of care when working with suicidal persons and the implications of the research presented in the book on the standards of practice. Attention will be given to the intertwined issues of malpractice and negligence, competence and hospitalization, and guidelines for protecting oneself from ethical and legal charges. The final set of data to be presented is from one of the national surveys that demonstrates that although many participants personally accepted a terminally ill person's decision to suicide, they would be hesitant to allow the person to follow through because of concerns with legal and ethical repercussions. The chapter examines the potential impact on the practice of mental health professionals if the current standards of care were changed to be more contextual instead of absolute when faced with a client who is suicidal.

The final chapter provides a synthesis of the information presented in the book and offers some predictions for the future. Additional implications for mental health professionals, the mental health field, and clients are noted. This discussion is put in the context of the role of the counselor when working with clients who are rationally suicidal.

The appendix is devoted to activities for reflection and discussion. These activities may be useful for individuals or for small groups. Both specific and general questions about the topic of rational suicide are offered as is another case example and references for additional cases that will allow mental health professionals to practice using the criteria for rational suicide.

If nothing else, I hope reading this book will make readers more aware that there are no absolutes when working with suicidal individuals. If mental health professionals agree that this is true, then their job will only become more difficult. In the past, mental health professionals did not have to think about what to do when faced with a person considering suicide—stop her or him from following through, no matter what it takes. By accepting that some individuals may have made a rational choice to suicide an added burden of evaluating rationality is placed on the professional. Yet, however large they may consider that burden, it is nothing compared to what individuals like Alan will have to live with if they are forced to endure their misery because mental health professionals refuse to allow them to end their suffering.

1

Introduction to Rational Suicide

Graduate students in the mental health professions often receive some training about how to assess and handle clients who are having suicidal ideation. The likely reasoning behind this attention is twofold. First, when providing counseling either during training or after graduation, a therapist probably will have at least one client who considers suicide (H. N. Brown, 1987; Chemtob, Bauer, Hamada, Pelowski, & Muraoka, 1989; Kleespies, Penk, & Forsyth, 1993; Kleespies, Smith, & Becker, 1990). In fact, since the potential for having a client suicide is an "occupational hazard" for mental health professionals, students should have training to help them deal effectively with clients who are having suicidal ideation (Bongar & Harmatz, 1989; Chemtob et al., 1989; Kleespies, 1993). Second, the imperative to do whatever is reasonably and feasibly possible to prevent a client from suiciding has been built into mental health workers' ethical and legal standards of care, which find their foundation in the ethical principles of the various professional organizations (e.g., American Counseling Association [ACA], 1988; American Psychological Association [APA], 1992). Thus, therapists-in-training are apt to have a client with whom they would be obligated to coerce into "choosing" life or to physically prevent from following through with a stated intention.

A few mental health workers have stated that they object to the assumption of the responsibility to prevent suicide in general (e.g., Szasz, 1986) or do not feel it is appropriate to intervene in certain types of cases (e.g., Kjervik, 1984; Werth, 1992; Widiger & Rinaldi, 1983). Nonetheless, at present, counselors are faced with the decision to either follow the general guideline of allowing clients the autonomy and independence to select their directions and goals in therapy and in life (Amchin, Wettstein, & Roth, 1990; Kitchener, 1984) or the specific ethical standard of not allowing harm-to-self to occur. This ethical conundrum may be one reason why suicide is one of the most difficult issues facing professionals (Clements, Sider, & Perlmutter, 1983). Further complicating this already difficult situation is the possibility of "rational suicide" (e.g., Battin & Mayo, 1980; Beckerman,

1995; Maris, 1982, 1983; Siegel, 1982a, 1986; Werth, 1992, 1995; see McIntosh, 1985, for a bibliography).

ACCEPTABILITY OF SUICIDE

In describing rational suicide, Siegel (1986) stated:

The defining characteristics of a rational suicide are: (1) the individual possesses a realistic assessment of his [or her] situation, (2) the mental processes leading to his [or her] decision to commit suicide are unimpaired by psychological illness or severe emotional distress, and (3) the motivational basis of his [or her] decision would be understandable to the majority of uninvolved observers from his [or her] community or social group. (p. 407)

Although criteria one and two must be assessed on an individual basis, the third criterion can be examined on a societal level. Public surveys have found increasing approval for allowing terminally ill people to end their own lives, either with or without the assistance of a physician (e.g., Deluty, 1988, 1989; Domino, Gibson, Poling, & Westlake, 1980; Droogas, Siiter, & O'Connell, 1982; Huber, Cox, & Edelen, 1992; Humphry & Wickett, 1990; Johnson, Fitch, Alston, & McIntosh, 1980; Klopfer & Price, 1978; Malcolm, 1990; Minear & Brush, 1981; Roper Organization of New York City, 1988; Singh, Williams, & Ryther, 1986).

Experimental research has also found attitudes reflecting acceptance of the idea that some individuals should be allowed to end their lives if they so decide. Most of these studies have presented undergraduate students with one or more written cases describing individuals who either have already suicided or are contemplating taking this action. Two of the relevant findings are (1) suicides by people who are in a great deal of pain are more acceptable than those by people suffering little pain and (2) terminal illness is a significantly more acceptable reason to suicide than physical pain, and both of these cases are significantly more acceptable reasons than psychological pain and a control condition (Deluty, 1988, 1989; Droogas et al., 1982; Lo Presto, Sherman, & DiCarlo, 1995; Martin & Range, 1991; Range & Martin, 1990). In two studies (Deluty, 1989; Lo Presto et al., 1995) the gender of the suicidal person was varied and in both cases women considering suicide were viewed more negatively than men in identical situations.

MENTAL HEALTH PROFESSIONALS' ATTITUDES TOWARD SUICIDE

There are a few studies that have examined the beliefs of therapists about suicide (e.g., Domino & Swain, 1986; Gurrister & Kane, 1978; Hammond, 1991; Swain & Domino, 1985). Two recent studies, which will be discussed in more detail in chapter 4, further add to the understanding of mental health professionals' attitudes toward men who are contemplating suicide (Werth, 1994b; Werth & Liddle, 1994). Werth and Liddle surveyed members of the APA's Division of

Psychotherapy through vignettes in which the cause of the suicidal ideation varied among terminal illness, chronic physical pain, psychological pain, and bankruptcy and was crossed with the ideator being portrayed as a client of the participant or as a member of the general public.

Results indicated that suicidal ideation in the terminal illness condition was significantly more acceptable than ideation in the physical pain or psychological pain conditions and all three of these were more acceptable than ideation as a result of bankruptcy. However, the physical and psychological pain conditions did not differ significantly from each other in acceptability. The study also investigated the amount of action the respondents would take to prevent the suicide. Respondents to the terminal illness condition indicated they would take significantly less action than did respondents to any of the other three scenarios. Physical pain required significantly less action than either psychological pain or bankruptcy, which did not differ significantly from each other. There were no significant interaction effects, nor was the main effect of client status (client versus nonclient) significant. Of the participant demographic variables examined, only number of years in practice was significant, with more experienced psychotherapists being more accepting and advocating less action. Belief in the concept of rational suicide was also related to greater acceptance and less action. A final finding of the Werth and Liddle (1994) study was that 81% of the respondents to the item asking about their belief in "rational suicide" indicated they believed in this concept.

The second study (Werth, 1994b) involved a survey of practicing psychologists and used a format similar to the Werth and Liddle (1994) investigation described above. In this study, psychologists received vignettes that varied in terms of the condition precipitating the decision to suicide (terminal bone cancer, AIDS, and endogenous depression), the sexual orientation of the suicidal man (gay or heterosexual), and whether or not the suicidal person's friends and family agreed with the decision to suicide (support present or absent). Results indicated that there were no interactions among the independent variables and that neither the sexual orientation nor the support variable produced significant results. However, the precipitating condition variable was significant.

Werth (1994b) found no significant differences between AIDS and terminal bone cancer on any of the independent variables (the same measures of acceptance and preventive action used by Werth & Liddle [1994] and three measures of stigma associated with the suicidal man). However, both terminal illness conditions were rated as significantly more acceptable reasons to suicide and deserving of significantly less preventive action than the depression condition. Furthermore, the men who were considering suicide due to depression were stigmatized more than the men who were suicidal as a result of a terminal illness. Finally, 86% of Werth's respondents indicated that they believed in rational suicide, and 20% stated that they had had at least one client whom they considered to be rationally suicidal.

The results of both studies (Werth, 1994b; Werth & Liddle, 1994) associated with the degree of acceptance and amount of action required supported a hypothesis made by Werth (1992; see also Jackson, 1957) that "intensity of suicide intervention" can be placed on a continuum. In this article Werth surmised that a person with AIDS could represent an example of a person whose suicidal ideation may not require a manipulative and/or coercive intervention; a person in constant pain but not terminally ill was used as an example of a person falling more in the middle of the continuum, warranting more intensive and extensive exploration and possibly intervention; finally, a person in a psychotic state was hypothesized to be representative of a case when potentially restrictive intervention could be necessary.

Both the Werth and Liddle (1994) and the Werth (1994b) studies provided support for the placement of various causes of suicidal ideation along this intervention continuum. The results indicated that the terminal bone cancer and AIDS scenarios are examples of conditions that psychologists believe warrant less direct intervention than physical pain, psychological pain, or bankruptcy, all of which demand more intensive and perhaps restrictive intervention. In addition, the studies showed that acceptance of suicidal ideation can also be placed on a continuum with bankruptcy representing the low acceptance pole and terminal bone cancer and AIDS illustrating the high acceptance end of the continuum (see also Werth, 1995).

In an investigation that complemented the Werth and Liddle (1994) study, Werth and Cobia (1995a) did a qualitative analysis of psychotherapist responses to open-ended questions about beliefs in rational suicide. They then generated the first empirically based set of criteria for rational suicide. Their definition had three components, which will be delineated in detail in chapter 5. First, the person should have an unremitting hopeless condition, such as a terminal illness. Second, the person must make the decision free from external coercion. Finally, the person needs to have engaged in a "sound decision-making process," consisting of five subcomponents: (a) nonimpulsivity, (b) consideration of all alternatives, (c) consideration of the congruence with one's values, (d) consideration of the impact on significant others, and (e) consultation with objective others (including a mental health professional who could do an assessment of psychological competence) and with significant others. In a follow-up study, which will also be described in chapter 5, Werth and Cobia (1995b) solicited feedback on the proposed set of criteria from ethicists, psychologist–attorneys, and suicidologists and also asked them to, in their expert opinions, provide feedback concerning the ethical or legal repercussions of a case scenario in which the treating mental health professional applied the criteria and then allowed the client to suicide.

Werth (1994b) essentially replicated the criteria enumerated by Werth and Cobia (1995a), with the only major difference being that his respondents indicated that if clinical depression was present then a suicide could not be rational. The conditions listed by both Werth and Cobia (1995a) and Werth (1994b) resemble others in the literature (e.g., Siegel, 1986) but they are more inclusive and descriptive.

Thus, there appears to be wide support for the idea that suicidal ideation by a person with certain conditions may be acceptable and require less intervention than similar thoughts by someone who is experiencing other circumstances. Given this apparent acceptance both by the general public and by therapists that there are some cases when it is acceptable for a person to suicide, it may be necessary to revise the restrictive demand present in the current standards of care that a mental health worker is always ethically and legally obligated to intervene when faced with any actively suicidal client.

STANDARDS OF CARE

Although changing the standards of care may appear to be an extreme reaction to these data, the logic behind the proposal can be seen if one considers the intertwined issues of standards of care, negligence, and malpractice. Since these issues will be discussed in more detail in chapter 7, only an overview will be presented here. There are four basic elements to malpractice (e.g., Meyer, Landis, & Hays, 1988; Van Hoose & Kottler, 1985). First, there must be a professional relationship implying a duty to care:

> This duty is often discussed in terms of standards of care, and is usually defined by the courts as reasonable professional practices followed by others in the same discipline and either considered standard practice or at least accepted by a significant minority of professionals. (Meyer et al., 1988, p. 15)

The second element involves a breach of the duty described above. "'Negligence' is defined as a departure from usual practice; that is, acceptable standards were not followed, and due care was not exercised" (Van Hoose & Kottler, 1985, p. 63). For example, "a failure to take some direct precautions with a potential suicide would almost certainly be ruled negligent" (Van Hoose & Kottler, 1985, p. 67). The third element is that the plaintiff suffered or was caused harm or injury. Finally, the practitioner's negligence must be proven to be the proximate cause of the injury.

The traditional standard of care with suicidal clients, and therefore the yardstick upon which mental health workers are measured in terms of gauging negligence, has been intervention and prevention at all costs—"once suicidality is noted, the therapist must take reasonably prudent steps to prevent harm" (Meyer et al., 1988, p. 39). Given a widespread acceptance of rational suicide under certain conditions, it seems reasonable that the ethical and legal standards of care should be changed to allow mental health workers the *option* to not coercively interfere with *some* clients who choose to die. Such a change is necessary before mental health workers can safely act as they believe is appropriate (Werth, 1994b; Werth & Liddle, 1994).

The dichotomy between personal beliefs and professionally and legally prescribed actions was illustrated by several respondents in the recent study involving psychotherapists (Werth & Liddle, 1994, p. 446). For example, one respondent said she would take no action to prevent the client who had a terminal illness from suiciding, "Unless ethics code required [otherwise]," while another said "I would consider whether I am in legal jeopardy by doing nothing." Meanwhile two respondents said they would involuntarily hospitalize the terminally ill client with one of them adding, "Only to protect myself! Otherwise [nothing]!" and the other saying, "This is due to legal considerations rather than ethical/humane [ones]." In terms of acceptability, all these respondents said that suicide in these circumstances would be nearly completely acceptable. These results indicate that some therapists may be acting against their beliefs due to their fear of ethical or legal reprisal. In a more formal investigation of this phenomenon, Werth (1994b) also found that many of his respondents stated that they believed in and accepted rational suicide but would be hesitant to allow a client to follow through with such a decision because of their fear of repercussions. These concerns about negative consequences may explain results (Gurrister & Kane, 1978; Hammond, 1991) in which even though many participants believed some suicides could be rational, these participants would still intervene to prevent virtually all suicides (Werth, 1994b; Werth & Liddle, 1994).

Both the Werth (1994b) and the Werth and Liddle (1994) studies revealed that a majority of the practicing psychologists who responded believed that it is acceptable for a person with a painful terminal illness to consider and then to suicide. However, given the recency of the results, they have not yet been extensively discussed among mental health workers and hence not translated into the standards of care. Thus, because counselors are judged in relation to their peers, these opinions must be discussed among professionals and, once the specifics are agreed upon, then be included in revisions of the ethical and legal standards regarding the handling of suicidal clients (Werth, 1994b; Werth & Liddle, 1994).

RECENT VIEWS OF RATIONAL SUICIDE

A person with terminal cancer has been the prototypic case of an individual whose suicide may be considered acceptable and therefore rational; however, some have suggested that the person with AIDS may soon supplant the person with cancer as the paradigmatic case of rational suicide (Martin & Range, 1991; Werth, 1992). It has even been argued that the HIV disease epidemic has brought the issue of rational suicide to the cutting edge of ethical and legal issues for mental health professionals (e.g., Bongar & Werth, 1994; Mayo & Werth, 1994; see also Beckerman, 1995). Along these lines, in 1987 the American Association of Suicidology (AAS) established a task force to study AIDS and suicide (McKinney, 1987) and in that same year there were two presentations at the AAS national convention on AIDS and rational suicide (Jonsen, Lo, Luce, Yarnell, & Younger, 1987; Saunders & Bunchingham, 1987). In 1994 the AAS sponsored a panel discussion regarding the Werth and Cobia (1995a) criteria and during that symposium all agreed that the discussion of rational suicide had turned the corner—instead of debating whether or not there was such a thing as rational suicide, the attention was focused on acknowledging that it was a reality and that guidelines for dealing with that reality must be established (Mayo & Werth, 1994; see also McIntosh, 1993b).

Other organizations comprised of mental health workers are also taking a close look at rational suicide. For example, an informal survey of the membership of the Association of Death Education and Counseling in 1991 found respondents fairly evenly split on many right-to-die issues (Chapman Dick, 1991). In addition, the National Association of Social Workers (1994) set forth guidelines concerning "Client Self-Determination in End-of-Life Decisions," and this document addresses social workers' attendance at client suicides. In essence, the guidelines state that the social worker cannot assist in the suicide but, if legally permissible, he or she is not required to intervene to prevent a suicide that appears to be rationally motivated and can be present at the suicide if the client requests this. The guidelines also set forth the circumstances that must be considered before a social worker could feel justified in not interfering (see chapter 5). These conditions closely parallel those outlined by Werth (1994b) and Werth and Cobia (1995a).

The APA has also begun exploring the issue of rational suicide in general (Bongar & Werth, 1993) and specifically with persons with AIDS (Barret, 1993; Bongar & Werth, 1994; Hoffman, 1992) during symposia at its annual convention. In addition, the APA Office on AIDS is convening a special committee to assemble a resource manual with materials related to ethical issues that commonly arise when working with clients who are infected with the human immunodeficiency virus (HIV) or have been diagnosed with AIDS (APA Committee on Psychology and AIDS, 1994). One of the topics that will be covered is rational suicide (see also Werth & Carney, 1994).

Although AIDS has gained increasing prominence in discussions about rational suicide, it is important to note that recent commentaries have also acknowledged that a terminal diagnosis should not be the sole condition under which a suicide could be considered rational. For example, Werth and Cobia (1995a) reported that their respondents listed physical and/or psychological pain, physically or mentally debilitating and/or deteriorating conditions, and an unacceptable quality of life as potential reasons for a rational suicide. These additional conditions have been elaborated upon in different contexts. For example, Bongar (in Bongar & Werth, 1993) presented a hypothetical case of a person with schizophrenia in remission as an example of a situation that would fall outside the traditional parameters but that could actually be considered a rational suicide. In a discussion of the criteria for rational suicide proposed by Werth and Cobia, Maris (in Mayo & Werth, 1994) said that the point of reference for the hopelessness and the unbearableness of the condition must be the person who is suffering; in the same symposium, Motto (1994b) reiterated this point and offered other conditions that may be unbearable to the person in distress.

Many writers (e.g., Barrington, 1980; Portwood, 1978; Prado, 1990) have suggested that suicide should be acceptable for the elderly. One set of researchers (Courage, Godbey, Ingram, Schramm, & Hale, 1993) investigated what older adults themselves believed about suicide. In a qualitative study, this group found that their interviewees "had given considerable thought to the ending of their lives" (p. 28). The participants varied in their views of how much control they had over the timing of their deaths and in their acceptance of suicide. Summarizing their results, the authors stated:

> The primary cause of suicide in this study was intolerable life circumstances. These circumstances comprised a single catastrophic problem—such as terminal illness—or an accumulation of problems and losses—such as pain, poor health, loss of financial resources, loss of purpose and contribution to society, and loss of independence. (p. 30)

The participants apparently indicated they wanted to talk about death and dying, including suicide, which led the authors to suggest that professionals initiate conversations about older adults' end-of-life decisions and expectations. The authors concluded that "Although social taboos interfere with discussion of suicide, this does not mean that the elderly do not consider some form of suicide as a means to control death" (p. 31). These results indicate that rational suicide may indeed be an apt consideration for some older adults.

However, one of the concerns with expanding the criteria for who may be eligible to suicide rationally beyond only those who are terminally ill is that this will lead to an unstoppable tide of people who would qualify as being rationally suicidal. This line of thinking has been called the "slippery slope" argument because the belief is that once any condition is considered a legitimate reason for a rational suicide, it will be easy for people without this condition to make a case that they should have the same right to kill themselves as the people who meet a narrowly defined set of criteria. Responses to this point of view and to other arguments against rational suicide will be presented in chapter 3, so for the time being the only rejoinder will be that such a slide down the slope has not occurred in other instances, such as when to stop life-sustaining medicine and machinery in hospitals and when killing another person is permissible (e.g., war, self-defense).

ADDITIONAL CONSIDERATIONS

As will be discussed in chapter 6, it must be emphasized that the final words about rational suicide are not contained in this book. There is much more work that needs to be done. For example, even though Werth (1994b) took a preliminary look at the issue of stigma and its impact on the acceptability and preventive action related to a suicidal ideator, he only examined two of the many different ways that prejudice may be involved in the assessment of rationality. Studies have yet to manipulate variables such as the ideator's gender, race, age, or disability status to assess the impact of any one or a combination of these qualities on professionals' judgments about rationality.

The issues of prejudice and stigma are not the only ones of importance when considering how rational suicide may have important implications from a multicultural standpoint. For example, Backer (1994) noted that important considerations for the Latino communities revolve around family, sacrifice, and religion. He also noted that there may be variation within different Latino communities as well. Similar concerns may be raised about other cultural groups, such as American Indians, Asians, and African Americans.

Religion in and of itself, within any community, is a topic of great importance in this discussion. Although research has indicated that no particular religious group is significantly more or less likely to support the idea of the right to die (e.g., Johnson et al., 1980; Roper Organization of New York City, 1988), different religious denominations have come out with strong opposition to the ideas of rational suicide and physician aid-in-dying. It has been hypothesized that it was the financing by some large religious organizations that caused the defeat of physician aid-in-dying initiatives in Washington and California (Battin, 1994d; "Public Actions," 1992).

However, a recently approved initiative in Oregon attempted to address some of the procedural concerns raised by those who opposed earlier efforts (Oregon Right to Die, 1994; "Public Actions," 1992). The passage of this measure (although it is in court for an evaluation of its constitutionality [Judd, 1995]), the fact that 12 other state legislatures are examining physician aid-in-dying bills (Larson, 1995), and a court ruling in Washington state that asserted that "a terminally ill adult has a 'constitutionally guaranteed right' under the 14th Amendment to medical assistance in committing suicide" (Leo, 1994, p. 22; see also Levy, 1995; Shapiro, 1994) indicate that an important shift may have occurred. These events have brought the United States closer to the society Zinner (1984) projected for the year 2010 in which a Supreme Court decision appeared to provide permission to suicide.

The Oregon act explicitly states that a mental health professional should be consulted if a person who requests aid-in-dying appears to be unable to make a reasoned choice (Oregon Right to Die, 1994). A similar provision was in the set of recommendations by the Michigan Association of Psychologists, which was forwarded to the state's Commission on Dying (Pantano, 1994). The guidelines for Compassion in Dying, an organization that supports terminally ill people asking for assistance in dying, state that a mental health professional should be involved if there are concerns about the requestor's mental status (Dunshee, 1994). It should be obvious that in order for a counselor to make such an evaluation she or he must have a set of guidelines with which she or he can gauge competence and rationality. However, until recently there has not been a set of criteria for the assessment of rational suicide. As has been noted, Werth (1994b) and Werth and Cobia (1995a, 1995b) have attempted to establish and refine criteria that could be used by therapists who are called upon to do assessments in medical settings or who, with their own clients, find themselves faced with individuals whose motivation to suicide appears rational. Some (e.g., Peterson, 1985; Smith, 1989) put a different twist on the need for criteria by noting that since courts have determined that one of their tasks is to prevent "irrational self-destruction" there must be a way to assess for rationality. Specifically, Peterson noted that "The question which naturally arises is whether a proper inquiry can be made into the rationality of the [client's] decision without specific guidelines designed for that purpose" (p. 117).

CONCLUSION

Several authors have attempted to explain why rational suicide and the entire issue of the right to die have become such hot topics in recent years. Two issues appear to be mentioned consistently. First is the societal move away from a religious view of life toward a more secular view (e.g., Barrington, 1980; Battin, 1982, 1992; Engelhardt, 1989; Heyd & Bloch, 1981; Szasz, 1976). The second reason is the vast improvement made in the medical field; not only the advances in technology and machination but also changes due to effective treatments of formerly fatal illnesses such as pneumonia—the combination of these developments have led to the possibility of prolonging life beyond the point of what many would consider to be a life worth living (e.g., Battin, 1994d; Colt, 1991; Engelhardt, 1989; Heyd & Bloch, 1981; Siegel, 1986; Werth, 1992; for the opposite view see R. L. Barry, 1994).

Because of a number of converging factors, including the two mentioned earlier, professionals will be seeing more people (both inside and outside of hospitals) who will want to discuss the idea of ending their own lives, with or without the assistance of others. Unfortunately, counselors have traditionally disregarded and discarded the possibility that a person could make a rational decision to suicide, thereby leaving such individuals with nowhere to turn. In order for therapists to be prepared for the eventuality of working with people who wish to assert their right to die it is imperative that counselors engage in intensive introspection regarding their own personal and professional values.

The arguments supporting the paternalistic view that all suicides must be prevented have, for the most part, been unexamined for so long that they are unthinkingly accepted as fact. What is presented in this book is an alternative view based on the idea that a contextual approach should be taken when evaluating suicidality. Research indicates that, even though this position is not presented in the literature, a majority of mental health professionals may subscribe to the point of view that some people may be able to make rational decisions to suicide. This evidence has implications for the standards of care in the treatment of suicidal clients, and it is time for professionals to begin openly discussing the issue at length. Battin (1994d) has stated that "the right-to-die issue . . . will become *the* major social issue of the next decade . . ." (pp. 8–9, emphasis original). If her contention is true then it is imperative that counselors be deeply involved in discussions about the right to die, including rational suicide, instead of being merely bystanders (Mayo, 1993), as happened to psychiatrists in the Netherlands (Huyse & van Tilburg, 1993).

2

The History of Suicide

Currently, suicide is predominantly seen in the mental health community and by the lay public as a by-product of mental illness. That is, if someone is suicidal, this is evidence of an underlying mental disturbance. In addition, suicide is seen by many counselors, and members of the public, as being immoral. Naturally, if one believes that suicide is evidence of mental illness and/or is immoral then one would be inclined to try to prevent all suicides.

However, the current predominant views of suicide are just that, *currently* predominant. This was not always the case. For example, Allen stated:

Historically, society's attitudes toward suicide and the suicidal act reveal a wide range between a rational one of acceptance, an irrational one of superstition, and a hostile one of punishment. Suicide is now regarded as an act whose empirical and theoretical dimensions can be investigated scientifically. (1977, p. 1; see also Colt, 1991)

Since the premise of this book is that there can, and should, be a shift in the currently articulated attitudes about suicide held by counselors, it is important to demonstrate that this shift would be neither radical nor novel. Therefore, the purpose of this chapter is to provide an overview of how suicide has been viewed over the ages and how these views have influenced current thinking. Because of space limitations, the focus will be on European and American views of suicide; however, other cultures such as those in Japan (e.g., hara-kiri in order to avoid capture or disgrace; Iga & Tatai, 1975) and India (e.g., suttee by a Hindu woman when her husband died; Rao, 1975) also have a long and storied history with suicide and, more specifically, with rational suicide (see, e.g., R. L. Barry, 1994; Cavan, 1928; Colt, 1991; Dublin, 1963; Farberow, 1975). Readers interested in more in-depth discussions of the eras described in this chapter should see the original sources; readers who would like information on how suicide is viewed in societies other than those described here should refer to R. L. Barry (1994), Cavan (1928), Colt (1991), Dublin (1963), Farberow (1975), Fedden (1938), and Humphry and Wickett (1990).

ANCIENT VIEWS OF SUICIDE

Ancient Greek views of suicide, although not totally accepting, were much more tolerant than views in later periods (R. L. Barry, 1994; Cavan, 1928; Choron, 1972; Colt, 1991; Dublin, 1963; Fedden, 1938; Marzen, O'Dowd, Crone, & Balch, 1985). Winslow (1840) said that Greek suicides usually involved people who wanted to avoid physical or mental suffering, wanted to avoid dishonor, or sacrificed their life as an example for others (see also Choron, 1972; Fedden, 1938). He stated:

the first class is the most excusable of the three. Pain, physical or mental, puts a [person's] courage severely to the test. [She or] he may have to choose between the alternative of years of unmitigated anguish, or an immediate release from torture. (pp. 2–3)

There is evidence that when suicide was acceptable to the state, the magistrates would then provide the means for the death: "Whoever no longer wishes to live shall state his [or her] reasons to the Senate, and after having received permission shall abandon life. If your existence is hateful to you, die; if you are overwhelmed by fate, drink the hemlock" (Humphry & Wickett, 1990, p. 4; see also R. L. Barry, 1994; Colt, 1991; Fedden, 1938; Portwood, 1978; Winslow, 1840).

Humphry and Wickett argue that the Greeks, "elevated [suicide] as a subject—and practice—worthy of rational discourse and consideration. It was, given certain circumstances, a worthy and reasonable choice. Not least important, it was often the most humane thing to do" (1990, p. 5).

However, at times suicide was not acceptable. These prohibitions were related to situations in which the suicide could be viewed as acting against the best interests of the state. Aristotle defined suicide, in some instances, as an offense against the state, Pythagoras saw it as an offense against God, and Plato (for the most part) saw it as both (R. L. Barry, 1994; Battin, 1994g; Cavan, 1928; Choron, 1972; Colt, 1991; Dublin, 1963; Fedden, 1938; Heyd & Bloch, 1981; Humphry & Wickett, 1990; Marzen et al., 1985; Pretzel, 1977; Williams, 1968). The early Greeks also had laws that allowed the maltreatment of the body of someone who had suicided, although these laws fell into disuse (Cavan, 1928; Fedden, 1938; Williams, 1968; Winslow, 1840).

For the Romans, only irrational suicide was punishable (Allen, 1977; Colt, 1991; Fedden, 1938; Humphry & Wickett, 1990). However, suicide due to terminal illness and/or pain was acceptable (Choron, 1972; Fedden, 1938). For Romans, suicide was apparently subject to neither moral condemnation nor legal action (Cavan, 1928; Colt, 1991). The major consideration for the Romans seems to have been how the suicide would affect the state, especially the treasury; therefore, suicide was not acceptable for slaves, soldiers, or one accused of a crime (R. L. Barry, 1994; Choron, 1972; Colt, 1991; Fedden, 1938; Morgan, 1979; Smith, 1989; Williams, 1968; Winslow, 1840).

When examining views on suicide one inevitably comes across the Greek and Roman philosophical school called the Stoics (e.g., Battin, 1994g; Choron, 1972; Marzen et al., 1985; Smith, 1989; Williams, 1968). The Stoics chose suicide when life was not "in accordance with nature—because of pain, grave illness, or physical abnormalities" (Humphry & Wickett, 1990, p. 4). Suicide was a "natural means of ending life that had become intolerable" (Cavan, 1928, p. 16), "providing the act is one of reason, will, and integrity" (Pretzel, 1977, p. 389; see also Dyck, 1977). The Roman Stoic Seneca said:

> It makes a great deal of difference whether [one] is lengthening [one's] life or [one's] death. But if the body is useless for service, why should one not free the struggling soul? Perhaps one ought to do this a little before the debt is due, lest, when it falls due, [one] may be unable to perform the act. (quoted in Humphry & Wickett, 1990, p. 5; see also Fedden, 1938)

Similarly, he stated:

> I will not relinquish old age if it leaves my better part intact. But if it begins to shake my mind, if it destroys my faculties one by one, if it leaves me not life but breath, I will depart from the putrid or tottering edifice. I will not escape by death from disease so long as it may be healed, and leaves my mind unimpaired. . . . But if I know that I must suffer without hope of relief, I will depart, not through fear of the pain itself, but because it prevents all for which I would live. (quoted in Lecky, 1898, p.220; see also R. L. Barry, 1994; Colt, 1991; Dublin, 1963; Pretzel, 1977; Williams, 1968)

Finally, he also said "mere living is not a good, but living well. Accordingly, the wise [person] will live as long as [she or] he ought, not as long as [she or] he can" (quoted in Choron, 1972, p. 116; see also Heyd & Bloch, 1981; Mayo, 1986; Rauscher, 1981; Smith, 1989). Laertius similarly stated that "A wise [person] will quit life when oppressed with severe pain, or when deprived of his [or her] senses, or when laboring under desperate diseases" (quoted in Winslow, 1840, p. 22; see also Rosen, 1975). Epictetus apparently was more cautious in his support of suicide: "If you like not life, you may leave it; the door is open; get you gone! But a little smoke ought not to frighten you away; it should be endured, and will thereby be often surmounted" (quoted in Dublin, 1963, p.114; see also Choron, 1972; Winslow, 1840). In addition, when discussing the existence of mental and emotional disorders, Rosen (1975) said that Epictetus took notice of a "death wish among young men and felt obliged to restrain it, urging them not to commit suicide" (p. 8). Similarly, Pliny the Younger said:

> to rush to death under the influence of an impulse and an instinctive feeling is no more than what many have done[;] but deliberately to weigh the motives for and against and then, as reason advises, to accept or reject the policy of life or death, that is the conduct of a great soul. (quoted in Mair, 1922, p.32)

In keeping with Pliny's idea, Dublin (1963) noted:

> Although the Stoics were so receptive to the idea of suicide, it must be pointed out that they were emphatic in teaching that it was not to be the rash act of a momentary impulse or a temporary confusion of values. It was to be accepted or rejected only after due deliberation and after all arguments for and against it had been carefully weighed. (p.114; see also Colt, 1991)

Suicide was condoned by other philosophical schools as well (Choron, 1972; Fedden, 1938; Smith, 1989; Williams, 1968). For example, several of the followers of Epicurus apparently died by suicide (for examples of people who suicided, see Choron, 1972; Colt, 1991; Fedden, 1938; Rosen, 1975; Winslow, 1840); a Cyrenaic named Hegesias (called "the orator of death") reportedly influenced many to suicide through his arguments; and Diogenes, the Cynic, believed that "A wise man will quit life, when oppressed with severe pain, or deprived of any of his senses, or when laboring under desperate diseases" (quoted in Dublin, 1963, p. 116; see also R. L. Barry, 1994; Colt, 1991).

RELIGION ENTERS

"The various religions [of the world] have taken every conceivable view of suicide; some have endorsed it, even recommended it under certain circumstances, while many others have opposed it resolutely and uncompromisingly at all times" (Dublin, 1963, p. 83). However, only Christianity will be mentioned in detail in this chapter since it has had the most direct effect on current views of suicide in the United States (see Battin, 1994f; readers interested in other religious views of suicide are encouraged to read Dublin, 1963 and Portwood, 1978).

"At first the [Christian] church approved certain forms of suicide: to procure martyrdom, to avoid apostasy, or to retain virginity" (Cavan, 1928, p. 19; see also Battin, 1994f, 1994g; Choron, 1972; Colt, 1991; Dublin, 1963; Fedden, 1938; Maris, 1981; Pretzel, 1977; for the opposite view see R. L. Barry, 1994). Dublin wrote that "The early Christians apparently accepted the prevailing attitudes of their time on suicide . . . for several centuries the leaders of the Church did not condemn the practice, which apparently was quite common" (1963, p. 118).

It is worthwhile to note that there does not appear to be a Biblical term related to "self-destruction" or "self-killing." The Old Testament of the Bible contains only a few cases of suicide, and in none of the incidents is there mention of condemnation for the individual's actions (Baelz, 1980; Battin, 1994f, 1994g; Choron, 1972; Colt, 1991; Dublin, 1963; Fedden, 1938; Humphry & Wickett, 1990; Maris, 1981; Marzen et al., 1985; Pretzel, 1977; Rosen, 1975; Smith, 1989; Valente, 1984; Williams, 1968; Winslow, 1840; for the opposite view see R. L. Barry, 1994). Similarly, the description in the New Testament of Judas Iscariot's hanging himself is done in a morally neutral manner (Baelz, 1980; Battin, 1994f; Colt, 1991; Dublin, 1963; Marzen et al., 1985; Pretzel, 1977; Rosen, 1975; Valente, 1984). It was only later that Judas was said to have doubled his sin by suiciding and, further, that the suicide was his greater sin (Battin, 1994g; Cavan, 1928; Heyd & Bloch, 1981).

However, the view of suicide changed so that, for Christians, one's life and death was believed to be solely in the hands of God. Suicide was viewed as adversely affecting one's soul after death because one owed everything to God and killing oneself before one's time usurped God's power and plan.

St. Augustine put forth the arguments upon which the Christian church's position was thereafter based (R. L. Barry, 1994; Battin, 1994f, 1994g; Cavan, 1928; Choron, 1972; Colt, 1991; Dublin, 1963; Fedden, 1938; Heyd & Bloch, 1981;

Humphry & Wickett, 1990; Marzen et al., 1985; Morgan, 1979; Pretzel, 1977; Smith, 1989; Williams, 1968). In order to stem the tide of people attempting to be martyred through acts that could be considered suicide, he set forth several arguments that still stand today. First, killing oneself was breaking the Sixth Commandment—thou shalt not kill. Second, suicide is a greater sin than anything one may wish to avoid through killing oneself. Third, suicide was interfering with the functions of the state and the church. Fourth, one's life—with its pleasures and sufferings—was divinely ordained by God and therefore must be experienced.

Because of his strong antisuicide bias, St. Augustine was put in an awkward situation regarding cases of people who had suicided but had already been canonized by the church. He resolved the dilemma by stating that such individuals had received divine inspiration and therefore were not subject to mortal laws (Baelz, 1980; Battin, 1994f; Choron, 1972; Colt, 1991; Dublin, 1963; Fedden, 1938; Marzen et al., 1985; Pretzel, 1977; Smith, 1989; Williams, 1968).

Augustine's arguments apparently soon led to official positions (coming out of the Council of Arles in 452 A.D.; the Council of Orleans in 533 A.D.; the Council of Braga in 563 A.D.; and the Council of Toledo in 693 A.D.) that denied funeral rites to someone who suicided and that supported excommunication of anyone who attempted suicide (R. L. Barry, 1994; Colt, 1991; Fedden, 1938; Smith, 1989; Williams, 1968). Furthermore, the church's opinions became laws, and the costs to the individual and her or his family members were great. The person was denied a Christian burial and instead was buried at a crossroads, impaled by a stake, and/or suffered numerous other indignities. In addition, the person's belongings and property were confiscated by the state. These legal punishments for suicide persisted well into the eighteenth and even nineteenth centuries (Colt, 1991; Dublin, 1963; Fedden, 1938; Humphry & Wickett, 1990; Marzen et al., 1985; Pretzel, 1977; Rosen, 1975; Smith, 1989; Williams, 1968). Yet, juries found that the presence of a physical illness or belief that the person who died was "insane" made a suicide not punishable (Colt, 1991; Kushner, 1989; Rosen, 1975; Valente, 1984; Williams, 1968). Kushner (1989) suggested that this policy of treating the body of a person considered insane with respect led to the belief that suicide was the result of mental illness (see also Colt, 1991; see the section, Suicide and the Sciences later in this chapter).

St. Thomas Aquinas, centuries later, set forth his own ideas about suicide (see Beauchamp & Perlin, 1978, pp. 102–105 and 111–121). Like Augustine, Aquinas saw suicide as breaking the Sixth Commandment, but he went even further. Aquinas held that because suicide left no time for repentance, it was the worst of all sins (Battin, 1994f; Dublin, 1963; Humphry & Wickett, 1990). He believed suicide was contrary to the natural law (struggling to maintain life is normal), moral law (suicide injures others in the community), and divine law (only God has the right to take life) (R. L. Barry, 1994; Battin, 1994f; Cavan, 1928; Choron, 1972; Colt, 1991; Fedden, 1938; Heyd & Bloch, 1981; Humphry & Wickett, 1990; Marzen et al., 1985; Smith, 1989; Williams, 1968).

Kushner (1989; see also Marzen et al., 1985; Williams, 1968) described the views of suicide in the United States. He noted that in the early years the attitudes in America paralleled those in Europe, especially England. For example, he quoted a sermon made by Increase Mather in 1682 in which the reverend stated "self-murder is the worst kind of murder. [A person] cannot disgrace himself [or herself] more than by committing such a sin" (p. 15).

Yet, even with the strong church opposition to suicide, which apparently did reduce the overall number of suicides, there reportedly were still were "epidemics of suicide." Specifically mentioned were those resulting from infection with deadly diseases, such as the plague or Black Death (Choron, 1972; Dublin, 1963; Fedden, 1938).

Thus, "in a few centuries [suicide] had gone from being a passport to paradise to being the shortest route to hell" (Colt, 1991, p. 158). Colt also remarked that "an act that had been a rational end to the Greeks, an honorable end to the Romans, and a means to heaven to the early Christians was now damned by God and despised by man" (p. 160; see also Heyd & Bloch, 1981; Humphry & Wickett, 1990).

THE RENAISSANCE BRINGS CHANGE

Beginning in the fourteenth century and continuing through the eighteenth century, attitudes toward suicide changed and opinion began to move away from the condemnation of suicide (Choron, 1972; Colt, 1991; Dublin, 1963; Humphry & Wickett, 1990; Marzen et al., 1985). In fact, there was a movement back toward the views of the Greeks and Romans in that suicide was, in some circles, seen not as a sin but rather as an acceptable option (R. L. Barry, 1994; Battin, 1994g; Cavan, 1928; Fedden, 1938; Humphry & Wickett, 1990; Pretzel, 1977). Sir Thomas More's *Utopia*, published in 1516, exemplified this shift in opinion. He wrote of a society in which if someone had an incurable disease and was suffering, priests and government officials would visit the individual and would, if the person voluntarily agreed, provide the person with the means to die (Battin, 1982; Choron, 1972; Colt, 1991; Fedden, 1938; Humphry & Wickett, 1990).

John Donne wrote one of the most important early responses to the church's prohibitions on suicide—*Biathanatos: A Declaration of that Paradoxe or Thesis that Self-homicide is not so naturally Sin that it may never be otherwise. Wherein the nature, and the extent of all these Lawes, which seem to be violated by this Act are diligently surveyed*—published posthumously in 1644 (R. L. Barry, 1994; Battin, 1994f, 1994g; Choron, 1972; Colt, 1991; Dublin, 1963; Fedden, 1938; Humphry & Wickett, 1990; Marzen et al., 1985; Williams, 1968; Winslow, 1840; see also Alvarez, 1971). Donne took issue with the idea that suicide was the worst of all sins and, in the end, he concluded that suicide was neither a violation of the law nor of reason.

One of the most far-reaching actions in the eighteenth century was the publication of David Hume's essay "Of Suicide" (R. L. Barry, 1994; Battin, 1994f, 1994g; Choron, 1972; Colt, 1991; Dublin, 1963; Fedden, 1938; Marzen et al., 1985; Williams, 1968; see also Alvarez, 1971). He wrote, "when life has become a burden, both courage and prudence should engage us to rid ourselves at once of existence" (quoted in Humphry & Wickett, 1990, p. 9). He also systematically addressed the points raised by Aquinas (see also Beauchamp & Perlin, 1978, pp. 105–121), specifically stating that

1. *If God is omnipotent and governs the world down to the minutest detail, then the act of suicide must also be seen as conforming to [God's] laws and will, and not as an encroachment upon [God's] power. And if suicide is a disturbance of the natural order of the universe, so must be any act of saving life from natural destruction, and this is absurd.*

2. *Suicide does no harm to society because death absolves [a person] from all his [or her] social duties which are reciprocal and binding only as long as the individual benefits from society. Indeed, sometimes an act of suicide may reduce the burden borne by society and hence be even laudable.*

3. *Suicide is not necessarily against the agent's interests. Misery, sickness, and misfortune can make life not worth living. The fact that people commit suicide despite the "natural horror of death" proves that in some cases it is not unnatural. (Heyd & Bloch, 1981, p. 192)*

Hume further provided a different interpretation of the Sixth Commandment—thou shall not kill—from that given by the Church. Hume contended that it only referred to murder (Battin, 1994f; Dublin, 1963).

Meanwhile, in France, several thinkers questioned prevailing attitudes about suicide. Montaigne, Montisquieu, Voltaire, and Rousseau led the way in viewing suicide as an acceptable and even merciful act when a person was suffering (R. L. Barry, 1994; Choron, 1972; Colt, 1991; Dublin, 1963; Fedden, 1938; Marzen et al., 1985; Rosen, 1975; Williams, 1968). Voltaire called for the repeal of laws that allowed the body of a person who had suicided to be degraded (Dublin, 1963).

Over time the laws in Europe were changed (Fedden, 1938). In 1770, the government in Geneva officially abolished negative actions toward the body and property of a person who died by suicide. In 1870 the government in France forbade discrimination in burial, but by that time the public had already become more forgiving of suicides—between 1700 and 1789 there were only 18 times that negative action was taken against a person who suicided (Humphry & Wickett, 1990). In 1824, England's Parliament lessened the strictures set forth centuries before: a person who suicided could be buried in a churchyard, but only between 9:00 p.m. and midnight (Humphry & Wickett, 1990).

In opposition to the above movement, Kant held that life must be preserved at all costs (Battin, 1994g; Choron, 1972; Dublin, 1963; Marzen et al., 1985; for a response to Kant's arguments see Battin, 1982; Engelhardt, 1989). Goethe's views followed from Kant's for the most part; however, he granted that suicide was at times permissible (Dublin, 1963). Although some state that Schopenhauer has incorrectly been cited as a supporter of suicide (e.g., Choron, 1972; Dublin, 1963; Pretzel, 1977), Cavan (1928) related that Schopenhauer said:

We have to hear, accordingly, that suicide is the greatest cowardice, that it is only possible in madness, and similar twaddle, or even the entirely senseless phrase that suicide is "wrong," whereas obviously no one has a greater right over anything in the world than over his [or her] own person and life. (p. 23; see also Choron, 1972; Fedden, 1938)

Nietzsche provided many examples of his affirmative view toward suicide; for example: "The thought of suicide is a strong consolation: it helps to get over many a bad night" and "Prevention of Suicide: There is a justice according to which we take a [person's] life, but there is none whatsoever when we deprive him [or her] of dying: this is only cruelty" (quoted in Choron, 1972, p. 134; see also Battin, 1994g). He also was an early advocate of the idea that people could "die at the right time" (quoted in Choron, 1972, p. 134).

Overall, it appears as if the move toward re-viewing suicide as an acceptable option was fueled, at least in part, by a renewed acceptance of individualism and individual rationality (Cavan, 1928; Humphry & Wickett, 1990). This new view led to a repeal of the laws punishing suicide, so that suicide was no longer a sin nor a crime (Cavan, 1928). Cavan summed up the changes in the view of suicide to this point in history:

> The dependence of suicide upon attitudes regarding it is clear. When death was re-garded as a natural event leading on to a desirable phase of life, as it was regarded in pagan Greece and Rome, suicide was easily justified. The Christian attitude that life belongs to a superhuman power and that death may lead to suffering made suicide repulsive and almost nonexistent. The individualism of the Renaissance again placed the right to die in the hands of the individual. (p. 24)

SUICIDE AND THE SCIENCES

The nineteenth century brought a new way of viewing suicide (Allen, 1977; Battin, 1994g; Colt, 1991; Dublin, 1963; Fedden, 1938; Kushner, 1989; Mayo, 1986; Rosen, 1975; Szasz, 1986). In essence, the change appears to have been from viewing suicide in theological, moral, philosophical, and legal terms to see-ing suicide as a social, medical, psychological, and statistical problem. An off-shoot was the removal of responsibility from the person who suicided (Szasz, 1986). Colt (1991) said that "although Enlightenment writers had fought to estab-lish the right to suicide as a moral, rational act, the argument in the nineteenth century was not whether suicide was moral but whether suicide could *ever* be rational" (p. 187, emphasis original).

Rosen (1975) noted that the link between suicide and mental illness actually predated 1800, quoting from the book *A Treatise on Madness* that was written by Battie and published in 1758, and also citing a book by Auenbrugger published in 1783 in which the author saw suicide as a result of mental illness. Colt (1991) mentions that in 1763 Merian said that people who suicided were "deranged." Rosen also cited examples of published works in the early 1800s in which suicide was seen as a form of insanity. And Kushner (1989) quoted William Blackstone, an English jurist, as stating in 1809 that "the very act of suicide is evidence of insanity" (p. 27; see also Colt, 1991, p. 179). Kushner also said that "by the 1830s melancholy [depression] and suicide, no longer religious or legal issues, had become almost exclusively the concern of medical men. . . . This transformation of consciousness signalled the medicalization of suicide that had emerged unchallenged by the 1840s" (p. 34). Colt (1991) described numerous unortho-dox treatments practiced by these medical professionals to "cure" the suicidal person.

Esquirol wrote *Mental Maladies: A Treatise on Insanity* in 1838 and he devoted more than 50 pages to suicide and its relationship to insanity. His treatment of the relationship prompted Dublin (1963) to state that "in spite of necessary crudities due to the state of knowledge at the time, the point of attack is along strictly modern lines" (p. 130). Rosen (1975; see also Colt, 1991) stated that Esquirol's position was different from other writers of his time because he saw suicide as a symptom of mental illness but not a mental illness in and of itself. In essence, as Colt (1991) noted "A suicide was a lunatic until proven rational" (p. 187).

Winslow's *The Anatomy of Suicide* (1840) provides an example of how medical professionals of this era viewed suicide. He discarded the idea that suicide can be a rational act by saying that suicide occurs in someone in a "depraved state of mind" (p. 31). He appealed to the idea of self-preservation being a basic law of nature and then cited several of his contemporaries' views on the subject, all of whom insisted that suicide is the result of insanity. For example, a Dr. Rowley reportedly said,

> *As no rational being will voluntarily give himself pain, or deprive himself of life, . . . it follows that every one who commits suicide is indubitably* non compos mentis, *not able to reason justly, but is under the influence of false images of the mind; and therefore suicide* should ever be considered an act of insanity. *(p. 222, emphasis original)*

Winslow even noted that no objective evidence of effects on the brain is necessary to prove that the person who suicided is insane (see also Kushner's [1989, p. 49] discussion of Isaac Ray's views):

> *Insanity results from a disease of the brain. Although after death, in many cases, no appreciable structural lesion can be detected in the structural mass, it would be illogical for us to conclude that the sentient organ has not been physically affected. (pp. 227–228)*

Furthermore, there need not even be subjective evidence prior to the suicide that the person was mentally ill: "In forming an estimate of the presence of derangement in cases of suicide, . . . we must not hastily conclude, because insanity is not *self-evident*, that it does not exist" (p. 231, emphasis original). Later he reinforced this point by saying, "it is important to remember that *the attempt at self-destruction is OFTEN the FIRST distinct overt act of insanity*" (p. 235, emphasis original; see also p. 336). Yet he then made the puzzling comment that if a person makes an unsuccessful attempt at suicide and regrets her or his actions, then it can be concluded that the person was sane when the suicide was attempted or that the person was insane during the attempt but became sane immediately afterward (p. 235). In the end, however, he summed up his overall view by stating, "It is a safe doctrine always to presume the presence of insanity in those who have exhibited a desire to commit suicide" (p. 237).

Kushner (1989) said that the first volume of the *American Journal of Insanity*, published in 1844, contained many articles using a disease model to explain the link between depression and suicide. In detailing attitudes toward suicide in the United States Kushner states, "The transformation of suicide from a crime to a disease coincided with the growth of institutional psychiatry in antebellum America" (p. 37).

Some exceptions to the predominant view that suicide was a result of insanity have been discovered, although these apparently were few and far between (Humphry & Wickett, 1990). Kushner (1989) said that "In the 1840s a few physicians argued that although suicide generally was connected to insanity, sane suicides were also possible" and he provided quotes from an 1847 article authored by an anonymous physician (p. 45). Rosen (1975) provided a example of a study conducted by Brierre de Boismont and published in 1856, in which, "On the basis of a detailed analysis [the author] denied that all suicides are due to insanity, even though a large number are caused by mental illness" (p. 25; see also Choron, 1972; Colt, 1991). Kushner noted that a reviewer of this book in the *American Journal of Insanity* "admitted that 'there are occasionally circumstances in life in which suicide, without ceasing to be reprehensible and culpable in a moral sense, can, however, be readily accounted for by a state of mind far removed from insanity'" (p. 46). Griesinger, a German physician, wrote in 1867 that

In fact, whatever certain scientific authorities may assert, we are not warranted in coming to the conclusion that suicide is always a symptom or a result of insanity. There is no insanity present where the feeling of disgust with life is in exact relation to the actual circumstances; where evident moral causes exist which sufficiently account for the act; where the resolution has been deliberately made, and might have been abandoned had the circumstances changed; and in which we discover no other symptoms of mental derangement. (p. 253)

In the 1870s John Gray stated that "in the large proportion of cases, if not the majority, [suicide] is committed by sane people" (quoted in Kushner, 1989, p. 50).

Dublin (1963) discussed Durkheim's 1897 book *Le Suicide*, which examined suicide from a sociological point of view. Durkheim concluded that "suicide is a normal, not an abnormal reaction. Since it is always present, it must be expected" (Dublin, 1963, p. 133; see also Alvarez, 1971; Choron, 1972; Colt, 1991; Kushner, 1989; Maris, 1992a).

Morgan (1979) summed up the influence of the end of the nineteenth century with the following:

Our present day understanding of suicide appears to have polarized into two divergent approaches, arising out of development of thought in the nineteenth century when sociologists such as Emil Durkheim emphasized the importance of environment, yet at the same time the concept of mental illness as a disease with neuropathological correlates became elaborated. On the one hand, we have the statisticosocial search for causative situational factors and, on the other, a medicopsychiatric concern with factors in the individual, particularly the role of mental illness. (p. 7; see also Kushner, 1989; Rosen, 1975)

In the early twentieth century, there were some individuals who broke from their peers and viewed suicide as something other than a result of mental illness. For example, in 1919 Alfred Hoche wrote of "balance-sheet suicide" in which a person could weigh the pros and cons of living and decide that death was preferable to continued life (Choron, 1972; Colt, 1991; Humphry & Wickett, 1990; Portwood,

1978). Portwood (1978) claims that in balance-sheet suicides "health entries, both physical and mental would come first . . . family and friends might come next, and economic factors after that" (p. 37).

Cavan (1928) asserted that suicide results from both "sociological and psychological causes" (p. 9). She later noted that "not all suicides [are] psychotic" and explained that "the discussion of the relation of insanity to suicide is . . . to present current views of psychiatrists . . ." (p. 112). On the basis of a study that she conducted, she concluded that less than 20% of the people who suicided in Chicago in 1923 were insane at the time of the act. She then said that "the insane group probably contributes more than its proportion to the suicide list, but cannot be held accountable for all the suicides" (p. 113). After summarizing the studies on the coexistence of "insanity" and suicide, she concluded that "in spite of some contradiction, the preponderance of evidence available at present indicates that the majority of actual suicides probably cannot be traced to insanity . . ." (p. 115).

In her following chapter, "Suicide Among Normal People," Cavan (1928) began by explaining:

There has been all too great a tendency to explain suicide as the result of a diseased mind. Studies made of psychotic people who have attempted or committed suicide show (1) that a large group of suicides are not insane, and (2) that even among the insane and the psychopathic the suicide is usually precipitated by some real or imagined crisis. (p. 141)

However, views such as those by Hoche and Cavan were apparently rare in the early twentieth century, as psychoanalysis was beginning to take root. Heyd and Bloch (1981) asserted that "the development of psychiatry and clinical psychology in general and psychoanalysis in particular contributed to the process of 'demoralization' of contemporary attitudes to suicide even to a greater extent than sociology and epidemiology have done" (p. 193). Furthermore,

After Freud's exploration of the unconscious, it was no longer possible to attribute suicide to simple causes such as poverty, loss of a job, or disappointment in love. The act of suicide was instead understood to be the end result of a complex variety of forces, conscious and unconscious. (Colt, 1991, p. 201; see also Litman, 1976)

Specifically, Sigmund Freud said,

Probably no one finds the mental energy required to kill himself [or herself] unless, in the first place, in doing so he [or she] is at the same time killing an object with whom he [or she] has identified himself [or herself] and, in the second place, is turning against himself [or herself] a death-wish which had been directed against someone else. (quoted in Valente, 1984, p. 10; p. 161; see also Alvarez, 1971; Choron, 1972; Colt, 1991; Dublin, 1963; Fedden, 1938; Kushner, 1989; Litman, 1976; Maris, 1992a; Morgan, 1979; Valente, 1984)

Other leading psychoanalysts (e.g., Zilboorg, Menninger) followed Freud's original lead regarding aggression turned against oneself, although Freud later modified his view by postulating the "death instinct" (Choron, 1972; Fedden, 1938; Heyd & Bloch, 1981; Jackson, 1957; Litman, 1976). For example, Menninger believed that there were "three main components to suicide: the wish to kill, the wish to be killed, and the wish to die" (Allen, 1977, p. 11; see also Alvarez, 1971; Choron, 1972; Colt, 1991; Jackson, 1957; Kushner, 1989; Maris, 1992a; Marzen et al., 1985; Morgan, 1979; Portwood, 1978). Later analysts apparently built upon the belief that early loss was crucial to the development of suicidal impulses (Adam, 1990; Alvarez, 1971; Kushner, 1989). It is worthwhile noting that Freud reportedly died from an injection of morphine he requested from his physician (Colt, 1991; Humphry & Wickett, 1990; Litman, 1992; Quill, 1994; Siegel, 1982b; Yarnell & Battin, 1988).

The view that suicide can be traced solely to internal causes—primarily due to irrationality or mental illness—had become so widely accepted that by the 1950s neuropsychiatrists believed that "depression and resultant suicidal behavior have an exclusively organic etiology" (Kushner, 1989, p. 82, emphasis original). The focus of recent work has been on neurotransmitters in the brain, especially serotonin (Colt, 1991; Kushner, 1989).

Growing out of the focus on internal (and increasingly biological) mechanisms for suicidality is the view by current mental health professionals of seeing "suicide as a manifestation of emotional illness. Rarely does he [or she] view it in a context other than that of psychiatry" (quoted in Szasz, 1976, p. 163; see also R. L. Barry, 1994). Szasz (1976) asserted that the pervasiveness of this belief is such that "it is difficult to find [a] 'responsible' medical or psychiatric authority today [who] does not regard suicide as a medical, and specifically as a mental health, problem" (p. 163). He went on to provide numerous quotations to reinforce his assertion and he attempted to show that a similar view had also been embraced by the legal system.

Similar changes have occurred in the theological arena as well. Colt (1991) described a symposium at a meeting of the American Association of Suicidology in the 1980s in which a priest stated that "I don't think anybody who is perfectly normal will commit suicide" and that "even with terminally ill suicides, deep down you'll find disturbance in makeup of personality" (p. 198; see also R. L. Barry, 1994). Colt noted that the statements in this symposium provided a glimpse of how the theological discussion of suicide has changed over the years so that "in the twentieth century suicide has been seen not as a moral, ethical, or theological issue but almost entirely as a medical-psychological problem" (p. 198; see also Valente, 1984). In other words, the effect of the theorizing about the underlying causes of suicide led to a shift so that "treating has replaced preaching!" (Heyd and Bloch, 1981, p. 193).

Heyd and Bloch (1981) went on to say that

Like many other phenomena in our culture (madness is a good example) suicide has undergone a deep process of medicalization. This process has . . . significant ethical implications, and it is by no means universally agreed that the medicalization of suicide has created a more enlightened and humane moral approach. (p. 193; see also Szasz, 1976)

Perhaps in reaction to this medicalization of suicide, writers in recent years have stated that suicidal behavior is complex and cannot be clearly defined, described, or understood by a single theory of causation; although, as will be described later, there are several formulations that assert the primacy of a particular cause. Generally speaking, four or five large domains have been identified as combining to influence suicidal ideation and behavior. Different authors use different terms but the most comprehensive formulation may be Blumenthal and Kupfer's (1986).

Blumenthal and Kupfer (1986; Blumenthal, 1990; Vaillant & Blumenthal, 1990) have identified five overlapping areas that they argue contribute to the presence of suicidal thoughts and behavior in different people. First is the psychosocial milieu, which includes life events, environmental factors, and medical illnesses and places special emphasis on the interpersonal support system. Second is biological vulnerability, which is tied to developmental changes across the lifespan and includes recent research involving serotonin levels. The third, or psychiatric area, includes diagnoses that have become associated with suicidal behavior—affective disorders, conduct disorders, schizophrenia, and organic mental disorders. The next area is personality, which is linked intimately with the previous three domains. The authors specifically note hostility, impulsivity, and depression as crucial facets of personality related to suicide. Finally, there is family history and genetics that the authors note needs more research to determine fully its impact. One last note is that substance use is an important variable that cuts across several of the domains. (see also Maris, Berman, & Maltsberger, 1992; Stillion & McDowell, 1991).

In addition to the multidimensional model proposed above, there have been several singular views of the etiology of suicide presented in the literature. Shneidman (1987, 1992a; see also Battin, 1994g; Bongar, 1991) provided a brief overview of many major approaches including literary and personal document, philosophical and theological, demographic, sociocultural, sociological, dyadic and family, psychodynamic, psychological, psychiatric or mental illness, constitutional and genetic, biological and biochemical, legal and ethical, preventional, systems theory, and political. Obviously, many of these approaches have been incorporated into more comprehensive models such as Blumenthal and Kupfer's (1986).

Shneidman's influential approach falls within the psychological category. According to Shneidman (1992a), the fundamental aspects of all suicides include

a sense of unbearable psychological pain . . . *traumatizing* self *denigration . . . a marked* constriction *of the mind and an unrealistic narrowing of life's actions . . . a sense of* isolation . . . *an overwhelmingly desperate feeling of* hopelessness . . . *a conscious decision that* egression—*leaving, exiting, or stopping life—is the* only *(or at least the best possible) solution to the problem of unbearable pain. (pp. 51–52, emphasis original)*

He also said that "it is undeniable that all persons—100 percent—who commit suicide are perturbed and experiencing unbearable psychological pain" (1992b, p. 889; see also 1993, p. 148). Finally, of direct relevance to this book, he stated that mental health workers "are well advised to minimize, if not totally disregard, the probably well-intentioned but shrill writings in this field which naively speak of an individual's 'right to commit suicide' . . ." (1981, p. 347).

CONCLUSION

The purpose of this chapter has been to provide a brief overview of how the attitudes toward suicide have changed over the years and, consequently, how current views of suicide were developed. A quotation from one of the books cited previously illustrates the reason this chapter needed to be included before presenting the rest of the text. Winslow (1840) wrote,

> *No inferences deduced from the consideration of the suicides of antiquity can be logically applied to modern instances. . . . Our notions of death, of honour, and of courage, are, in many respects, so dissimilar from those which the ancients entertained, that the subject of suicide is placed entirely on a different basis. (p. 2)*

Attitudes have shifted again and, for a variety of reasons, today's world is much closer to the ancients in our attitudes about suicide than to when Winslow was practicing (see also Battin, 1982, 1992).

3

Arguments Against Rational Suicide

The goal of this chapter is to provide an overview of some of the common arguments against rational suicide that have been offered in the mental health literature. The biases and traditional beliefs of some therapists will be implicit within the arguments, which will be grouped herein as based on religious beliefs, mental health issues, and societal concerns. After relating different traditional positions, responses to these arguments will be discussed (for more detailed arguments see R. L. Barry, 1994; for more detailed replies see Battin, 1982). The offering of responses is not meant to imply that the arguments do not contain valid points, but merely to show that suicide need not necessarily be viewed as immoral, irrational, or antisocial.

RELIGION-BASED ARGUMENTS

As noted in chapter 2, religion-based arguments serve as the foundation upon which the current suicide prevention and intervention culture is built. Because many mental health professionals have spiritual beliefs, the ideas that life is sacred, that one's life belongs to a higher power, that suicide is a sin, and other religion-based tenets serve as reasons for arguing against the possibility that suicide could be a rational choice (Baelz, 1980; R. L. Barry, 1994; Battin, 1994f; Colt, 1991; deCatanzaro, 1981; Drinan, 1977; Early, 1992; Fedden, 1938; Hauerwas, 1981; Maguire, 1975; McIntosh, 1993a; Moskop & Engelhardt, 1979; Rauscher, 1981).

An obvious response to religion-based arguments, particularly those attached to a particular denomination, is that they have no bearing on people who hold to a different belief system (Battin, 1994f; Engelhardt, 1989; Engelhardt & Malloy, 1982; Fedden, 1938; Humphry, 1987; Lebacqz & Engelhardt, 1977; Moskop & Engelhardt, 1979; Williams, 1968). Thus, because of the diversity of opinions about the views, desires, and even existence of a higher power, it is inappropriate and unwise to try to use religion-based views as arguments that suicide is *always* wrong for *everyone*. R. L. Barry (1994) conceded to this point when he stated, "were the state after suicide simply and certainly annihilation . . . then the dictates of religion concerning suicide would be irrelevant" (p. 196).

The view that the Sixth Commandment prohibits suicide is controversial (see also Baelz, 1980). Hook (1927) discarded the debate by saying that since there is nothing specific in the Bible regarding suicide the point could be, and has been, argued either way and therefore the issue is moot. Fletcher (1977) contended that it is absurd to apply this commandment to suicide but not to other acts such as self-defense or self-sacrifice:

> *You may end your neighbor's life for your own sake but you may not do it for his [or her] sake! And you may end you own life for your neighbor's sake, as in the act of sacrificial heroism, but you may not end your life for your own sake. (p. 357; see also Barrington, 1980; Battin, 1994f; Lebacqz & Engelhardt, 1977)*

In addition, exceptions appear to have been made for capital punishment and killing in wars (Amchin et al., 1990; Baelz, 1980; Battin, 1982, 1994f; Colt, 1991; Maguire, 1975). Battin (1994f) pointed out:

> *In recent years a committee for the New York Presbytery has concluded that the Bible does not prohibit suicide; rather, "it is clear that for some Christians, as a last resort in the gravest of situations, suicide may be the act of their Christian conscience." (p. 213)*

Another religion-based argument against allowing suicide is that one should not interfere with a "natural death" by hastening it through suicide (Baelz, 1980; R. L. Barry, 1994; Battin, 1982, 1994f; Colt, 1991; Early, 1992; Fedden, 1938; Lebacqz & Engelhardt, 1977; Maguire, 1975; Rauscher, 1981). However, several have argued that if one should not hasten death by killing oneself, then one also should not take action to lengthen one's life such as through taking medicine or having an operation and, similarly, if suffering is good then anesthesia should be withheld (Baelz, 1980; Battin, 1994f; Colt, 1991; Moskop & Engelhardt, 1979).

A related contention is that suicide is a cowardly act or an easy way out of the suffering that life entails and that one is required to endure (Baelz, 1980; R. L. Barry, 1994; Battin, 1982, 1994f; Colt, 1991; Early, 1992; Fedden, 1938; Lebacqz & Engelhardt, 1977; Maguire, 1975; Rauscher, 1981). In regard to suffering, Rauscher (1981) said,

> *[suicide] does not allow for any working of the power of redemptive suffering in the life of the individual, his or her friends, or his or her family. And, if there be such a thing as rational suicide, it is by far the most selfish and the most arrogant for the very reason that it does not (cannot?) rationally consider the Christian teaching of redemptive suffering for others. (p. 102, emphasis original)*

Several authors have questioned the view that suffering is honorable and necessary (B. Barry, 1984; Battin, 1994f; Colt, 1991; Fedden, 1938; Hook, 1927; Kohl,

1975; Maguire, 1975; Williams, 1968). First, as mentioned previously, this argument would not pertain to those with different beliefs about suffering. Second, many authors note that most people do not choose suicide at the first sign of suffering but, rather, after they can stand no more pain (Humphry, 1987; see also Cappon, 1962). Third, it is argued that just because life inherently involves pain does not mean that any level of pain must be endured indefinitely. (R. L. Barry [1994] even mentioned that Pope Pius XII said that at times suffering could be "evil" [p. 262].) Further, many authors question the idea that a higher power would require people to endure agony and prohibit taking action to alleviate the pain (Baelz, 1980; B. Barry, 1989; Fletcher, 1977; Humphry, 1987; Kjervik, 1984; Maguire, 1975; Moskop & Engelhardt, 1979). Finally, Battin (1994f) asserted that the view that suffering was valuable would lead, logically, to the imposition of suffering on others.

In conclusion, although arguments against rational suicide based on religious beliefs are pertinent, the important fact is that they are relevant only to particular people. This is especially important in today's diverse and multicultural society where the counselor will frequently be working with clients who have different backgrounds, beliefs, and values. Those who adhere to different value systems should not have their choices restricted because of the spiritual beliefs of their counselors.

MENTAL HEALTH-BASED ARGUMENTS

In chapter 2 it was shown that only around the end of the eighteenth century was suicide viewed as either a mental illness in and of itself or a manifestation of a mental illness. After reviewing this development, Szasz (1976) asked, "What was discovered in the nineteenth century that required removing suicide from the category of sin or crime and placing it into that of illness?" (p. 164). He then answered, "Nothing. Suicide was not *discovered* to be a disease, it was *declared* to be one" (p. 164, emphasis original). It may be argued that this declaration is still biasing investigators and clinicians.

The Presence of Mental Illness

There are many interrelated concerns about rational suicide that are based on the view that suicide results from one or more types of mental disturbances. The chief argument that suicide is the result of mental illness comes from studies that report approximately 80% of all suicides are related to depression and/or alcoholism and that over 90% of all people who suicided had a psychiatric disorder when they killed themselves (Adam, 1990; R. L. Barry, 1994; Black & Winokur, 1990; Blumenthal, 1990; Bongar, 1991; Buda & Tsuang, 1990; Clark, 1992; Dublin, 1963; Heyd & Bloch, 1981; Leonard, 1967; Maris, 1992b; Marzen et al., 1985; Morgan, 1979; Tanney, 1992; Winokur & Black, 1992; Winslow, 1840). These findings have led to suicide being viewed solely, and perhaps even necessarily, as the result of a psychological disturbance, which therefore leads directly to an absolutist intervention view (Ahia & Martin, 1993; Amchin et al., 1990; Battin, 1982;

Black & Winokur, 1990; Callahan, 1994; Clark, 1992; Greenberg, 1974; Harris, 1994; Heyd & Bloch, 1981; Lester, 1969; Maris, 1981; Martin, 1980; Mayo, 1986; Murphy, 1973; Murphy & Robins, 1968; Ringel, 1980; Siegel, 1982b; Szasz, 1976; Victoroff, 1983; Widiger & Rinaldi, 1983; Yarnell & Battin, 1988). For example, Black and Winokur (1990) in their review of the literature state that "few suicides occurred in persons judged not mentally ill, suggesting that the 'rational' suicide is uncommon" (p. 136).

However, these data may be misleading, for even accepting the data as reported, the studies have shown that from 3 to 12% of people who have killed themselves had no mental illness (Black & Winokur, 1990; Clark & Horton-Deutsch, 1992) and others (e.g., Maris, 1981; Meerloo, 1962; Patel, 1973) report on studies in which greater than 25% of the respective samples of suicide completers did not have a mental disorder and could be considered rational. For example, after studying suicide notes, Tuckman, Kleiner, and Lavell (1959) stated that they "were impressed with the possibility that in a number of cases the suicide could have resulted from a conscious, 'rational' decision reached by weighing the pros and cons of continuing to live . . ." (p. 62; see also Jacobs & Teicher, 1967).

Furthermore, some studies suggest the data linking suicide and mental illness may be oversimplified. Tanney (1992) noted that dramatic differences appear when studies of the association between mental illness and suicide are broken down into general population surveys and hospital surveys. He reported that, on the average, only 38% of completed suicides in the general population had a known history of mental disorder while, on the average, over 80% of people who suicided in hospital-based surveys had a psychiatric disorder or history of care. Similarly, Temoche, Pugh, and MacMahon (1964) reported that all the highest estimates (47%–94%) of the percentage of suicides who had displayed prior evidence of mental illness occur in studies that were done *after* the suicide had occurred; in studies dependent upon objective criteria prior to the suicide, estimates were much lower (5%–22%).

There are other reasons to question the strength of the relationship between mental illness and suicide. For example, it has been noted that psychological autopsy studies of suicides (where investigators work backward from the death to try to identify causal factors), which provide much support for the presence of psychopathology, are flawed because the people being interviewed about the death are not blind to the cause of death (Choron, 1972; Cotton, 1993; Leonard, 1967; see also Temoche et al., 1964; see Clark & Horton-Deutsch [1992] and Tanney [1992] for additional points and responses to criticisms). This is crucial for several reasons. The widespread assumption that suicide is a result of mental illness may influence what the interviewee tells the interviewer and/or what she or he focuses on as she or he tries to make sense in her or his own mind why the suicide occurred (Choron, 1972; Tanney, 1992). As Nisbett and Ross (1980) noted, "people tend to seek out, recall, and interpret evidence in a manner that sustains beliefs" (p. 192) and therefore, as Wortman and Silver (1989) stated, "the interpretation of data tends to be strongly biased by the expectations researchers, clinicians, and laypersons may hold" (p. 355). It should be noted that this bias affects both interviewee and interviewer (Kobler & Stotland, 1964; Leonard, 1967; Lester, 1969; Lowenthal, 1976; Maris, 1981; Siegel, 1982b; Temoche et al., 1964). In regard to clinical situations, it is worth highlighting that most mental health professionals are indoctrinated into seeing and/or assuming pathology (Ennis & Litwack, 1974; Garmezy, 1982; Siegel, 1982b), especially with a suicidal client. Thus, the same social psychological factors, which may lead to self-fulfilling prophecies about links between mental illness and suicide, that are operating on researchers are also present with clinicians (Ennis & Litwack, 1974; Leonard, 1967; Lester, 1969; Lowenthal, 1976; Temoche et al., 1964).

Tanney (1992) questioned the strength of the link between mental illness and suicide in another, though related, way. He said that if the cause of death is uncertain and the person has a history of a mental disorder, the pressure of the prevailing professional opinion may lead to a declaration that the person had suicided. This result would inflate the statistical link between suicide and mental illness, which would make it more likely that the next uncertain death by someone with a mental disorder would be classified as a suicide and so the cycle feeds on itself.

It would be pointless and circular to argue that the psychological turmoil generated in deciding about suicide is mental disorder, and that this mental disorder is itself one of the factors that at some earlier time led to the very consideration of the suicide option. It is even less appropriate to use the observation of mental disorganization near the time of suicide to infer that mental disorder has contributed to the decision for death. (p. 304, reprinted with permission; see also Amchin et al., 1990; Shneidman, Farberow, & Litman, 1961; Widiger & Rinaldi, 1983)

Many authors (Amchin et al., 1990; Battin, 1982; Choron, 1972; Moskop & Engelhardt, 1979; Tanney, 1992; Widiger & Rinaldi, 1983) note the obvious fact that just because someone who has a mental disorder suicides does not mean that the mental illness was related to the cause of death—the old correlation does not prove causation argument; and, conversely, just because someone suicides does not mean the person had a mental illness. On the basis of his examination of the issue, Tanney (1992) concluded that "the diagnosis of a mental disorder is not a sufficient explanation for suicidal behavior" (p. 309). Similarly, several authors (Amchin et al., 1990; Battin, 1982; Choron, 1972; Dublin, 1963; Maris, 1981, 1986, 1992a; Moskop & Engelhardt, 1979; Pohlmeier, 1985; Pokorny, 1968; Shneidman, 1987, 1993) have emphasized that not all people who suicide have a mental disorder, even if the data presented above was accepted at face value. Illustrating this point, investigators from the Los Angeles Suicide Prevention Center have examined over 700 suicide notes from the standpoint of the reasoning, judgment, and logic expressed in the notes and found that "A large minority of suicides, usually older persons in physical pain, are logical and rational and not psychotic" (Shneidman et al., 1961, p. 13; see also Leenaars, 1992; Shneidman & Farberow, 1976; Tuckman et al., 1959; see Jacobs & Teicher [1967] for a discussion of rationality in the suicide notes of adolescents).

Szasz (1976), of course, went even further and asserted that mental disorders are irrelevant and that all forms of coercive suicide prevention and intervention are wrong. Finally, others (e.g., Battin, 1982, 1994f; Choron, 1972; deCatanzaro, 1981; Maris, 1981; Pokorny, 1968; Siegel, 1982b) point out that in some societies suicide is seen as socially acceptable (e.g., with the Eskimos; Humphry & Wickett, 1990) or even required in certain situations (e.g., for samurai in Japan; Iga & Tatai, 1975), which makes it difficult to consider these suicides due to mental illness.

Depression and Suicide

Moving from mental disorders in general to specific diagnoses, in the following discussion only concerns related to depression will be mentioned, although research has shown that other conditions such as alcohol and other substance abuse or dependence and schizophrenia are also statistically linked to suicide (e.g., Black & Winokur, 1990; Blumenthal, 1990; Bongar, 1991; Buda & Tsuang, 1990; Farberow, Shneidman, & Leonard, 1976a; Flavin, Franklin, & Frances, 1990; Lester, 1992; Tanney, 1992) as are certain personality disorders or traits (Blumenthal, 1990; Goldsmith, Fyer, & Frances, 1990). The link between depression and suicide is so dominant and explicit that suicidal thoughts, plans, and/or attempts are a criterion for Major Depressive Disorder (American Psychiatric Association, 1994) and numerous authors report that a large percentage, perhaps as many as two-thirds, of people who suicide were clinically depressed at the time of death (R. L. Barry, 1994; Black & Winokur, 1990; Blumenthal, 1990; Bongar, 1991; Buda & Tsuang, 1990; Choron, 1972; Clark, 1992; Cotton, 1993; Maltsberger, 1994; Maris, 1992b; Marzen et al., 1985; Marzuk, 1994; Morgan, 1979; Tanney, 1992).

One of the primary reasons professionals argue that rational suicide is not possible is because suicidal people are depressed and therefore their cognitive functioning is impaired. Of specific concern is that depression may lead to "tunnel vision" or an inability to see available options (Bongar, 1991; Brandt, 1975; Clum, 1987; Erard, 1994; Hendin, 1982; Maris, 1992b; Marzen et al., 1985; McIntosh, 1993a; Richman, 1988, 1992; Siegel, 1982a, 1982b, 1986; Snipe, 1988). This relates to Beck and his colleagues' work on hopelessness (Weishaar & Beck, 1990, 1992). Finally, some mental health professionals (e.g., Rogers & Britton, 1994; Snipe, 1988) go so far as to state that a suicidal client, whom the counselor will probably view as depressed, may appear competent, but the therapist should not believe such competence exists.

Several concerns have been raised about the apparent tie between depression and suicide. First and foremost, the link between suicide and depression and certain other psychiatric conditions may be exaggerated somewhat because suicide-related behaviors are part of the criteria for these conditions (Maltsberger, 1994; Tanney, 1992; Widiger & Rinaldi, 1983). Such reasoning is circular, which leads to the idea that at least part of the association is an "artifact of definition." This may harken back to the comparatively recent view that mental illness, specifically depression, is linked to suicide (Szasz, 1976; Tanney, 1992). Other authors have noted that the data presented still show that there is a large percentage of people who suicide who are not depressed (Kobler & Stotland, 1964; Leonard, 1967; Pokorny, 1968).

Furthermore, in regard to psychological autopsy findings that a large majority of people were reportedly depressed, one should not be surprised that many people appear distraught immediately prior to killing themselves (Tanney, 1992; Widiger & Rinaldi, 1983). This state of being is not necessarily the same as a clinical depression; the lack of differentiation between the presence of depressive symptoms or syndromes and the presence of depressive mental disorders is problematic (Greenberg, 1974; Kobler & Stotland, 1964; Maltsberger, 1994; Tanney, 1992; Widiger & Rinaldi, 1983).

Physical Illness and Suicide

Just as there is a statistical link between mental illness and suicide, there is also a link between physical illness, especially terminal or chronic illness, and suicide. Estimates are that up to 40–50% of all people who suicide have a significant physical illness, with the illness believed to be a significant factor in roughly 25% of all suicides; this is especially true for painful illnesses such as AIDS, particular forms of cancer, epilepsy, some gastrointestinal problems, and certain musculo-skeletal disorders (Blumenthal, 1990; Bongar, 1991; Cavan, 1928; Dorpat, Anderson, & Ripley, 1968; Farberow, Shneidman, & Leonard, 1976b; Leonard, 1967; Mackenzie & Popkin, 1990; Maris, 1981, 1992b; Marshall, Burnett, & Brasure, 1983; Marzen et al., 1985; Marzuk, 1994; Pokorny, 1968; Saunders & Valente, 1988; Vaillant & Blumenthal, 1990; Whitlock, 1986).

However, the majority of authors in the mental health field disregard, downplay, or otherwise ignore the possibility that physical illness may be important in and of itself in the suicidal ideation and/or completed suicides of many people. Specifically, several state that most people with physical illness could be diagnosed with depression, the implication being that 'therefore, they are irrational in their suicidality' (R. L. Barry, 1994; Blumenthal, 1990; Brown, Henteleff, Barakat, & Rowe, 1986; Callahan, 1994; Clark, 1992; Colt, 1991; Dorpat et al, 1968; Farberow et al., 1976b; Mackenzie & Popkin, 1990; Marzen et al., 1985; Marzuk, 1994; McCartney, 1978; Morgan, 1979; Saunders & Valente, 1988; Siegel, 1982a, 1986; Siegel & Tuckel, 1984; Whitlock, 1986). Mackenzie and Popkin (1990) even state that, at most, only 5% of all suicides could be considered rational because of the link between suicidal thoughts and depression even among terminally ill people. Yet, Mackenzie and Popkin (1990) conclude by stating that

> *little research on the psychiatric histories of persons who commit suicide in relationship to medical illness has been conducted. The literature describes some suicides as having a positive neuropsychiatric history, often alcoholism, but these studies are a minority. Some patients who suicide are noted to be demanding and difficult when confronted with a medical illness. Apparently few have made prior suicide attempts. How many have had full-blown depressive episodes well in advance of their medical illness or have a positive family history of suicide or affective disorder is unknown. (p. 227)*

These conclusions regarding the research are interesting for several reasons. Most importantly, the authors repeatedly admit that the literature documenting a strong relationship between terminal illness and mental disorders prior to the physical illness is scant (see also Quill, 1994). Thus, the notion that terminally ill people who are suicidal are mentally ill is subject to all the criticisms cited previously (see also Huyse & van Tilburg, 1993). One additional point that is striking is the mention that those who suicided were demanding when faced with their illness (see also Farberow et al., 1976b). Perhaps these individuals may have had a greater need for control over their lives and perhaps their attempts at asserting themselves or trying to regain some semblance of control were viewed negatively by staff who did not like their routine disrupted (see also Angell, 1982). Seeing this trait of being demanding as evidence of a desire for control would tie in with the view that suicide can be the final act of control and choice (Humphry, 1987; Motto, 1972; Victoroff, 1983). In any event, just being demanding is not evidence of a mental illness (see also Widiger & Rinaldi, 1983).

Mackenzie and Popkin (1990) also made the observation that, in regard to the relation between physical illness and suicide, "for some clinicians, death related to nonadherence to a medical regimen is considered suicide; for others, lethal non-compliance must be accompanied by symptoms of depression to be judged suicide" (p. 220). Similarly, Hendin (1982) said, "The person facing imminent death who is in intractable pain and arranges to end his life may be a suicide in the dictionary definition of the term, but not in the psychological sense" (p. 215). In regard to this state of affairs, Tanney (1992) says that "if suicide is defined as a life-ending event occurring only during a state of mental disorder ('all suicides are insane [or depressed]'), any appraisal of the contribution of mental disorders to assessing and predicting suicide becomes frivolous" (p. 304; see also Green & Irish, 1971). Marzuk (1994) noted that many of the signs of depression overlap with symptoms of physical illness, which obviously has the potential for depression to be overdiagnosed. Quill (1994) asserted that the suggestion that a choice to die by a person who is terminally ill is the result of unrecognized mental illness is "absurd and infuriating to those who have spent time at the bedsides of dying patients who are suffering severely with no good choices" (p. 317). He continued by saying that the fact that some individuals who want to die have distorted judgment "argue[s] for a careful, open exploration rather than a blanket prohibition" (p. 317). Similarly, Jackson (1957) stated nearly 40 years ago that "it is possible that the victim of a painful, crippling illness, for example, is mentally healthy rather than masochistic in arranging [her or] his own demise. We need to know more about so-called 'rational' suicide" (p. 19). In an attempt to learn more, Jones and Dilley (1993) surveyed 39 persons infected with HIV concerning their opinions about rational suicide. They reported that 67% of their sample had considered rational suicide and that suicidality and depression, as measured by the Beck Depression Inventory, were not directly related.

There is also the view that suicide is not appropriate because of the availability of hospice care and better pain-management techniques (R. L. Barry, 1994; McIntosh, 1993a). A reason related to this point is that suicide is wrong because, even in the face of what is today a painful, incurable, terminal illness, one never knows what discovery will be made tomorrow (Amchin et al., 1990; Battin, 1982; Colt, 1991; Drinan, 1977; Erard, 1994; Lebacqz & Engelhardt, 1977; Maguire, 1975; Yarnell & Battin, 1988).

Although it is true that hospice care can be helpful to some people, others may decide that they do not want to linger on (Humphry, 1987; Quill, 1991, 1994; see also Barrington, 1980), and hospice care is not always available (Humphry & Wickett, 1990). It is true that there have been remarkable advances in pain control; however, few physicians would claim that all pain can be controlled, especially without negative side effects (e.g., Quill, Cassel, & Meier, 1992; see also Mesler, 1995). Further, pain is not the only condition that leads to the perception of an unacceptably low quality of life (Battin, 1982, 1994e; Humphry & Wickett, 1990; Mesler, 1995; Quill, 1991, 1994; Rees, 1972). In addition, some authors have stated that optimism in the form of 'a cure may be found tomorrow' comes across as Pollyannaish or as a reliance upon miracles and condemns the person to suffer indefinitely while others hang on to what could be considered to be irrational hope (Amchin et al., 1990; Battin, 1982; Hook, 1927; Maguire, 1975; Slater, 1976; Yarnell & Battin, 1988). Others have noted that people often make important decisions in the absence of complete knowledge about the future (Brandt, 1975; Lebacqz & Engelhardt, 1977; Mayo, 1983, 1986; Soll, 1979). Hook (1927) pointed out that by saying a person should hold out hope for a better existence, the advocate "concedes the main point at issue, since it is tacitly admitted that it is not the sacredness of life but the hope of attaining a certain order of life which should determine the specific recommendation" (p. 180).

Cappon (1962) studied the attitudes of four different groups (nonpatients, psychiatric patients, somatic patients, and dying patients) and found that the length of the dying process and the amount of pain involved were important factors for a large number of respondents from all groups and that the dying patients were most supportive of euthanasia. Also, the more physically sick the person the less willing she or he was to part with life in exchange for avoiding pain, which leads to the inference that those dying individuals who are wanting to die must be truly suffering. As an interesting side note to the above discussion, Cappon (1962) noted that "the amount of education received by the subject increased the (imagined) pain threshold in the intact subject; but this relationship was reversed in the presence of somatic illness or death" (p. 695). This indicates that those most likely to be doing the evaluations of the person in pain are least likely to be sympathetic to the degree of pain the person is experiencing—which could then increase the amount of suffering the person is forced to endure (Cassell, 1982; see also Slater, 1976; Smith, 1989).

Other Mental Health Arguments

It is often stated as a fact that people who are suicidal are ambivalent (Baelz, 1980; R. L. Barry, 1994; Battin, 1982; Clum, 1987; Erard, 1994; Green & Irish, 1971; Hendin, 1982; Hoff, 1989; Knuth, 1979; Leonard, 1967; Maris, 1986; Martin, 1980; Marzen et al., 1985; McIntosh, 1993a; Motto, 1972, 1981; Nelson, 1984; Shneidman, 1981, 1992a; Shneidman et al., 1961; Siegel, 1982a, 1982b, 1986; Snipe, 1988). That is, they want to die and they want to live, both at the same time. This is seen as related to the irreversibility of the decision to kill themselves. The question is whether they would choose suicide at another point in time. In fact, the mere presence of the suicidal person in the office of a therapist is viewed as evidence of ambivalence. The line of thinking appears to be 'Since this person is in my office talking about suicide he or she obviously is ambivalent and therefore wants to be talked out of it or prevented from doing it.' In a double-bind manner, Snipe (1988) stated that the absence of ambivalence is also a sign that the person needs help. The issue of ambivalence is related to viewing suicidal ideation or attempts as a cry for help or request for support and intervention (Amchin et al., 1990; Battin, 1982; Dublin, 1963; Erard, 1994; Farberow & Shneidman, 1961; Kobler & Stotland, 1964; Marzen et al., 1985).

However, the suicidal person in the therapist's office may have a need to have another person evaluate the rationality of the plan, not a need to be prevented from acting on the plan (B. Barry, 1984; Battin, 1982, 1992; Brandt, 1975; Cotton, 1993; Maguire, 1975; Portwood, 1978; Roy, 1988; Werth, 1994a; for other arguments related to the inappropriateness of using ambivalence as a reason to prevent suicide see Martin, 1980 and Widiger & Rinaldi, 1983). Similarly, although she was arguing against rational suicide, Snipe (1988) wondered if there could be times in which it would be appropriate to help a rationally suicidal person "work through ambivalent feelings about her or his decision to suicide, say his or her good-byes, and prepare for death" (p. 135). B. Barry (1984) contended that "counselors who choose to equate helping the suicidal individual with preventing suicide would have nothing to offer [those who are looking for an objective listener]. This could be a real disservice" (p. 18).

In sum, to quote Shneidman (1987, p. 160): "the plethora of studies relating suicide to psychiatric disorders . . . look formidable, almost overwhelming, until one steps back from them and views them in a broader perspective." Similarly, viewing the suicidality of those with terminal illnesses through "psychiatric lenses" will prevent seeing any rational reasoning.

SOCIETAL-BASED ARGUMENTS

Impact on Significant Others

Since few people are completely without social ties, other individuals often suffer a loss when someone suicides. The argument goes that although the dead person's pain is ended, the pain and perhaps a legacy of guilt, blame, and shame are left for others to bear (Baelz, 1980; B. Barry, 1984; R. L. Barry, 1994; Battin, 1982; Dyck, 1977; Fedden, 1938; Greenberg, 1974; Holmes, 1987; Hook, 1927; Lebacqz & Engelhardt, 1977; Leonard, 1967; Mather, 1987; Mayo, 1983; McIntosh, 1993a; Rauscher, 1981; Werth, 1992, 1994a, 1995). Thus, the suicide may make rational sense to the person but it leaves an irrational burden for the survivors. Further, the survivors may now have a role model for how to act when faced with adversity (see, e.g., Silverman, Range, & Overholser, 1994). In sum, "a rational person would not want to inflict such agony on people who care for her or him; thus, someone who wants to commit suicide is not rational" (Werth, 1994a, p. 10).

This argument does bear some weight. However, it is not a deterrent for those who do not have close ties to anyone else (Hook, 1927; Lebacqz & Engelhardt, 1977; Moskop & Engelhardt, 1979; Williams, 1968). In addition, one could argue that if a person should not kill herself or himself because it hurts others, then suicide would be obligatory if it helped others (Amchin et al., 1990; Baelz, 1980; Battin, 1982, 1994g; Lebacqz & Engelhardt, 1977). Some question delaying the inevitable (death) at the cost of the continued suffering of the person who is considering suicide (Brandt, 1975; Cantor, 1973; Greenberg, 1974; Moskop & Engelhardt, 1979; Williams, 1968).

Furthermore, the argument is predicated on the assumption that the death will cause the survivors pain; however, this is not necessarily the case (Battin, 1982; Cantor, 1973; Fedden, 1938; Greenberg, 1974; Kjervik, 1984; Lester, 1977; Maguire, 1975; Ness & Pfeffer, 1990; Shepherd & Barraclough, 1974; Werth, 1992). For example, Shepherd and Barraclough (1974) in their survey of spouses of people who suicided found that "outcome was evenly divided between better and worse" and they concluded that "the greater the burden the greater the relief in being released from it and the greater the energy to invest in the future" (p. 602). A corollary to this, which makes intuitive sense and follows from case reports of rational suicides, would be that better outcome for survivors might follow if the person who suicided made a rational choice, given her or his life circumstances (see also Kjervik, 1984; Shanfield, Benjamin, & Swain, 1984). Finally, the negative effects on survivors may be caused, primarily, by the negative view of suicide in society and if the views of suicide were changed then the effects on survivors would not be as bad (Battin, 1982; Portwood, 1978).

Impact on Society

Some claim that when an individual suicides society loses the skills and knowledge the individual possessed (Amchin et al., 1990; Baelz, 1980; R. L. Barry, 1994; Battin, 1982; Fedden, 1938; McIntosh, 1993a). This argument appears to relate to the idea that individuals have an obligation to society. One response to this argument is that not everyone who suicides has anything left to offer society and, in fact, may provide some benefit to society by dying (Baelz, 1980; Battin, 1982; Colt, 1991; deCatanzaro, 1981; Fedden, 1938; Greenberg, 1974; Hook, 1927; Kjervik, 1984; Williams, 1968; see also the discussion of Hume's views in the previous chapter). An example of this is the Eskimo who directly suicides or allows himself or herself to be abandoned when he or she cannot contribute to the family's welfare (Battin, 1994f). Another reply is that, according to the political tradition of the United States, the state is subordinate to individuals (Baelz, 1980; Engelhardt & Malloy, 1982; Moskop & Engelhardt, 1979; Sullivan, 1980) so people do not need to continue living for the sake of the state.

Another concern is that if suicide were seen as permissible, then some individuals—especially the old and/or the disabled—might feel pressured or obligated or might be manipulated by others into suiciding (Barrington, 1980; R. L. Barry, 1994; Battin, 1994e; Erard, 1994; Finnerty, 1987; Francis, 1980; Gill, 1992; Humphry & Wickett, 1990; Maguire, 1975; McIntosh, 1993a; Moore, 1993; "Public Actions," 1992). Often this issue is discussed in terms of older adults because of ageism—the devaluing of the older adult (Barrington, 1980; Clark, 1992; Colt, 1991; Hendin, 1982; McIntosh, 1993a; Moore, 1993; Richman, 1988, 1992; Ringel, 1980; see Bromberg & Cassel [1983] for a different view). There is concern that decisions about the acceptability for suicide might hinge on economic scales, especially regarding medical resources (Battin, 1982, 1994c, 1994d; McIntosh, 1993a; "Public Actions," 1992; Siegel, 1986; Yarnell & Battin, 1988). This leads to the fear that suicide may become viewed as an obligation, especially if one believes that her or his illness is putting a heavy emotional and financial burden on family members—then she or he may feel that suicide is necessary to save her or his family (Battin, 1982; Colt, 1991; Siegel, 1982a, 1982b).

The issue of manipulated or obligated suicide is intimately related to the primary social argument against allowing suicide, which is called the "wedge" or "slippery slope." In essence, the view is that if suicide is permitted under some circumstances, this will open the door to allowing suicide under many other conditions (R. L. Barry, 1994; Battin, 1982, 1994c, 1994d; Colt, 1991; Dyck, 1977; Humphry & Wickett, 1990; Lebacqz & Engelhardt, 1977; Leo, 1994; Maguire, 1975; Mayo, 1983; McIntosh, 1993a; Smith, 1989; Werth, 1994a). Following this argument, it will be difficult to draw a line between who is and who is not allowed to suicide. For example, the idea of suicide in the face of terminal illness might be expanded to chronic but not life-threatening illness; or disability might in and of itself become an acceptable reason to suicide. Then it might extend to people who are not considered competent to make decisions for themselves, so people who are profoundly mentally retarded or severely and persistently mentally ill would then be encouraged to suicide or have their death more directly assisted. Siegel (1986) extends the slope in another way (for a related view see B. Barry, 1989, p. 189). She said that if suicide became acceptable the "the means for successfully completing suicide would inevitably become much more readily obtainable. As a result many tragic deaths might occur among individuals for whom the suicidal urge was transitory and irrational" (p. 411).

Weber (1988; see also R. L. Barry, 1994; Marzen et al., 1985) argued the slippery slope would occur if the right to die was legalized because the courts would not be able to restrict this right to solely, for example, the terminally ill. Battin (1988, p. 192; see also Battin, 1994d) dismantled this claim and stated that court cases have pointed to the "state's compelling interest in the preservation of life . . . but the state's interest recedes as the medical likelihood of recovery becomes increasingly small, and one's right to die emerges from this eclipse." She said Weber's mistake "is in conceiving of the right to die as an *absolute* right, overridable in no way. Were this the case, it would indeed spread as he fears. But this is not the case" (p. 193, emphasis original).

There are two ways to respond to the slippery slope argument (Battin, 1994d; Engelhardt, 1989; Lebacqz & Engelhardt, 1977; Mayo, 1983). First, one can attack the empirical claim that such a slope—"a continuum of cases between which it is difficult to draw clear moral lines"—does indeed exist (Mayo, 1983, p. 339). Second, one could show that whatever slope might exist will not necessarily lead to an inability to set limits. Engelhardt said that Nazi Germany is held up as an example of what could happen in this area (most authors reference Alexander, 1949). However, he countered this by citing the fact that until 1973 Texas did not forbid either suicide or aiding suicide and that there is not evidence of Texas having an inordinate number of suicides or murders (see also Engelhardt & Malloy, 1982). Maguire (1975) pointed out that if Nazi Germany was to be used as a slippery slope argument in the case of euthanasia (and suicide) then it should also be used to argue against war in general, sterilization, using humans in medical experiments, and killing in self-defense. Others counter the comparison to Nazi Germany by stating that the different motivations behind the actions of the Nazis and of the people currently advocating for "death with dignity" make the analogy inappropriate (Battin, 1994c; Colt, 1991; Humphry & Wickett, 1990; Kohl, 1975; Maguire, 1975; Yarnell & Battin, 1988; for the opposite view see Dyck, 1977). Maguire (1975) added that "the fact that something can be abused does not mean that it should not be used" (p. 137; see also Smith, 1989).

Engelhardt (1989) proceeded to turn the argument around by saying that "if one worried about slippery slopes, perhaps one should worry about policies that would forbid voluntary euthanasia and rational suicide because of a concern for the sanctity of life" because this may lead to policies that "presume that the state has the power to impose by force particular views of the good life and good death on the unconsenting innocent" (p. 266; for a related view related to aging see Barrington, 1980). He also mentioned that the Netherlands has allowed euthanasia in certain circumstances and "significant abuses and untoward consequences are hard to document" (p. 273; see also Battin, 1994c; Colt, 1991; see R. L. Barry [1994] for the opposite view). He concluded that the experience in both Texas and the Netherlands should help show "that widespread horrors will not occur if the rights of competent individuals are respected with regard to suicide, assisting suicide and voluntary euthanasia" (p. 275). In other words, killing—oneself or others—is not "contagious" (Kohl, 1975).

In documenting other responses to the slippery slope argument, Mayo (1983) said that those who claim that the slope is so slippery that tragedy is inevitable may actually "*facilitate* the slide down the slope" since there is no attempt to delineate boundary lines (p. 342, emphasis original). Mayo concluded by stating that the difficulty related to drawing lines around suicide and euthanasia points out the "importance of avoiding the kind of taboo mentality which the slippery slope argument feeds by insisting we cannot, and therefore must not, act on policies which require the drawing of fine moral lines" (p. 343; see also Cotton, 1993).

Thus, although concerns about rational suicide based on fears of how suicide may impact significant others and potentially society as a whole are strong, they are not completely convincing nor completely unanswerable. There are ways to take such concerns into account and work around them so that the person who is suffering is not disregarded and forgotten.

CONCLUSION

Several writers have conceded the possibility of rational suicide (especially in the case of a painful terminal illness), although they claim the numbers of individuals for whom suicide could be rational or who actually do suicide are small—even negligible (Brandt, 1975; Callahan, 1994; Clark, 1992; Hendin, 1982; Marzen et al., 1985; Ringel, 1980; Siegel, 1982a, 1982b, 1986). Thus, they seem to imply that counselors should not worry about the issue of rational suicide. Yet, in apparent response to these contentions, Rangell (1988), when talking about the issue of "rational or voluntary suicide," said that "although it may occupy a small percentage and an atypical segment of the total suicide problem, [it] must be worked through theoretically, as clinical and life situations become more complex" (p. 42; see also Jackson, 1957; Widiger & Rinaldi, 1983). Similarly, Quill (1994) noted that "we cannot possibly address a problem that we don't even acknowledge exists" (p. 320). Furthermore, other authors note that, actually, it is difficult to determine the number of suicides that could be considered rational (Choron, 1972; Jones & Dilley, 1993; Marzuk, 1994; Morgan, 1979; Pohlmeier, 1985; Portwood, 1978; Quill, 1994). However, even if the estimate of 3 to 12% of the people who suicide are mentally healthy (Black & Winokur, 1990; Clark & Horton-Deutsch, 1992) is accepted, this amounts to a substantial number of people who may be being treated as if they were mentally ill for no reason other than the fact that they considered suiciding.

4

Research on Mental Health Professionals' Attitudes

Chapter 3 outlined many of the common arguments against rational suicide that are present in the mental health literature. These arguments are often imbedded within the current general belief systems surrounding suicide. Reading only this literature would lead one to conclude that virtually all mental health professionals believe that suicide has its foundation in one or more mental illnesses and, therefore, is an irrational act. Although, as was noted earlier, some authors have questioned these assumptions, arguments, and conclusions regarding suicide, the predominant view is that suicide should be prevented, forcibly if necessary. Thus, logically, suicide prevention has been incorporated into therapists' legal and ethical standards of care.

However, digging a little deeper leads to some interesting findings. Surveying the front-line service providers allows a shockingly different view to become amazingly clear: Rational suicide is accepted and acceptable to a majority of respondents and a substantial minority have worked with rationally suicidal clients. The goals of the current chapter are to review the literature on recent empirical studies of attitudes toward suicide and to discuss in depth two recent surveys that call into question the presently articulated party line that requires suicide prevention in all cases.

ACCEPTANCE OF SUICIDE

Pope, Tabachnick, and Keith-Speigel (1987, 1988) surveyed psychologists about a large number of ethical issues. Two of their questions are of direct relevance here. When asked about the acceptability of breaking confidentiality if a client is suicidal, 57.5% of the respondents stated that this was "unquestionably" ethical (Pope et al., 1987) and 45.6% stated that it was a "good" practice (Pope et al., 1988). In response to a question about accepting a client's decision to suicide, 48% stated that this was "poor" practice (Pope et al., 1988) and 45.2% said it was "unquestionably not" ethical (Pope et al., 1987). In the older article Pope and his colleagues reported that 73.9% of the respondents said that they had "never" accepted a client's decision to suicide. In discussing these specific pieces of data the authors state,

> *Whether to accept a client's decision to commit suicide is likewise a difficult and painful dilemma for many psychologists. . . . Only about one in five of the respondents has accepted, either rarely (16.4%) or more frequently (4.1%), a client's decision to kill himself or herself. Almost half (45.2%) believe it to be unethical. An additional 36.6% believe it to be unethical under most circumstances. (Pope et al., 1987, p. 1003)*

Although these authors downplay the size of the numbers demonstrating support for rational suicide, their findings are significant. More than 20% of the respondents indicated that they had "accepted" a client's decision to suicide. This figure is far from negligible and points out that the literature cited in chapter 3 may underestimate the prevalence of rational suicide and the amount of experience counselors have with clients who are rationally suicidal. Also, over half of the respondents believed that it is sometimes ethical to accept a client's decision to suicide.

Swain and Domino (1985) found that the largest factor in their analysis of the attitudes of seven types of mental health professionals about suicide was "acceptability, which involves the theme that suicide is an acceptable and sometimes preferable act, particularly suicide in response to old age, disease, or enduring problems of living" (p. 459). Later, Domino and Swain (1986) investigated the relationship between attitudes toward suicide and recognition of suicide lethality. They found that respondents who recognized more "signs of suicide tend to perceive suicide as acceptable and as a reaction to a harsh world and external circumstances rather than as a manipulative ploy or as a self-destructive drive" (p. 306).

In an earlier study, Gurrister and Kane (1978) examined the attitudes of therapists at a community mental health center. During their in-depth interviews, the participants provided evidence of some dissonance concerning their roles when working with suicidal clients. On one hand, a majority stated that they would try to prevent clients from deciding to suicide, yet a large number also conceded that they believed terminal illness was an acceptable reason to decide to suicide. Gurrister and Kane summarized these attitudes by stating, "almost all therapists believed they would always make an effort to help the [client] decide against suicide, yet a growing recognition that suicide could be a reasonable, viable alternative was also present" (p. 12).

Similarly, Hammond (1991) found that the majority of her psychologist, psychiatrist, and oncologist respondents believed that people have a right to die and that there can be rational suicides. Yet the participants also stated that they would do virtually anything to deter a client considering suicide from dying. Hammond found that terminal illness was significantly more acceptable to the respondents than chronic physical illness and both were significantly more acceptable reasons for considering suicide than chronic psychiatric illness. The majority of the respondents believed suicide to be wrong not because of moral or religious reasons but because of its effects on the survivors. Finally, although most respondents said that they did not feel a significant amount of personal responsibility for attempted or completed suicides by clients, they did feel more culpable for such suicides than for those by family members or friends.

RECENT EMPIRICAL RESEARCH

At this point, two of the studies that provide some of the evidence for the overall focus of this book—that many mental health professionals appear to believe that suicide can be rational at times and that criteria for assessing rationality can be delineated (the second half of this statement will be reviewed in the next chapter)—will be introduced more formally. However, since this book is not intended to read as a research study and is not intended solely for an academic audience, the specific statistical analyses and results of the different studies will not be discussed in depth. Tables will be used periodically to display numbers that will be useful in comparisons between the two investigations. Readers interested in the exact results of the analyses are encouraged to review the original sources.

Psychotherapists' Attitudes

Procedure. The first study involved a survey of 400 members of the Division of Psychotherapy of the American Psychological Association (Werth & Liddle, 1994—hereinafter Psychotherapy Study). Participants were mailed a questionnaire that contained a vignette describing a middle-aged suicidal man. The vignettes were identical except that they varied in terms of the circumstances precipitating the suicidal ideation: bankruptcy, chronic endogenous depression ("psychological pain"), a painful nerve condition ("physical pain"), and terminal bone cancer. This study was a refinement over previous research in that the psychological pain condition was defined better and there was not an ambiguous "ideation for reasons unspecified" condition operating as a pseudo-control. The scenarios also varied by whether or not the man described was assumed to be a client of the participant. Below is the vignette for a man with terminal bone cancer who is a client of the participant:

> *Carl, a 45 year old factory worker who is currently a client of yours, has been suffering from severe physical pain related to malignant bone cancer. Despite having received a wide variety of therapies, the cancer is spreading. Carl feels that both you and his physicians have already done all you can, and he has no hope that his symptoms will be reduced. Carl is currently experiencing a great deal of pain and is very upset over the fact that his condition is draining the emotional and financial resources of his family and friends. Carl feels that the quality of his life now is very poor and will only get worse, and he fears that he will be an increasingly large burden to his loved ones. Despite protests from his family and friends, Carl has decided to kill himself.*

Participants then filled out the Suicide Semantic Differential Scale (SSDS; Droogas et al., 1982), which is designed to assess acceptance of suicidal ideators.

This instrument has 10 items (e.g., brave/cowardly, wise/foolish, unselfish/selfish) that are rated on seven-point Likert scales. Higher scores indicate more negative reactions. Reliability estimates (Werth & Liddle, 1994; Werth, 1994b) for this instrument are above .90. Following the SSDS were two evaluative questions, which also used seven-point scales, the first designed to assess acceptance for the decision to suicide ("Acceptance") and the second focusing on the amount of action that would be taken to prevent the suicide ("Action"). On these items, higher scores meant less acceptance and more action. Participants were also asked demographic items.

Results. In the Psychotherapy Study the 186 respondents (a 50.5% usable response rate, taking into account undeliverable questionnaires and responses that were unusable due to missing data) were not unevenly spread across the eight different types of scenarios. Statistical analyses revealed that there was not an interaction between precipitating circumstance and client status, nor was the client status variable significant. However, the precipitating circumstances variable was significant for all three dependent variables (SSDS, Acceptance, Action). The results are summarized in Table 4.1.

Table 4.1 shows that on the SSDS, the terminal cancer condition had scores significantly lower (indicating more acceptance) than any of the other three conditions. Physical and psychological pain did not differ from each other, but both had significantly lower scores than the bankruptcy condition. This pattern is mirrored in the results of the single Acceptance question. On the Action question a different hierarchy emerged. Again the terminal condition had significantly lower scores (indicating less action would be taken to prevent the suicide) than the other three conditions but this time the physical pain condition had significantly lower scores than both the psychological pain and bankruptcy conditions, which did not differ significantly.

There were two other significant results in the Psychotherapy Study, based on an analysis of the possible effects of demographic characteristics (see Table 4.2). First, respondents who had been in practice for more than 30 years had signifi-

Table 4.1 Means and standard deviations for condition

Condition	SSDS		Acceptance		Action	
	M	SD	M	SD	M	SD
Terminal	30.37[a]	10.73	2.63[a]	1.72	3.41[a]	1.80
Physical	38.12[b]	9.77	4.23[b]	1.67	4.86[b]	1.91
Psychological	42.23[b]	11.33	4.93[b]	1.77	5.86[c]	1.62
Bankruptcy	51.94[c]	8.68	5.84[c]	1.48	6.52[c]	0.61

Source. From Werth & Liddle (1994, p. 444). Reprinted with permission.

Note. Column means with differently lettered superscripts indicate differences of at least $p < .05$. SSDS = Suicide Semantic Differential Scale, lower scores indicate more acceptance of suicide (range: 10–70). Acceptance = "How acceptable to you is Carl's decision to kill himself?" Lower scores indicate more acceptance (range: 1–7). Action = "How much action would you take to prevent Carl from killing himself?" Lower scores indicate less action should be taken (range: 1–7).

Table 4.2 Means and standard deviations for years in practice and belief in rational suicide

Group	SSDS M	SSDS SD	Acceptance M	Acceptance SD	Action M	Action SD
			Years in Practice			
0–15	43.11[a]	10.95	4.68[a]	1.94	5.35[a]	1.82
16–29	41.78[a]	11.75	4.49[a]	1.94	5.43[a]	1.66
30+	34.97[b]	16.37	3.76[b]	2.34	4.29[a]	2.51
			Belief in Rational Suicide			
Yes	39.16[a]	12.49	4.16[a]	2.02	5.05[a]	2.02
No	48.21[b]	11.70	5.50[b]	1.80	5.76[b]	1.48

Source. From Werth & Liddle (1994, p. 445). Reprinted with permission.

Note. Column means with differently lettered superscripts indicate differences of at least $p < .05$. SSDS = Suicide Semantic Differential Scale, lower scores indicate more acceptance of suicide (range: 10–70). Acceptance = "How acceptable to you is Carl's decision to kill himself?" Lower scores indicate more acceptance (range: 1–7). Action = "How much action would you take to prevent Carl from killing himself?" Lower scores indicate less action should be taken (range: 1–7).

cantly lower scores on both the SSDS and the Action question (but not on the Acceptance question) than respondents with fewer years of experience. It should be noted that the authors stated that, because of the large number of statistical tests performed on the demographic variables, this result may have been due to chance. Second, respondents who believed in rational suicide (146 individuals; 81%) scored significantly lower on all three variables than those who said they did not believe in rational suicide (34 respondents; 19%).

Health Service Providers in Psychology

Procedure. In a subsequent study Werth (1994b—hereinafter Register Survey) extended these results by examining additional suicidal ideator characteristics. This study will be described in more detail here since it has not previously been reported in the literature. This study involved 480 randomly selected members of the National Register of Health Service Providers in Psychology. Of the 480 packets mailed out, 30 were returned as undeliverable and 21 were returned blank by psychologists who did not wish to participate in the study. There were 215 usable surveys received, for a response rate of 48%.

The intent of the Register Survey was to replicate and extend the results of the Psychotherapy Study. Specifically, the focus was on how the presence of a stigmatized condition might affect ratings of action and acceptance. The author reasoned that before he could call for acceptance of rational suicide he needed to determine if this change would have a negative effect on some groups of people who might be suicidal. For example, he was concerned about the fact that, currently, the majority of persons with AIDS in the United States are members of disenfranchised groups (injectable drug users and/or men who have had sex with men) and therefore seen by some as undesirables (see, e.g., Herek, 1990; Herek & Glunt, 1988). Thus, it is possible that the acceptability of a suicide by a person with AIDS would be partially a function of the presumed demographics or habits and activities of the ideator (see also Beckerman, 1995; Rogers & Britton, 1994). In other words, some people who accept a suicide by a person with AIDS may be viewing it as one less undesirable in America rather than as the best option the person has given his or her medical, social, and/or personal condition. Consistent with this line of thinking, Martin and Range (1991; see also Range & Alliston, 1995) found that their participants considered a suicide by a man with AIDS as more acceptable than a suicide by a man with cancer *and* the students also viewed men with AIDS more negatively than men with cancer.

Recent reports (e.g., Herek, 1990; Herek & Glunt, 1988) have described persons with AIDS as being "stigmatized." Stigmatized individuals are members of social groups "about which others hold negative attitudes, stereotypes, and beliefs, or which, on average, receive disproportionately poor interpersonal and/or economic outcomes relative to members of the society at large due to discrimination against" them (Crocker & Major, 1989, p. 609).

Kelly and his colleagues have studied how members of several professional groups stigmatize persons with AIDS. They used a vignette that varied in terms of whether the person with whom the respondent would be interacting socially was diagnosed with either leukemia or AIDS and was either a heterosexual or gay man (Kelly, St. Lawrence, Smith, Hood, & Cook, 1987 [physicians]; Kelly et al., 1988 [nurses]; St. Lawrence, Kelly, Owen, Hogan, & Wilson, 1990 [psychologists]; see also, Crawford, Humfleet, Ribordy, Ho, & Vickers, 1991 [psychologists and social workers] and Fliszar, 1993 [psychologists-in-training]). The consistent findings have been that the man with AIDS was stigmatized more than the man with leukemia and that the gay man was perceived more negatively than the heterosexual man (however, St. Lawrence et al. [1990] did not find a significant difference in attitudes based on sexual orientation). Govin (1989) found that mental health service providers were more willing to counsel a heterosexual man who was not infected with HIV than each of three other men, who did not significantly differ from each other (an uninfected gay man, a heterosexual man who was infected with HIV, and a gay man who was infected with HIV). Hayes and Gelso (1993) found that male counselors experienced greater discomfort with an HIV-infected male client than with a noninfected male client, though they also found that male client sexual orientation did not affect counselor discomfort. Finally, an examination of mental health care providers' attitudes toward persons with AIDS found that "the general tone of responses [to questions about interacting professionally or personally with persons with AIDS] indicates reluctance at best and possibly even stronger negative feelings toward those with AIDS" (Knox, Dow, & Cotton, 1989, p. 288).

Numerous studies have examined mental health professionals' attitudes toward persons who are gay. Most recently, the American Psychological Association Committee on Lesbian and Gay Concerns (1991) found compelling evidence that gay men and lesbians are stigmatized by practicing psychologists (see also Graham, Rawlings,

Halpern, & Hermes, 1984). Cantor and Pilkington (1992) found similar results when examining how lesbian and gay graduate students were treated by faculty members. Rudolph (1988) reviewed the literature related to counseling gay and lesbian clients and concluded that many counselors hold negative attitudes and, further, that the AIDS crisis may be making attitudes even more negative (Rudolph, 1989).

The potential implications of these studies examining attitudes toward men with AIDS and men who are gay on mental health professionals' acceptance of suicide become clear when viewed in combination with the results of Martin and Range's (1991; see also Range & Alliston, 1995) study. Professionals hold significantly more negative attitudes toward men who are gay and men who have AIDS than toward heterosexual men and men who do not have AIDS. These skewed perceptions may impact the assessment of the rationality of a man with AIDS and/or a gay man who is considering suicide. In other words, the negative prejudices held toward gay men and men with AIDS may lead to a less stringent or less complete investigation of the rationality of a decision to suicide by a man who is a member of one or both of these groups.

In order to examine if the presence of one or more stigmatized conditions affected ratings of acceptance and/or action, the Register Survey employed a vignette format similar to that utilized in the Psychotherapy Study. The scenarios utilized were combinations of vignettes used by researchers examining suicide (Deluty, 1988, 1989; Hammond, 1991; Range & Martin, 1990; Werth & Liddle, 1994) and investigators of stigma (Kelly et al., 1987; Crawford et al., 1991). For each vignette the suicidal ideator was presented as either a gay or heterosexual man; whose ideation is caused by endogenous depression, terminal bone cancer, or AIDS; and whose decision to suicide is either supported or protested by his family and friends. The case of the man with terminal bone cancer who is gay and whose decision to suicide is not supported by his family and friends is presented here:

John, a 53 year old grocery store manager, is a client of yours. During your 26 sessions together you have learned that John is the second of three children. He has a close relationship with his older brother but a conflictual one with his younger sister. He described his family life in positive terms and said that he has always been close to his parents. After graduating from community college at the age of 24 John moved out of his parents' home and accepted a job with his present employer. He has not had any problems at his place of employment.

John has been suffering from severe physical pain related to terminal bone cancer, which he has been diagnosed with for nearly two years. Despite having received a wide variety of interventions (several types of experimental and traditional medical treatments and intensive psychotherapy with two highly qualified psychologists before he came to you), his physical and psychological conditions have been getting progressively worse over the past three years. John feels that both you and his physicians have already done all you can, and he has no hope that his symptoms will be reduced. Though you have not deemed him an imminent risk thus far, throughout your six months working together, John has repeatedly talked about death and the possibility of suicide.

John is currently experiencing a great deal of physical pain and is very upset over the fact that his condition is draining the emotional and financial resources of his family and friends; he is especially concerned about the impact his condition is having on Steven, his longstanding romantic partner. John feels that the quality of his life now is very poor and will only get worse and he fears that he will be an increasingly large burden on his loved ones and is worried that Steven could not handle this strain. John has discussed his concerns with Steven and his family and, despite protests from his family and friends, John has decided to kill himself.

The Register Survey used six scales to measure amount of acceptance (two scales), action (one scale), and stigma (three scales). The acceptance and action scales were the same as those used in the Psychotherapy Study (the SSDS, Acceptance, and Action scales). An open-ended question then asked why the respondent answered as she or he had on the Acceptance and Action questions: "How did you decide what numbers to circle on the scales in questions 2 and 3 on the previous page (i.e., What were the bases for your decisions)?" The results from this item will be covered in chapter 7.

Three scales were used in the Register Survey to examine the amount of stigma placed on the suicidal ideator. The Prejudicial Evaluation Scale (PES; Kelly et al., 1987) is a 12-item scale designed to assess attitudes toward the person in the vignette. Each item is rated on a seven-point Likert scale with bipolar ends (1 = *very strongly agree*; 7 = *very strongly disagree*). An example of an item is: "John is responsible for his illness." On the basis of reliability analyses using Cronbach's alpha conducted on the pilot data ($N = 46$), five items were added to the PES to improve its reliability (initially .37; with added items .69).

The Professional Contact Questionnaire (PCQ; Crawford et al., 1991) is a six-item scale designed to assess the degree of comfort the respondent would have in working with the person in the vignette in a counseling setting; for example, "I would accept John for treatment." Each item is rated on a seven-point Likert scale with bipolar ends (1 = *very strongly agree*; 7 = *very strongly disagree*). This scale's reliability was initially .46. To increase reliability, one item ("I would have strong personal reactions to John") was dropped before analyzing the data, leading to a revised alpha of .54—higher, but still indicating that the results (both significant and nonsignificant) on this scale need to be viewed with caution.

The Social Interaction Scale (SIS; Kelly et al., 1987) describes seven potential social interactions, such as working in the same office with the person in the vignette. Respondents indicate their willingness to interact with the person on a seven-point scale, with lower scores indicating more willingness to interact with the person. This scale had a Cronbach's alpha reliability coefficient of .88.

Two questions were aimed at assessing the respondent's beliefs in the concept of rational suicide (Werth & Cobia, 1995a; Werth & Liddle, 1994): "Do you believe in the idea of rational suicide? Why or why not?" "If you believe that suicide in some cases may be rational, please give your definition of a 'rational suicide.'" The results related to these questions will be discussed in detail in the next chapter.

Finally, several demographic questions were asked: gender, age, race/ethnicity, type of degree, theoretical orientation, membership in APA divisions, type of graduate training program attended, work setting, length of time in practice, state practicing in, religiosity, political orientation, experience with clients in John's condition, experience with clients of John's sexual orientation, work with suicidal ideators and attempters, number of completed client suicides of which they are aware, number of suicidal clients who would meet their own definition of rational suicide, personal consideration of suicide, and exposure to the topic of rational suicide.

Hypotheses. The Register Survey involved hypotheses that there would be significant differences on all the scales among the three precipitating conditions. It was believed that AIDS would be viewed as a significantly more acceptable reason to suicide (on the SSDS and Acceptance question), would demand significantly less action (as measured by the Action question), and would be stigmatized significantly more (on the PES, PCQ, and SIS) than both terminal bone cancer and chronic endogenous depression. It was also thought that terminal bone cancer would be significantly more acceptable, demand significantly less action, and be significantly less stigmatized than chronic endogenous depression. In regard to sexual orientation, it was thought that suicidal ideation by gay men would be significantly more acceptable and demand significantly less action than ideation by heterosexual men and that gay men would be stigmatized more than heterosexual men. For the social support variable, it was thought the decision to suicide by men whose ideation was supported by family and friends would be significantly more acceptable, demand significantly less action, and would lead to significantly less stigma than a choice by men whose decision was not supported by family and friends.

Results. Before discussing the results of the statistical analyses, several points related to the demographics of the respondents deserve attention. First, 86% of the participants who answered this question stated that they believed in the concept of rational suicide. Second, only four of the respondents to the question on ethnicity (165 individuals) were non-Caucasian. Third, respondents had a broad range of experience with clients who had a condition similar to the case with which they were presented in the vignette. As would be expected, respondents had much more experience with clients who were depressed than with clients who either had bone cancer or AIDS. Similarly, respondents had much more experience working with heterosexual men than self-identified gay men. Fourth, there was also a wide range of experience with clients who had considered or attempted suicide, with 29 respondents indicating they had seen "hundreds" of suicidal ideators and attempters. The range was more restricted in regard to experience with client suicide (only three respondents stated they had had nine or more clients suicide) and with suicidal clients the psychologists had worked with whom they considered rational. Of note, 20% of the respondents had seen at least one rationally suicidal client. Finally, nearly one-third of the respondents had either done reading or attended presentations on rational suicide.

Statistical analyses (a multivariate analysis of variance) indicated that the interaction between the three independent variables was not significant, nor were the two-way interactions (sexual orientation by social support, precipitating condition by social support, precipitating condition by sexual orientation). Main effects could therefore be evaluated. The main effect of condition was significant but neither the main effect for sexual orientation nor the main effect for social support was significant. In other words, only the precipitating condition was important enough to the respondents to differentiate among the suicidal men.

In regard to the precipitating condition, results will be mentioned for each of the six scales (see Table 4.3 for means and standard deviations). On the SSDS, AIDS and terminal bone cancer did not differ from each other but both had significantly lower scores (indicating more acceptance of the decision to suicide) than chronic, endogenous depression. On the Acceptance question, suicidal ideation acceptance scores in the AIDS and terminal bone cancer conditions did not differ significantly from each other. Both of these conditions had significantly lower scores (indicating more acceptance) than the depression condition. For the Action question, there were no significant differences between responses to the AIDS or terminal bone cancer vignettes, but each of these two conditions had significantly lower scores than the depression condition (i.e., respondents would take significantly less action to prevent a suicide in each of the first two cases than in the latter).

In contrast to the results described thus far, there were no differences among

Table 4.3 Means and standard deviations for condition

Condition	SSDS		Acceptance		Action	
	M	*SD*	*M*	*SD*	*M*	*SD*
Depression	47.56[a]	8.53	5.65[a]	1.53	6.30[a]	1.12
Cancer	32.95[b]	10.04	3.18[b]	1.65	4.65[b]	1.75
AIDS	32.24[b]	8.85	3.19[b]	1.52	4.26[b]	1.77

Condition	PES		PCQ		SIS	
	M	*SD*	*M*	*SD*	*M*	*SD*
Depression	35.27[a]	9.36	14.39[a]	4.39	16.56[a]	8.27
Cancer	34.43[a]	9.03	12.37[b]	4.62	11.97[b]	6.50
AIDS	35.34[a]	9.18	12.68[ab]	5.32	11.82[b]	6.42

Source. From Werth (1994b, pp. 39–40).

Note. Column means with differently lettered superscripts differ significantly from each other at the .05 level as determined by post-hoc comparisons using Tukey's Honestly Significant Difference Test or, for the comparison between Depression and AIDS on the SIS, a two-tailed t-test. SSDS = Suicide Semantic Differential Scale. Lower scores indicate more acceptance of suicide (range: 10–70). Acceptance = "How acceptable to you is John's decision to kill himself?" Lower scores indicate more acceptance (range: 1–7). Action = "How much action would you take to prevent John from killing himself?" Lower scores indicate less action should be taken (range: 1–7). PES = Prejudicial Evaluation Scale. Lower scores indicate more positive general attitudes toward target person (range: 17–119). PCQ = Professional Contact Questionnaire. Lower scores indicate more positive attitudes toward having the target person as a client (range: 6–42). SIS = Social Interaction Scale. Lower scores indicate more willingness to interact with the target person in social situations (range: 7–49). Group sizes: Depression, *n* = 68; Cancer, *n* = 79; AIDS, *n* = 68.

the three conditions on the PES. That is, on this scale, no condition led to more stigma than any other group. On the PCQ only one of the expected three between-groups differences was found. Men with depression had higher scores (indicating more stigmatization) than did ideators with terminal bone cancer. Finally, on the SIS, it was expected that ideators with AIDS would receive higher scores (be viewed more negatively) than men with cancer, but this was not supported. Another component of this hypothesis was that ideators with depression would receive higher scores than those with cancer and this was supported. It was also expected that ideators with AIDS would receive higher scores than ideators with depression, but this was not the case. Visual inspection of means revealed that the reverse of the hypothesis may have occurred; a post-hoc test indicated that ideators with depression were given higher scores (viewed more negatively) than ideators with AIDS.

In order to determine whether demographic characteristics had an impact on how participants responded to the dependent variables, additional statistical tests were performed on 19 of the 21 demographic variables. (There was not enough variability in ethnicity to warrant an investigation of this variable. The APA membership/division question was included merely to determine whether respondent membership in Division 44—The Society for the Psychological Study of Lesbian and Gay Issues—was an important factor. But only two respondents indicated that they belonged to this division.) After correcting for the large number of tests, it was found that only belief in rational suicide had a bearing on respondents' answers (see Table 4.4). Specifically, respondents who believed in the concept of rational suicide scored significantly lower (indicating more acceptance) on the

Table 4.4 Means and standard deviations for belief in rational suicide

Dependent variable	Yes ($n = 170$)		No ($n = 28$)		t-value
	M	SD	M	SD	
SSDS	35.52	10.55	49.72	11.47	−6.57*
Acceptance	3.69	1.87	5.93	1.39	−6.07*
Action	4.81	1.84	6.43	0.79	−4.59*
PES	35.54	9.04	32.97	8.51	1.41
PCQ	13.12	4.82	12.75	4.83	0.37
SIS	13.40	7.14	12.62	7.11	0.53

Source. From Werth (1994b, p. 45).

Note. *$p < .001$. SSDS = Suicide Semantic Differential Scale. Lower scores indicate more acceptance of suicide (range: 10–70). Acceptance = "How acceptable to you is John's decision to kill himself?" Lower scores indicate more acceptance (range: 1–7). Action = "How much action would you take to prevent John from killing himself?" Lower scores indicate less action should be taken (range: 1–7). PES = Prejudicial Evaluation Scale. Lower scores indicate more positive general attitudes toward target person (range: 17–119). PCQ = Professional Contact Questionnaire. Lower scores indicate more positive attitudes toward having the target person as a client (range: 6–42). SIS = Social Interaction Scale. Lower scores indicate more willingness to interact with the target person in social situations (range: 7–49).

SSDS, the Acceptance question (again, indicating more acceptance), and the Action question (less action would be taken). However, the believers and nonbelievers did not differ significantly on the PES, PCQ, or SIS. The three nonsignificant results indicate that the two groups did not differ in the amount of stigma attached to the suicidal ideators. None of the other 18 demographic variables had a significant impact on any of the six dependent variables.

Previous research (e.g., Crawford et al., 1991; St. Lawrence et al., 1990) using the three stigma scales analyzed individual items. Item analysis was deemed to be too unreliable a method to be used extensively in the Register Survey. However, because of its direct relevance to the investigation, an analysis was performed on one question from the PES: "Suicide is the best option for John." This analysis revealed that among the independent variables, only the precipitating condition led to significant differences. Specifically, the mean response on this question for the bone cancer condition (mean = 3.95, standard deviation [sd] = 1.40) was significantly higher (indicating greater acceptance with the statement) than the mean for AIDS (mean = 3.38, sd = 1.55). The means for both of the terminal illnesses were significantly higher than the mean for the depression condition (mean = 1.76, sd = 1.24).

Discussion. Few of the hypotheses of the Register Survey were supported by the results. Only the independent variable of precipitating condition appeared to be important in differentiating among the different suicidal ideators. And, more specifically, the differences were primarily between the terminal illness conditions (AIDS and bone cancer) and the depression condition but not between the two terminal illness conditions. Both AIDS and bone cancer were seen as significantly more acceptable reasons to suicide than endogenous depression and respondents indicated they would take significantly less action to prevent a suicide by either a man with AIDS or a man with bone cancer than a man with endogenous depression. On two different scales the suicidal ideator with depression was stigmatized more than the ideator with bone cancer; respondents reported they would have less professional comfort working with, and would want to have less social interaction with, the depressed man. Contrary to expectations, respondents also indicated that they would interact less in social situations with a man with depression than a man with AIDS. One possible explanation for this unexpected finding is that participants may have believed that interacting with a depressed person socially might lead to the respondent herself or himself becoming depressed while a man with AIDS who is not depressed does not pose this threat.

None of an extensive list of demographic variables had a significant impact on participant responses. The only descriptive variable that made a significant difference in how respondents reacted to the different scales was belief in the concept of rational suicide. The differences between believers and nonbelievers were evident on the two measures of acceptance (the SSDS and the Acceptance question) and the Action question but not on the measures of general, professional, or social stigma.

The finding that the independent variable of sexual orientation was not significant implies that, although gay men have been viewed more negatively than heterosexual men by the general public and, at least historically, by mental health professionals, this general stigma did not make a difference when assessing suicidal ideation and intervention using vignettes and a mail survey design. The lack of significant differences attributable to sexual orientation may ease concerns that psychologists might be more accepting of, and take less action to prevent, a suicide by a gay man than one by a heterosexual man because they may view the death of the gay man as less of a loss. One possible explanation for these results is that the man's decision to suicide (and therefore his intention to die) may have overridden any negative attitudes the psychologist may have for the ideator because of his actual or perceived sexual orientation.

The lack of significant results related to the social support independent variable is confusing, especially given the qualitative analysis of the beliefs about rational suicide, which included consultation with significant others as an important component (reported in the next chapter). This apparent contradiction may be due to the fact that consultation with significant others was only one of several factors that respondents indicated should be present for a suicide to be considered rational. That is, in and of itself, this variable may not be powerful enough to sway psychologists' opinions about the acceptability of a suicide, the amount of action that would be taken to prevent a suicide, or the amount of stigma associated with the suicidal decision.

COMPARISONS OF STUDIES

The results from the Psychotherapy Study provide the best comparison for the Register Survey. The means for the SSDS, Acceptance, and Action scales in the depression condition of the Psychotherapy Study (see Table 4.1) were slightly lower than the comparable means in the Register Survey (see Table 4.3). Although the case scenarios were not identical, these figures indicate that the respondents in the Register Survey viewed ideation arising from depression a little more negatively and would take slightly more action to prevent a suicide due to this condition than respondents in the Psychotherapy Study.

Similarly, respondents in the terminal bone cancer condition of the Psychotherapy Study had slightly lower means on the SSDS, Acceptance, and Action Scales (see Table 4.1) than those in the Register Survey (see Table 4.3). Again, this indicates that the participants in the Register Survey were a little less accepting and would take slightly more action to prevent a suicide due to bone cancer. However, the pattern of responses was nearly identical in both studies for the two conditions on all three scales.

Comparisons may also be made in regard to whether or not the respondent believed in rational suicide. In the Register Survey, approximately 86% of the respondents to the question on this subject espoused a belief in rational suicide while the Psychotherapy Study reported a comparative figure of 81%.

Psychotherapy Study respondents who believed in rational suicide had higher average scores on the SSDS, Acceptance, and Action scales (see Table 4.2) than comparable respondents in the Register Survey (see Table 4.4). Those who did not believe in rational suicide in the Psychotherapy Study had lower average scores on the three scales (see Table 4.2) than nonbelievers in the Register Survey (see Table 4.4). Comparing these results, it appears as if respondents in the Register Survey who believed in rational suicide were a little more accepting of suicide and would take slightly less action to prevent it than those in the Psychotherapy Study. In contrast, those who did not believe in rational suicide in the Register Survey were a little less accepting and would take slightly more action to prevent suicide than the nonbelievers in the Psychotherapy Study. However, the means on the scales were very similar.

One last comparison of note is the number of respondents who reported having had one or more clients in their care suicide. Approximately one-third (34.2%) of the Psychotherapy Study (unpublished data) respondents had had at least one client suicide, with an average of 1.8 each. In the Register Survey, nearly one-third (31.6%) reported having had at least one client suicide, with an average of two clients each. In contrast, Chemtob and his coworkers (1989), who also surveyed members of the National Register, found that 22% of their respondents reported at least one suicide.

There was one notable difference in the comparative quantitative results between the Register Survey and the Psychotherapy Study. In the Psychotherapy Study, years in practice was found to be an important demographic variable. Specifically, respondents who had been in practice for 30 or more years had significantly lower scores on the SSDS (indicating more acceptance) and significantly lower scores on the Action question (indicating they would take less action to prevent the suicide) than those who had less experience. (There were no significant differences between the groups on the Acceptance question.) In the Register Survey this variable was not found to be significant in differentiating among the respondents. The authors of the Psychotherapy Study made a point of saying that this finding might have been the result of chance given the large number of comparisons they made on the demographic variables. The lack of a significant result in the Register Survey may indicate that their finding was, indeed, a chance occurrence.

Thus, even though there were some small differences between the figures reported in the Psychotherapy Study and those found in the Register Survey in regard to amount of acceptance of suicide and amount of action that would be taken to prevent suicide under two essentially equivalent conditions, the overall findings were very consistent. Similarly, comparing the two studies, the mean scores of those who believed versus those who did not believe in rational suicide were also fairly similar, as was the percentage of respondents who espoused a belief in the concept of rational suicide.

Although the stigma scales (PES, PCQ, and SIS) had been used with psychologists by other research teams in the past (e.g., Crawford et al., 1991; St. Lawrence et al., 1990), direct comparisons between the results of these studies and the Register Survey are not possible because the other researchers used item analysis. In the Register Survey only one item, "Suicide is the best option for John," was analyzed by itself. This analysis revealed that the mean for the bone cancer condition was significantly higher than the mean for the AIDS condition, meaning respondents agreed with the statement more for the cancer condition. Both of the means for the terminal illness conditions were significantly higher than the mean for the depression condition. St. Lawrence and colleagues (1990) found that psychologists were significantly more willing to accept this item for persons with

AIDS than for persons with leukemia. However, Crawford and his coworkers (1991) did not find a significant difference on this item. In regard to the Register Survey, it is noteworthy that this single item again provided support for the conclusions that terminal illnesses are significantly more acceptable reasons to suicide than depression and, further, that respondents did not single out persons with AIDS as the only or even the most appropriate group for suicide.

CONCLUSION

The studies reviewed in this chapter show strong support for the idea that suicide is not always seen as an irrational choice. Respondents indicated that there are some conditions in which suicide is seen as an acceptable option and when intervention is not seen as necessary and may even be inappropriate. Of equal, if not greater importance, is that approximately 20% of psychologists and psychotherapists report working with a suicidal client whom they considered rational. These investigations, therefore, are in dramatic contrast to the report by Litman (1965) who said that he had never interviewed a therapist who saw suicide as acceptable.

These studies argue powerfully for a different way of viewing suicide and the mental health professional's role when working with suicidal clients. Based on the results reported here, it appears as if many mental health professionals, perhaps even a majority, subscribe to the belief that suicides should not always be prevented. The question that logically arises out of this finding is when the professional should take an interventionist stance and when the role should be more of an exploration or assessment of the rationality of the decision. Answering this question is the focus of chapter 5.

5

Criteria for Rational Suicide

Chapter 2 reviewed how attitudes about suicide had shifted over time from seeing it as an act of dignity to a sinful act to evidence of mental illness. Yet, even though most of the mental health literature on suicide is heavily weighted toward viewing suicide as an irrational act, there have been some authors who have asked if prevention and intervention are always warranted (e.g., Amchin et al., 1990; Beckerman, 1995; Choron, 1972; Decker, 1977; Diekstra, 1986; Diggory, 1968; Heyd & Bloch, 1981; Hoff, 1989; Kjervik, 1984; Kobler & Stotland, 1964; Lester, 1969, 1970, 1977; Lowenthal, 1976; Mackenzie & Popkin, 1990; Maris, 1981, 1982, 1983; Morgan, 1979; Motto, 1972, 1981, 1983, 1994a, 1994b; Nelson, 1984; Pretzel, 1977, 1984; Rangell, 1988; Redlich & Mollica, 1976; Roy, 1988; Slater, 1980; Szasz, 1976, 1986; Werth, 1992, 1994b, 1995; Widiger & Rinaldi, 1983). Diekstra (1986) said, "Stated within the framework of suicide prevention, the question is not 'Should we or should we not prevent suicide?' but, rather, 'how and when should suicide be prevented?'" (p. 15; see also Choron, 1972). This revised question takes away the absolutist nature of the issue and promotes a more contextual climate (Kastenbaum, 1976; Maris, 1986; Nelson, 1984; Werth, 1995). The answer must be considered carefully because to be too strict is to continue the current paternalistic overcontrol and to be too lenient may lead to a missed opportunity to help someone who has not made a well-reasoned decision.

McIntosh (1993b), a former president of the American Association of Suicidology, said that "In my opinion, the public nature of the controversy [surrounding assisted and rational suicide] along with its immediacy, makes assisted suicide the single most significant issue in suicidology at this time" and "[a]mong the most significant of medical (as well as larger) issues will be the establishment of criteria" (p. 3). Over the past two decades several other authors have stated that there is a need for guidelines and criteria for rational suicide:

It seems inevitable to me that we must eventually establish procedures for the voluntary cessation of life, with the time, place, and manner largely controlled by the person concerned. It will necessarily involve a series of steps providing assurance that appro-

priate criteria are met. . . . (Motto, 1972, p. 188; see also Conwell & Caine, 1991;
Goldfarb, 1983; Kastenbaum, 1976; Lebacqz & Engelhardt, 1977; Motto, 1981, 1994a;
see R. L. Barry, 1994 for an alternate view)

Even those who do not believe in rational suicide, like McIntosh (1993a), have
implicitly provided criteria for when suicide can be rational. For example, Siegel
(1982a) argued that intervention is appropriate when it appears as if the person is
ambivalent and/or if the person does not have a realistic view of his or her life and
future. Pretzel (1977) noted that Shneidman and other intervention/preventionists
justify their actions because of ambivalence, impulsivity, and the potential effect a
suicide has on others. If these factors are what justify intervention, then it would
appear that if these concerns are attended to, then a decision to suicide could be
rational.

Although the topic of physician-assisted suicide is not the focus of this book, it
may be helpful to provide one list of suggested criteria in order to demonstrate the
apparent agreement about the criteria that should be involved when assessing a
person's decision to die. Quill and his colleagues' (Quill, Cassel, & Meier, 1992;
see also Quill, 1994) criteria include the following: an incurable (though not necessarily terminal) painful condition, ensuring that the desire to die is not arising
out of "inadequate comfort-care," the requests to die must be made "clearly and
repeatedly, of [the person's] own free will and initiative," "the physician must be
sure that the patient's judgment is not distorted," "the physician-assisted suicide
should be carried out only in the context of a meaningful doctor-patient relationship," "consultation with another experienced physician is required," clear documentation of the entire process is necessary, and "informing family members is
strongly recommended, but whom to involve and inform should be left to the
discretion and control of the patient" (p. 1382; see also Diekstra [1986], Heifetz
[1975], Humphry [1991, pp. 142–143], Humphry & Wickett [1990], Wanzer et al.
[1989], Wolhandler [1984], Yarnell & Battin [1988]; see Battin [1994a], Colt [1991],
Humphry & Wickett [1990], and Huyse & van Tilburg [1993] for a description of
the euthanasia guidelines for the Netherlands).

Quill, a physician who has been active in the fight for physician aid-in-dying,
acknowledged during a question-and-answer session at the Annual Conference of
the American Association of Suicidology that he would like mental health professionals involved when people are making decisions about physician aid-in-dying.
He noted that there is a link between depression and suicide and, further, that
medical professionals are notoriously poor at identifying and treating depression
in their patients (see also Blumenthal, 1990; Bongar, 1991; Buda & Tsuang, 1990;
Clark, 1992; Conwell & Caine, 1991). He then stated that it was for precisely
these reasons that he wants to have counselors involved in the process of evaluating dying patients. However, he followed by saying that at the present time he
could not ask a mental health colleague to evaluate the state of a patient requesting to die because the mental health worker would be obligated to take action to
prevent the act that Dr. Quill was wondering about facilitating, even if the patient
was competent, not depressed or otherwise mentally impaired (see also Battin,
1992).

However, in a development that may portend the face of things to come, the

National Association of Social Workers (NASW, 1994) issued a policy regarding "Client Self-determination in End-of-Life Decisions," stating:

> Social workers should be free to participate or not participate in assisted-suicide matters or other discussions concerning end-of-life decisions depending on their own beliefs, attitudes, and value systems. If a social worker is unable to help with decisions about assisted suicide or other end-of-life choices, he or she has a professional obligation to refer [clients] and their families to competent professionals who are available to address end-of-life issues. (p. 60)

The policy goes even further by stating that, "If legally permissible, it is not inappropriate for a social worker to be present during an assisted suicide if the client requests the social worker's presence" (p. 60).

The policy does not designate specific criteria that should be used to determine if the client is competent to make an end-of-life decision. However, there are several implicit messages about what the social worker should look for and what the social worker should do when working with someone who is dealing with an end-of-life decision. The person should have a "terminal and irreversible condition, a progressive chronic illness, or chronic intractable pain" (p. 59). Further, "self-determination assumes that the client is mentally competent" (p. 58). Following this assessment, "competent individuals should have the opportunity to make their own choices but only after being informed of all options and consequences" (p. 60). The policy noted:

> the appropriate role for social workers is to help [clients] express their thoughts and feelings, to facilitate exploration of alternatives, to provide information to make an informed choice, and to deal with grief and loss issues. . . . [They] should explore and help ameliorate any factors such as pain, depression, a need for medical treatment, and so forth. . . . [They] should act as liaisons with other health care professionals and help the [client] and family communicate concerns and attitudes to the health care team. . . . [They] should encourage the involvement of significant others, family, and friends in these decisions. (p. 60)

This policy statement by the NASW is a dramatic step forward in the consideration of how professionals can be involved in end-of-life decisions. The policy is setting forth in writing a distinction that professionals acknowledge exists but is not recognized in ethics codes or legal standards. Therefore, determination of who should be allowed to make end-of-life decisions and the role of the mental health professional in this process is still based upon the beliefs and experiences of a few individuals.

EMPIRICALLY BASED CRITERIA

In order to develop the first set of empirically based criteria for rational suicide, Werth and Cobia (1995a) analyzed the qualitative data collected during the Werth and Liddle (1994) study of psychotherapists described in chapter 4. The specific questions asked were: (1) Do you believe in the idea of rational suicide? Why or why not? (2) If you believe that suicide in some cases may be rational, please give your definition of a rational suicide. These questions were also used by Werth (1994b) in his study.

Procedure

Both Werth and Cobia (1995a) and Werth (1994b) analyzed the data using the following technique (Bogdan & Biklen, 1982; Weiss, 1994). Responses were typed and placed on separate 3-by-5-inch index cards. The cards were then examined for participant perspectives on their beliefs about rational suicide and were placed in piles when connections between cards became apparent (e.g., two respondents specifically referring to the *terminal* nature of John's condition would be placed in the same pile). If a card had statements that could place it in more than one stack each statement was copied onto different cards and these were placed either in an already existing stack or a new stack was created. This same procedure was followed if a card had statements that could not be placed in any stack created up to that point.

The cards in each stack were grouped and regrouped until it became evident, because two consecutive passes through the cards in each stack led to no changes in the stacks or placements of particular cards, that no more stacks were necessary to represent the data while remaining as true as possible to respondent meaning. In other words, after all the cards were examined and placed into tentative stacks, each stack was reviewed to determine whether the cards in the stack "held together" in a logical fashion or whether more than one theme was evident in the stack (e.g., the initial sort led to a stack of cards related to *pain*. Upon review this stack was divided into *physical pain* and *psychological pain*). Stacks were then examined to determine whether one or more could be combined to make a logical group. That is, the piles, which can be viewed as first order factors, were examined to see if they could be viewed as components of a larger category (second-order factors). For example, after one review there was a stack for *personal freedom*, a stack for *individual rights*, and a stack for *personal responsibility*; these three stacks were combined into one larger stack with the heading *free choice*. Finally, the remaining stacks, which could be first or second order factors, were examined to determine whether they could be classified as belonging within a particular category (i.e., second- or third-order factors). For example, the stacks *terminal illness* and *physical pain* (among others), were deemed to be members of a second-order category that was called *hopeless conditions*. Cards that could not be placed in any of the stacks (i.e., cards that represented idiosyncratic responses) were deemed unusable and removed from consideration (Bogdan & Biklen, 1982). Following the final sort, formal names for the themes were developed and representative examples were selected to elucidate the content of each category.

Because the results of the Werth and Cobia (1995a) and Werth (1994b) studies were nearly identical, the results of Werth's study will be presented in detail and then contrasted with the results from the Werth and Cobia study. In both investigations, although the respondents were asked two separate questions ("Do you believe in the idea of 'rational suicide?' Why or why not?" and "If you believe that suicide in some cases may be rational, please give your definition of a 'rational suicide.'"), a large number of respondents answered the second question by stating "see above" or "answered above." Therefore, although it may be argued that the reasons why one does or does not believe in rational suicide are different from definitions of rational suicide, to stay true to the data provided, responses to these two items were combined in the analyses of these questions.

Results

This section will be divided in two ways. There are divisions by broad categories of responses and then these groups are divided into components.

Suicide cannot be rational. A small number of respondents provided reasons to explain why they did not believe in rational suicide.

Moral principles. The most frequent reason for not believing that suicide could be rational involved moral principles, such as the idea that suicide "is morally wrong," or because the respondent was a "Christian therefore I don't believe in rational suicide."

Contradictory terms. The other reason was a belief that rational and suicide are contradictory terms. For example, "suicide, by definition, implies constricted options"; "by definition suicide is an irrational decision"; and "rational implies logic and reason; suicide seems to be just the opposite."

Suicide can be rational when the condition is hopeless. A much larger number of participants stated that they did believe in rational suicide. The largest category of reasons given for why the respondents think suicide can at times be rational was a category that will be called *hopeless conditions*. This title was chosen because the underlying theme appeared to be that the person was suffering from a situation for which no end could be foreseen: "no hope of improvement," "no hope for cure," and "minimal hope for meaningful recovery" typify some of the reasons given. These conditions may or may not necessarily be leading to imminent death.

Terminal illness. Many respondents said that the presence of a "terminal illness" or a "terminal and painful illness" was a satisfactory reason for suiciding.

Generalized pain. Similarly, a large number of respondents mentioned general pain and suffering. They made statements such as "unendurable suffering," "the person is suffering greatly," "given a choice between endless suffering and death some individuals can rationally choose suicide."

Physical pain. Others specified "physical pain," "intolerable incurable physical ailments," "in cases of extreme physical suffering."

Mental/emotional pain. Finally, there were some participants who mentioned mental or emotional pain in their responses. Examples include, "overwhelming emotional or physical pain," "ongoing physical or psychological pain that cannot be alleviated," and "in cases of terminal psychic or physical pain."

Generally debilitating or deteriorating condition. A related subcategory is that of disabling and/or deteriorating conditions. One respondent summed up this category by saying that if a "totally disabling, slowly progressive illness" was present then suicide could be rational. Other, responses included "a degenerative illness," "progressive deterioration," and "prolonged degradation."

Physical deterioration. There were some respondents whose answers were similar to the preceding subcategory except they specified physical deterioration, such as the participant who said "a progressive deteriorating physical illness."

Mental deterioration. Others mentioned deteriorating mental capabilities, such as "when [client] knows the dementia of Alzheimers [*sic*] is close to leaving him/her functionless."

Quality of life. The last subcategory in the hopeless conditions category is rather broadly called quality of life. A few of the respondents specified that the person must be experiencing low quality of life and death must be approaching. Most others did not mention the imminence of death. An example of the first of these types of responses is "if death is imminent and the person's quality of life is deteriorating" while an example of the second is "when the quality of life is so poor that the person derives no satisfaction out of it." It should be noted that these respondents did not specify that others had to necessarily agree that the person's quality of life was unbearable.

Other responses that were classified as being related to quality of life revolved around (a) a "condition that produces devastating financial loss" and "if physical illness is . . . costly"; (b) "when a person is 'truly' convinced that continuing to live serves no purpose" and "loss of value in living"; and (c) "pre-empt capture and torture in wartime," and "prisoners on death row."

Suicide can be rational because of personal rights. The second major category of pro-rational suicide responses was called personal rights because these respondents appeared to believe that individuals have the right to take their own lives. Examples include: "I respect an individual's desire to chart their [*sic*] own course," "I believe the person has a right to choose not to live," people have the "right to make this decision for themselves," "the choice to terminate one's existence must reflect the most fundamental right we possess," and "we should each have some degree of freedom to determine what happens with our lives."

Suicide can be rational if a sound decision-making process is followed. The third major category of reasons for belief in rational suicide was labeled sound decision-making process. There were several groupings of cards that appeared to be components of the larger decision-making process and therefore they were brought together under this larger heading. However, although some respondents listed several of the subcategories described below, few participants mentioned all of the subcategories.

Mental competence. The first subcategory, or component, within the decision-making process appeared to be that the suicidal person must be "mentally competent" or "of sound mind" and "capable of exercising reasonable judgment." More specifically, the decision should not be "based on mental illness or severe depression," and the person should be "non-psychotic" and should not be "suffering from an organic mental syndrome."

Not impulsive. When the desire to suicide is for a "prolonged period of time, not simply fleeting thoughts then acting on the impulse" then the person is not acting impulsively.

Consideration of all alternatives. An example of this subcategory is "when a person realistically considers their [*sic*] alternatives and decides that, for them [*sic*], suicide is their [*sic*] best option."

Consideration of personal beliefs and/or values. Many of these respondents specifically mentioned moral or spiritual beliefs. For instance, "rationally consider current life situation against spiritual beliefs" and "the decision to end one's *physical* life after carefully considering all the options and reconciling any spiritual beliefs" (emphasis original).

Consideration of the impact on others. The suicidal person should take into account "one's relationship with others and the impact the act will have on others," he or she should think about "the effects of [the] suicide on loved ones," and "consider the consequences of suicide upon their survivors and weigh the relief [versus the] extra guilt equations."

Consultation. Finally, in order to be rational, the decision should be made after consulting both significant others and professionals. "Consult with all loved ones, prepare affairs, say goodbye"; when significant others "have been involved in this assessment [of options] and have come to accept the [client's] decision (even if not necessarily approving of it)"; and when one has "conferred with family, and friends, and ends with people in her/his life before dying." Objective others, such as psychological and medical professionals should also be consulted. Some examples of this idea include, "Having consulted an expert mental health professional *and* appropriate medical specialists" (emphasis original), "hopeless by a [number] of medical opinions," and "individual has been determined competent by at least 3 professionals."

Summary

In sum, participants were asked open-ended questions about their reasons for believing or not believing in rational suicide and, if they did believe in the concept, they were asked to provide a definition. Most of the psychologists who did not believe in rational suicide cited reasons stemming from either moral principles or a belief that rational and suicide were contradictory terms.

Those participants who did believe in rational suicide gave a number of different reasons that were grouped into three categories: hopeless conditions, personal rights, and ability to conduct a sound decision-making process (see Table 5.1). The first and third categories were composed of several subcategories. It is important to note that few respondents actually listed all three of the categories in their responses; however, for the sake of comprehensiveness all these categories can be used to generate a set of conditions that would need to be met for a suicide to be considered rational. Based on a compilation of these responses, therefore, for a suicide to be deemed rational, the person must have a hopeless condition (e.g., a terminal illness, a painful condition, a disabling and/or deteriorating condition, or chronic low quality of life), he or she must have arrived at the decision through his or her own free will, and he or she must have engaged in a sound decision-making process (i.e., nonimpulsively consider all alternatives, consider his or her personal beliefs, consider the impact on others, and consult with significant others and with professionals—especially a mental health professional who can assess psychological competence that, for this sample, would include the absence of treatable major depression).

Table 5.1 Criteria for Rational Suicide

---

1. The person considering suicide has an unremitting "hopeless" condition. "Hopeless" conditions include, but are not necessarily limited to, terminal illnesses, severe physical and/or psychological pain, physically or mentally debilitating and/or deteriorating conditions, or quality of life no longer acceptable to the individual.
2. The person makes the decision as a free choice (i.e., is not pressured by others to choose suicide).
3. The person has engaged in a sound decision-making process. This process should include the following:
   a. Consultation with a mental health professional who can make an assessment of mental competence (which would include the absence of treatable major depression);
   b. Nonimpulsive consideration of all alternatives;
   c. Consideration of the congruence of the act with one's personal values;
   d. Consideration of the impact on significant others;
   e. Consultation with objective others (e.g., medical and religious professionals) and with significant others.

COMPARISON OF EMPIRICALLY BASED CRITERIA

The results of one other study can be directly compared to those arising from the current investigation. Werth and Cobia (1995a) did a qualitative analysis of psychotherapist beliefs about rational suicide and produced the first empirically based set of criteria for the concept. A comparison of the categories found in the present study with those listed by Werth and Cobia shows them to be virtually identical. The fact that the different categories of responses listed by Werth and Cobia essentially were replicated in the present study further validates the conclusions from both the investigations. However, since the author was involved in both surveys, additional studies on this topic by other researchers should be undertaken.

There were only two notable differences between Werth and Cobia's (1995a) criteria and the present one. The first was the inclusion in the present study of a moral principles reason for not believing in rational suicide. The second is that a large number of the current respondents specifically said that they would not consider depression a satisfactory reason to suicide. Werth and Cobia listed "severe physical or psychological pain" as an example of a hopeless condition; however, for the present study, such a statement could only be made as long as treatable major depression was ruled out during the assessment process since a large number of respondents would appear to agree with the participant who stated that "I cannot agree [that suicide is rational] with a severe case of depression because depression colors the judgment in a negative fashion."

This last point deserves additional attention. Although not stated explicitly in the quote, the idea that depression impacts decision making is related to competence. Depression may make a person temporarily incompetent to make a life-or-death decision (see Grisso & Appelbaum, 1995). Therefore, although "competence" is, technically, a legal term, it was used in the set of criteria. The decision to include an evaluation of competence into the criteria was also based on the fact that:

> Although competency is a legal concept and all individuals are presumed by the law to be competent until determined otherwise in a judicial hearing, the practical realities of clinical care often require that [mental health professionals] make their own assessments of whether a [client] is competent or not. We might call this a determination of "psychological capacity" rather than "legal competence," but the impact of the [mental health professional's] decision is often just as important as that of decisions emanating from the bench. (Appelbaum & Roth, 1981, p. 1462; see also Appelbaum & Grisso, 1988; Appelbaum & Gutheil, 1991; "Developments," 1974; Freedman, 1981; Maltsberger, 1994; Office of Technology Assessment, 1988)

Furthermore, as will be discussed in greater detail in chapter 7, competence is a crucial factor in determining whether or not a decision is legally valid. In addition, if a client is considered competent she or he should not be involuntarily hospitalized. Both of these factors have implications for the way the client and counselor work together.

Discussion Based on the Literature

Although the two studies mentioned above are the only ones to derive criteria through research and evaluation of a large number of respondents, the literature on rational suicide is replete with criteria developed by the author of a particular piece of writing. Because many of the aspects of the lists formulated intuitively by authors overlap with each other and with the empirically based criteria listed in Table 5.1, this section will place the criteria from these other authors in the framework provided by the research described above (see R. L. Barry [1994], Battin [1982, 1994b], Beckerman [1995], Decker [1977], Maguire [1975], and Peterson [1985] for alternate frameworks; see Tepper & Elwork [1984] for an overview of decision making as it relates to competence; see Motto [1994b] for commentary on the criteria developed by Werth & Cobia).

Hopeless condition. Discussed in many ways, this criterion is one of the most prevalent in the literature. Some authors put it in terms of the reason motivating the decision to suicide being "understandable" to other people (Choron, 1972; Lebacqz & Engelhardt, 1977; Prado, 1990; Saunders & Valente, 1988; Siegel, 1982b, 1986), but Battin (1982) said that the stigma surrounding suicide makes this wording difficult to accept. Decker (1977) used the general term "quality of life," Motto (1994b) used "unbearable conditions," while others are more specific in their sets of criteria, specifically listing terminal illness or a debilitating condition (Battin, 1982; Dunshee, 1994; Francis, 1980; Humphry, 1987; Maris, 1986; Mayo, 1993). Many list pain, physical or psychological, that cannot be alleviated (e.g., Battin, 1982; Diekstra, 1986; Francis, 1980; Goldfarb, 1983; Kjervik, 1984; Lebacqz & Engelhardt, 1977; Maltsberger, 1994; Mayo, 1983; Motto, 1972, 1981, 1983; Nelson, 1984; Slater, 1980; Widiger & Rinaldi, 1983). Several authors (e.g., Barrington, 1980; Kaplan & Adamek, 1995; Prado, 1990) specifically discuss rational suicide as it relates to the elderly.

Free from coercion. Diekstra (1986) put this in terms of a "free-will decision." Lebacqz and Engelhardt (1977) indirectly state that lack of coercion is important (see also Francis, 1980; Hoff, 1989; Mayo, 1983; Motto, 1981; Sullivan, 1980) but they also state that determining the presence of coercion may be difficult (see also R. L. Barry, 1994; Battin, 1994e; Gill, 1992). Battin (1982, 1994e) claimed that in some instances a decision to suicide could be rational even though coercion had occurred.

Sound decision-making process. *Mental Competence.* The absence of current mental illness or severe emotional distress and the ability to foresee consequences are vital aspects of many sets of criteria (e.g., Amchin et al., 1990; R. L. Barry, 1994; Battin, 1982; Choron, 1972; Clements et al., 1983; Conwell & Caine, 1991; Decker, 1977; Diekstra, 1986; Dunshee, 1994; Engelhardt, 1989; Francis, 1980; Heyd & Bloch, 1981; Kjervik, 1984; Lebacqz & Engelhardt, 1977; Mackenzie & Popkin, 1990; Mayo, 1993; Moskop & Engelhardt, 1979; Motto, 1972, 1983, 1994a; Prado, 1990; Saunders & Valente, 1988; Siegel, 1982b, 1986; Sullivan, 1980; Victoroff, 1983). However, Widiger and Rinaldi (1983) state that the absence of powerful affect in the face of a suicidal decision would be so rare as to effectively rule out the possibility of rational suicide while Maris (1986) notes that the presence of powerful affect need not preclude rationality. Many lists specifically state there should be no depression (Amchin et al., 1990; Dunshee, 1994; Motto, 1994a; Saunders & Valente, 1988; see also Clark, 1992), but Conwell and Caine (1991) try to refine this condition by asking "how severe must depression be before it precludes rational decision making? What factors facilitate rational thinking in the face of personal distress or clinical mood disturbance?" (p. 1102; see also Battin, 1982; Clark, 1992; Huyse & van Tilburg, 1993; Maltsberger, 1994). A tangential but related aspect to this criterion is that the person is either of the age of majority (Humphry, 1987; Lebacqz & Engelhardt, 1977; Moskop & Engelhardt, 1979) or judged able to decide for her or himself (Bednar, Bednar, Lambert, & Waite, 1991; Brody, 1988; Buchanan & Brock, 1989; Powell, 1984; Smith, 1989).

Nonimpulsive consideration of alternatives. Several authors say the decision should be deliberated and that other alternatives should be thoroughly considered (R. L. Barry, 1994; Battin, 1982; Decker, 1977; Dunshee, 1994; Engelhardt, 1989; Francis, 1980; Heyd & Bloch, 1981; Hoff, 1989; Humphry, 1987; Kastenbaum, 1976; Maltsberger, 1994; Mayo, 1983; Motto, 1981, 1994a, 1994b; Nelson, 1984; Saunders & Valente, 1988; Sullivan, 1980). Some theorists highlight the issue of time (Diekstra, 1986; Lebacqz & Engelhardt, 1977; Motto, 1972; see also Gill, 1992; Werth, 1995) and in one work (Werth, 1995) three months was suggested as a minimum time frame to explore the decision. Now, however, time per se is not viewed as the crucial factor but, rather, the consideration, and perhaps trials, of available alternatives is the important aspect. A variation of this criterion is that the person has made a realistic assessment of his or her life and the world (Amchin et al., 1990; R. L. Barry, 1994; Battin, 1982; Decker, 1977; Francis, 1980; Hoff, 1989; Kjervik, 1984; Martin, 1980; Mayo, 1993; Motto, 1972, 1981, 1994a; Saunders & Valente, 1988; Siegel, 1986; Sullivan, 1980; see also Gill, 1992). Widiger and Rinaldi (1983; see also Martin, 1980) note that a criterion that involves the absence of ambivalence (e.g., Motto, 1972) effectively eliminates the possibility of a rational suicide.

Congruence with personal values. Different authors put emphasis on variations of a common theme. Basically one should examine one's personal goals, interests, desires, philosophy, etc., and act in accordance with these factors (R. L. Barry, 1994; Battin, 1982; Brandt, 1975; Kjervik, 1984; Mayo, 1983, 1993; Motto, 1972, 1981, 1983, 1994a; Nelson, 1984; Prado, 1990).

Consideration of the impact on others. Numerous authors have advocated that the potential effect on others be considered (Battin, 1982; Dunshee, 1994; Engelhardt, 1989; Humphry, 1987; Kastenbaum, 1976; Kjervik, 1984; Maris, 1986; Motto, 1981, 1983, 1994a, 1994b; Slater, 1976) and that preventable harm to others should not occur (Diekstra, 1986; Mayo, 1983). Lebacqz and Engelhardt (1977) argue that the only reason a rational person should be prevented from suiciding is if the act will harm others.

Consultation with objective and significant others. Consultation specifically with physicians is important to Humphry (1987) while several others (Dunshee, 1994; Kastenbaum, 1976; Lebacqz and Engelhardt, 1977; Maltsberger, 1994; Maris, 1986; Martin, 1980; Slater, 1976) mention talking with significant others. Motto (1981, 1994a) mentions getting a second mental health professional's opinion, bringing in family members, and talking with other people like ministers. Victoroff (1983; see also Gill, 1992) broadly suggests getting a "second opinion." When evaluating the opinions of the general public toward euthanasia and suicide Johnson and colleagues (1980) interpreted the results that suicide appeared to be approved of less than euthanasia as being the effect of the suicidal decision being made in isolation. Thus, if the decision was made with others it may be more acceptable.

A Follow-Up Study

In summary, based on the results of the Werth and Cobia (1995a) and Werth (1994b) studies, a list of criteria for rational suicide was established that appears to encompass and expand upon most of the theoretical definitions presented in the literature. In order to further refine the criteria, Werth and Cobia (1995b) mailed their initial list (without the qualifier related to depression listed in criteria 3a of Table 5.1) to members of ethics committees of state boards of examiners for counselors, psychologists, and social workers; randomly selected members of the American Psychological Association Division of Psychology and the Law; and randomly selected members of the American Association of Suicidology. After the participants provided feedback about the criteria, they read the following vignette (or one with "Ms. Smith" instead of "Mr. Smith") and responded to a series of questions about what, if any, sanctions Dr. Johnson should experience:

Dr. Johnson saw the client in question, Mr. Smith, for approximately three months prior to the client's suicide. Dr. Johnson reports that Mr. Smith initially presented because he wanted to "work on some issues before I die." Mr. Smith stated that he had been diagnosed with acquired immunodeficiency syndrome (AIDS) approximately two years prior to initiating counseling. Mr. Smith stated that he had been taking one antiviral medication (AZT) until his T-cell count fell below 200, at which point he was diagnosed with AIDS, then he switched to combination therapy. He had also participated in several drug trials but saw no improvement in his condition. Mr. Smith and his physician, who had embarked on an aggressive Western medicine treatment campaign, also utilized alternate therapies (including acupuncture, meditation, and hypnosis) in an attempt to control Mr. Smith's pain. Mr. Smith contacted Dr. Johnson after his physician admitted that there was nothing more he (nor two other consulting physicians) could think of to try to alleviate Mr. Smith's pain. Further, Mr. Smith's physician made a referral to the local Hospice, indicating that he believed that Mr. Smith had at most six more months of life.

After talking with his family and friends, Mr. Smith tried Hospice care for approximately one month before contacting Dr. Johnson, during which he apparently saw himself begin to deteriorate and the time with pain started to outlast the amount of time in which he felt some relief from the suffering. When he initiated contact with Dr. Johnson, Mr. Smith evidently was already thinking about committing suicide when he felt the pain and loss of dignity to be more than he could bear.

Dr. Johnson agreed to discuss the possibility of suicide with Mr. Smith provided the client contract not to commit suicide until he and Dr. Johnson believed that all alternatives had been considered. Dr. Johnson referred Mr. Smith to a psychiatrist for an evaluation for psychotropic medications. Because of the possibility of HIV-related dementia or an opportunistic infection of the brain, Mr. Smith was also referred for neuropsychological testing. Neither the psychiatric consultation nor the testing revealed any indication of cognitive impairment or need for medication. Dr. Johnson discussed Mr. Smith's condition with the client's physician, who corroborated the client's reports.

During the second month of treatment, Dr. Johnson and Mr. Smith held three sessions with Mr. Smith's significant others—his parents, sister and brother-in-law, spouse, and two grown children, as well as three close friends. It became apparent to Dr. Johnson that Mr. Smith's friends and family, while saddened that Mr. Smith was in so much pain that he felt that he needed to consider suicide, supported his decision and believed that he had a "right" to take his own life. These sessions also apparently entailed discussions of Mr. Smith's, and his significant others', beliefs and values. The final four sessions between Dr. Johnson and Mr. Smith were spent putting Mr. Smith's affairs in order, which included a referral to an attorney, and additional consideration of alternatives to suicide.

Mr. Smith's physical condition reportedly deteriorated during the three months that Dr. Johnson saw the client. At the beginning of the eleventh session Mr. Smith declared that the pain was so intense and constant that he had made plans to commit suicide within the week, following a final evening involving his family and friends. Dr. Johnson made a second referral for neuropsychological testing, which again was negative, and during their final session, two days after the eleventh meeting, said goodbye to Mr. Smith. The next evening Mr. Smith took an overdose of medication after having a final meal with his family and died.

The discussion that follows is based on a preliminary analysis of the data received thus far. It must be stressed that as responses are added to the pool and as the ongoing investigation is expanded, the results and implications may change. To reduce the likelihood that changes will be significant the focus will primarily be on the trends that are overwhelmingly clear at present. The summary will be divided into three sections, one for each of the subgroups.

Ethicists. When questioned about the set of criteria, 7 of the 12 respondents said that it was acceptable as a means for assessing the rationality of a suicidal client, four said they would accept it with slight changes, and only one said it was unacceptable. When asked if they would add anything, four respondents said they would add nothing. Suggestions included requiring psychological pain to be present for more than two years, adding consultation with an attorney to criterion 3e, and providing for a means of verification that the criteria had been met. Seven respondents said they would delete nothing from the list; four had concerns about different conditions listed in criterion 1; and one suggested that criteria 3a, 3d, and 3e be optional. They were also asked for any additional comments and seven respondents did add remarks, none of which differed greatly from those mentioned previously.

The second half of the questionnaire related to the case presented above. For these responses, multiple answers were provided for some questions by many respondents so only those that were mentioned by a third or more of the group will be listed. In regard to the most important points in the case, seven mentioned the current condition and prognosis, six said the involvement of significant others, five specified considering alternatives and four said the consultations. Five also mentioned the promotion of, and respect for, the client's dignity.

The next item asked if Dr. Johnson had acted unethically. Seven participants said there was not ethical misconduct. Four mentioned, in various ways, not meeting the duty to protect (one did not answer). A follow-up question asked if the respondent would find Dr. Johnson guilty of violating the ethics code. Nine said no, one said yes, and two were unsure. Of note is that when asked what sanctions they would deem appropriate, even those who thought there were violations said no sanctions were warranted. The most important things Dr. Johnson did to prompt the nonsanctions were consulting (6) and pursuing alternatives (4).

The researchers also asked the participants to say how their responses would differ if the client's significant others had disagreed with the decision. Five said that more counseling with the client and family would be important, four insisted that it was still the client's choice, and four said that it was then the family's responsibility to prevent the suicide. Of note is that only two respondents said that they would then attempt to prevent the suicide.

Finally, the investigators asked them to discuss standards of care. Virtually all mentioned aspects of the process outlined in the criteria, three specifically said the standards of care are changing, and two said that the set of criteria should be the standard. One respondent said "this case presents a difficult dilemma that needs to be addressed with and within professional organizations that dictate ethical standards and standards of practice." An interesting and perhaps related side note is that Pope and Bajt (1988) surveyed ethicists about their own behavior and found that "three fourths of this select sample believed that psychologists should sometimes violate formal legal and ethical standards, and that a majority have actually done so. . . ." (p. 828).

When asked specifically if they believed in rational suicide 11 of the 12 respondents (92%) said yes, but only two individuals had actually seen suicidal clients who they considered rational (one reported seeing one client and the other reported seeing two). Only one respondent said that she had seen an ethics case related to failure to prevent suicide.

Suicidologists. Of the 35 members of the American Association of Suicidology whose responses have been analyzed, 14 said that they accepted the criteria without qualifications, nine accepted it with minimal comments, and ten said they did not accept it (two did not answer). Fifteen then said that they would not add anything to the criteria, eight mentioned (in one way or another) that a time period should be specified, eight wanted more specificity for criterion 1, and there were several idiosyncratic responses. In regard to aspects they would delete, 19 said nothing, 11 mentioned one or more aspects of criterion 1, three said the entire list, and there were a few other answers. Finally, several respondents chose to add further comments, which were split fairly evenly between supportive and negative.

The most often listed relevant points in the scenario for these respondents included the client's condition and prognosis (17), the involvement of family and friends (14), the psychological competence of the client (14), the client's pain (10), and the consideration of alternatives (10). The major concern of the respondents, in regard to potentially breaking ethical codes, was not preventing the suicide (10). Twenty-six respondents said that Dr. Johnson did not commit an ethical violation, five said that there was a violation, and the other four did not commit one way or the other. The only sanctions recommended were probation (1), additional training (1), board reprimand (1), and supervision (2). The most important reasons for minor sanctions were consultations (15), consideration of alternatives (11), and meeting with significant others (10).

When asked if their decisions would change if the client's significant others had objected to the decision, 13 said the decision is the client's, 10 said there should be more family counseling and there were several unique responses. The answers to the question about standards of care were wide and varied, with several stating or implying that the criteria would meet the standards and a few arguing that one should never accept suicide. One respondent replied:

> *The standard of practice is to protect oneself professionally—it should be as outlined in 1–3e. Professionals focus on their issues/responsibilities rather than patient/client wishes. We (professionals) encourage autonomous decision-making except when 'end-of-life' decisions are made and then we (and I do speak generally) move to protect ourselves rather than facilitate [the client's] decision-making process.*

Twenty-six of the 35 respondents (74%) said that they believed in rational suicide, seven (20%) said they did not, and two were undecided. Thirteen of the respondents (37%) reported having experience with rationally suicidal clients, with their amount of experience ranging from one (four people) to more than 10 (two people). The average number of rationally suicidal clients seen by these 13 individuals was approximately 4.25.

Psychologist–attorneys. The responses of 44 members of the Division of Psychology and the Law have been analyzed. Twenty-three participants accepted the criteria as adequate without changes, eight accepted it with minor changes, nine would not accept the list, and four did not answer. Similarly, 24 said there was nothing they would add, four would add a time frame, four suggested more specificity, and three would add consultation with another mental health professional (there were some unique responses). A comparable number, 26, would not delete anything, eight would want criterion number 1 changed, and a few added other comments. The most frequent additional comment was that the criteria needed to be more specific in several areas.

As would be expected, when asked to evaluate the case from the point of view of a legal consultant, these respondents listed numerous points of importance. Most often mentioned was the involvement of significant others (13), followed by the absence of cognitive impairment (11), prognosis (8), and the decision-making process (8). In terms of potential violations of mental health-related laws, 16 said not preventing suicide, 16 said none, and there were some idiosyncratic answers. Only seven respondents said they would find Dr. Johnson guilty of violating any laws. Possible sanctions included additional education (3), probation (2), suspended license (1), peer supervision (1), and professional review of practice (1). The most important reasons for these sanctions not being greater included the consultations (7; although 11 suggested more consultation) and the involvement of significant others (7); many respondents made comments that were mentioned only once.

If the significant others had disagreed with the decision to suicide, 15 respondents said it was still the client's decision, seven suggested talking to the client about the disagreement, six said that this would make things more difficult, and six also said that Dr. Johnson would then be open to a lawsuit. Finally, the question about standards of care elicited numerous answers, most of which were components of the criteria listed. Significantly, 17 said the set of criteria should be the standard of care but 12 mentioned that at present even if the criteria were followed, it would still be illegal in many states to allow a client to suicide.

Only three of these participants said that they did not believe in rational suicide, another three were undecided, and 38 (86%) said that they did believe in it. Seventeen of the 44 respondents (39%) had seen at least one rationally suicidal client (two reported seeing six, one reported seeing seven, and one reported seeing 10), with the average number among these respondents being 2.8. Six respondents said they had been legal consultants in cases involving failure to prevent suicide but only one was reported to involve rational suicide.

Synthesis. The results thus far demonstrate that the criteria outlined in this chapter may be acceptable to a majority of ethicists, suicidologists, and psychologist–attorneys. This is important for it is these individuals who will be deciding about ethical violations, establishing the standard of care, and providing legal consultation for and against cases of rational suicide.

Perhaps most significant is the overwhelming number of respondents who believed that Dr. Johnson did not violate any ethical standards and the even greater number who would not implement any negative sanctions (indicating that even those who thought a violation had been committed did not believe it was severe enough to warrant punishment). There was more of a split among the psychologist–attorneys regarding whether or not Dr. Johnson broke any laws but, once again, there were very few sanctions that would be handed down. It is also worth noting that several respondents in each of the groups declared that either the set of criteria or a less rigorous set of actions is or should be the standard of care. However, as some of the psychologist–attorneys noted, until things change and these criteria are accepted in practice, then someone who allowed a rational suicide might be in legal jeopardy. Finally, a large majority of respondents in each group said that they believe in rational suicide, and a high percentage also had experience with rationally suicidal clients.

Once again, however, it must be reiterated that the results reported above are preliminary and based on a small and potentially skewed sample. Yet, the results so far are compelling and warrant further investigation.

ADDITIONAL SCENARIOS

Many books and articles on suicide present and perhaps analyze case studies of persons who are either suicidal or have suicided (e.g., Farberow & Shneidman, 1961; Hendin, 1982; Maris, Berman, Maltsberger, & Yufit, 1992). However, as would be expected given most of these authors' views on suicide, the subjects of the cases are often clearly not rational in their consideration of suicide. Even authors (e.g., Pretzel, 1977; Snipe, 1988; see also Jackson & Younger, 1979) who purport to be examining whether or not suicide can be rational present cases that they then use to demonstrate that suicide cannot be rational (see Lester, 1969). There obviously is a need to include cases of arguably rational suicide in the mental health literature (see Saunders, Valente, & Berman, 1993; Vinogradov, Thornton, Levinson, & Callen, 1984 for examples).

In the brief discussion of the preliminary results of the second Werth and Cobia (1995b) study, the vignette that was included in the surveys was reproduced. One of the participants in the study said, "This is a clear-cut case, I could think of much more difficult ones." It is the purpose of this section to provide examples of three additional types of more difficult cases of suicidal persons, drawn from the literature, who could be evaluated with these criteria. A fifth scenario will be provided in the appendix along with references for others.

Adolescent Suicide

In his discussion of ethical issues related to counseling adolescents, Powell (1984) briefly discussed his beliefs regarding a minor's right to die. He presented two cases, the second of which is recounted here, along with some of his evaluation of the case. It should be noted that the case, as presented, is different from Powell's only in that the woman dies from an overdose instead of a protracted death (over nine days) from uremic poisoning. This minor change should not, however, alter the analysis that follows (see also Smith, 1989; see McCartney [1978] for a different view):

> Karen was a 16 year old with a three year history of chronic and acute kidney failure. Surgery was performed to remove both her kidneys and she received a transplant from her father. Despite initial apparent success the kidney failed to function after some months and Karen once again began the treatment regime which involved hemodialysis three times a week. The family exhibited signs of stress with the father trying to "lose himself" in his work and the mother evidencing other signs of stress reaction. Karen was assessed as suffering from a reactive depression which the psychiatrist judged to be appropriate to the situation.

Some time after the failure of the transplanted kidney, both Karen and her family began to speak with staff about a desire to discontinue treatment, and let the natural consequences occur. Staff generally were distressed at this and tried to persuade Karen and her family to continue. The helping professionals involved attempted to have the whole family process the decision as fully as possible, including its significance. Karen did continue treatment.

Six weeks later a high fever developed and Karen was hospitalized again and the transplanted kidney removed. At this time it was ascertained from pathology reports that there was virtually no hope of a future successful transplant. Shortly after, the shunt in Karen's arm, used for dialysis, became infected and had to be surgically altered. Although reluctant to allow the surgery, Karen agreed to have it done. When the shunt closed again three days later, the family and Karen refused to have any further surgery on the shunt area and refused to continue dialysis.

Karen died after taking an overdose of medication with her parents by her bedside. In the time between the refusal of further treatment and her death a psychiatrist had seen her and judged that her decision was carefully thought out and that she was aware of the consequences. It was later learned that she had made a will, chosen her burial spot, and had been of considerable support to her parents in the final days. (Powell, 1984, pp. 65–66; see also Schowalter, Ferholt, & Mann, 1973)

Powell's (1984) analysis will be placed within the context of the criteria outlined earlier and displayed in Table 5.1. Criterion 1 is a hopeless condition. Powell states that "Karen is not dying but she *is* terminally ill. Hemodialysis cannot cure her, though it can prolong her life" (p. 67; see also McKegney & Lange, 1971; Neu & Kjellstrand, 1986). Criterion 2 specifies that the person is not coerced into deciding to suicide. Powell remarks that "There is no suggestion that her parents have exerted their wills over Karen" (p. 66).

The third criterion has several components, which will be examined individually. The criterion first specifies an assessment of competence by a mental health professional. Powell (1984) devotes much space to the consideration of Karen's competence. First he notes Karen's depression and her parents' stress. However, he then states that "we cannot rule the decision as incompetent *simply because* it is made under conditions of stress or depression. If this were so we would be ruling out people's right to autonomy under all such conditions" (p. 66, emphasis original). He then looks at the decision through a mental status exam. He states that there were no hallucinations; that she appeared to be functioning adequately intellectually; that she had the capacity for abstract thought; that there is no evidence that her memory or ability to concentrate and attend were significantly impaired; and that her thought processing, speech, appearance, and motor behavior did not indicate lack of competence; and, finally, she appeared to have insight regarding the consequences of her decision. He concluded that "there appears to be virtually no reason to doubt her competence" (p. 66).

The next part of the decision-making process involves nonimpulsive consideration of alternatives. On this account Powell noted that "the decision to stop treatment remained firm for a period in excess of six weeks" and that all the hospital had to offer her was *more of what she apparently decided is too painful, too undignified, too hopeless. Of course, they can extend her life, but it is uncertain for how long and it is apparent that she doesn't want her life as it is to be extended. They can offer no hope that her extended life will differ in quality from life as it is now for her. (pp. 66–67, emphasis original)*

Powell (1984) did not address Karen's values directly, so one cannot adequately ascertain how her values impacted her decision, except as they relate, as noted above, to her perception of her current and future quality of life. The fourth and fifth components of criterion 3 can be combined since Karen's parents had been involved in her decision-making process from the outset. Powell notes that "it is important that Karen's decision is in accord with her parents'. What seems apparent is that the family has talked about this decision, something many families in similar positions might avoid" (p. 66). It is also evident from the case itself that her different hospital personnel have been consulted concerning her care.

Given the above analysis of Powell's (1984) position and the application of the criteria for rational suicide, it would appear that Karen's decision to die was one that could be rational. However, the sticking point is Karen's age. She was only 16, still a minor. This point is of concern to Powell as well and he notes that courts have sometimes seen adolescents as competent to make decisions that may threaten their lives. He concludes his short analysis of court decisions by stating:

even though Karen is legally a minor, there is precedence for taking her wishes into consideration, even for allowing her to make the life-determining decision, provided there is some basis for assuming her to be competent to make this decision. (p. 66)

Due to developmental considerations, Powell stated that it is important to assess an adolescent's understanding of the permanence of death. He concluded that, given her actions such as making a will, she had awareness of the consequences. He further noted that mental health professionals had been involved in helping Karen and her family discuss the decision. The fact that Karen's parents supported her decision is also important, since they are the ones the court would appoint as surrogate decision makers if Karen had been considered incompetent to make this decision.

In summary, Powell concluded that Karen, even though she is legally a minor, should be allowed to die and that her decision was rational. It is noteworthy that his analysis of Karen's decision could, fairly easily, fit into the criteria outlined above. The only aspect that was missing was a clear examination of Karen's values, although some of her relevant beliefs could be assumed given her assessment of her quality of life.

Suicide Prompted by Disability

The issue of perceived quality of life is relevant when the idea of suicide is raised in the context of physical disability. It is certainly true that many individuals are either born with or acquire significant disabilities and live happy, productive, high quality lives. However, there are others who, for any number of reasons, may be unable to cope with such changes in their views of themselves. In the case that follows there are two changes. First, the client's age is changed from 16 to 23 (and high school is changed to college) since decision making by a minor was covered above. Second, the original case presented what would have amounted to a "mercy killing"; instead here there is a potential death by suicide. These changes do not alter the interpretation of Brody's (1988) analysis but, instead, put it in the context covered here—rational suicide:

> The [client] in this case, Nancy, is a 23-year-old junior at a local college. Before her accident, she was an outstanding student. Her grades were at the top of the class, she represented the school in swimming and in track and field, and she was an outstanding folk dancer. Three months ago, Nancy was in a serious automobile accident that left her paralyzed from the neck down. For the first week or two, there was serious doubt about whether she would survive. Now her medical condition has stabilized. She has a good understanding of her condition and what she must face for the rest of her life. She is totally unwilling to accept what fate has dealt her. When people talk about rehabilitative therapy, she expresses absolutely no interest in what they have to say. Her standard response is to ask to be left alone. She expresses great regrets that her physicians pulled her through her immediate crisis after the accident, and she believes that she would be better off had she been allowed to die. She has been living with her older brother since both of her parents died some years ago. She wants to go home to his house, and he is willing to take her home as soon as possible. One of the nurses heard them talking and heard the older brother promise that he would follow her wishes and not prevent her from killing herself after they left the hospital. The nurse reported this to the attending physician, who believes that this conversation best explains why Nancy wants to go home now and why the brother wants to take her home. (Brody, 1988, p. 233)

Brody has his own framework for analyzing this case; however, in his analysis he addresses many of the points that are to be covered in the present set of criteria (see Table 5.1). The "hopeless condition" criterion for this case could be either physically debilitating condition and/or quality of life unacceptable to the individual. Without doubt, she has little hope of seeing the paralysis reduced or eliminated. The evaluation of her quality of life, as will be discussed below, is intimately connected with her personal values and views of herself and her life. Therefore, given her paralysis and her repeated statements about her perceptions of herself, it can tentatively be said that this criterion is met, from her point of view. On this issue, Brody (1988) specifically said:

> She clearly thinks she is better off dead. Having now lived for some months with her tremendous physical disabilities, she is in a better position than most to evaluate whether her continued living is a gain or a loss to her. (p. 235)

The coercion of others is not touched upon directly in the case as presented. However, it appears as if the only person who is in the position to coerce her has agreed with, rather than (as far as the data shows) initiated the discussion of suicide. Now, for the criteria outlined in this chapter, this matter needs additional exploration; however, Brody does not examine the possibility of coercion further, limiting the analysis at this point to mere speculation. If discussions with Nancy revealed no evidence that her brother had, for his own self-interest, pressured her into suiciding then this criterion would be considered satisfied. If there were hints of coercion then personal and/or family counseling would be warranted.

Brody (1988) examines criterion 3a—competence—in detail since that is a foundation of his model too. He noted, "Everyone who discusses the case with her is impressed by how much careful thought she has given to her situation" (p. 234). He continued by ruling out diagnosable depression by noting that although she is obviously (and naturally) saddened by her circumstances, this did not mean she is clinically depressed and, in fact, he found no evidence of a depression that would render her incompetent. Next is criterion 3b—nonimpulsive consideration of alternatives—to which Brody also devotes considerable attention. He stated that Nancy "may simply be overlooking at this point the various possibilities (as limited as they are) which are open to her. . . ." (p. 236). It therefore appears as if Brody believed she has not nonimpulsively examined all her options, which as a result would lead to the advice that this aspect of her decision making should be evaluated further. This is especially relevant here since it has only been three months since the accident and she may not have given herself the opportunity to adjust to her new style of living and relating to others and the environment.

In regard to considering her values (criterion 3c), Brody (1988) argued that Nancy's desire to leave the hospital (and apparently then die) "is rooted in her fundamental conception of what she values and how she sees herself as a person" (p. 235). He continues by saying, "given her current values . . . she believes that she would find the life she is living unacceptable" (p. 236). However, he then says that the values she may potentially hold if forced to live are more important than the values about her life she holds now. Brody's explanation of this is different than the author's but the outcome is the same. One could say that because she has not considered all her alternatives she does not know how they fit within her current values and therefore cannot come to a fully informed and rational decision to suicide. There is no information about her spiritual beliefs or other values and, consequently, one cannot evaluate how her decision relates to them.

As was mentioned in the brief discussion of criterion 2, her brother (the only significant other mentioned in the case) appears to accept her decision to suicide. This issue would need to be examined further, preferably (as criterion 3e would indicate) with both Nancy and her brother. Further consultations with other professionals would only be warranted if she desired to involve someone, since additional medical consultations do not appear warranted.

In sum, the present set of criteria would warrant holding Nancy in the hospital as attempts are made to discuss additional options, examine her values, and converse about the role her brother is playing in her decision making. Brody (1988) similarly decided she should be kept in the hospital with the hope that she will find an alternative acceptable. However, he concluded:

> At the end, she must be discharged, and we cannot permanently prevent Nancy and her brother from carrying out their plan. But if it persists, that may tell us that the consequences for Nancy of continued existence are truly undesirable, and that may justify the [suicide]. (p. 236)

Suicide in the Presence of Alzheimer's Disease

One additional special type of case that deserves attention is that of a person who has been diagnosed with a condition that primarily affects the brain. To demonstrate the difficulties associated with assessing for rationality with this type of client, a person with Alzheimer's disease will be used (see Table 5.1 for the criteria). Humphry and Wickett (1990; see also Battin, 1994c; Cassel & Goldstein, 1988) state that Alzheimer's disease poses the most complex question for euthanasia advocates, and rational suicide advocates as well. The difficulties lie in the progression of the disease from a point in the early years where one's life is only minimally affected to a time when life as one used to know it no longer exists; at this later time the person is not competent to make most everyday decisions, let alone a life-or-death choice. The scenario presented below is adapted from information provided in the Office of Technology Assessment Task Force report (OTA; 1988) and Gruetzner (1988):

Thomas is a 55 year old physician. For years he has been a distinguished surgeon with a thriving private practice. He has been a leader in his suburban community as well, serving on the school board and the board of directors of the area homeless shelter (where he also volunteers two nights a week). In addition to advocating for better treatment of the homeless, he has worked tirelessly to educate his community about "the necessities of having a living will and durable power of attorney instituted before you find yourself in the hospital."

During his speeches on advance directives he often used himself as an example, explaining why he has filled out these forms. Many times he has said that "All too often I see people kept physically alive by medicine and machinery well past the point when they are mentally alive. I do not want that to happen to me." With some audiences he has talked about watching his parents "deteriorate slowly with Alzheimer's disease" and said that witnessing them wither away "made me vow to myself that I would never let that happen to me nor would I force my family to watch me fade away physically and mentally."

Given his prior experience with Alzheimer's he was attuned to the fact that he had recently begun to have difficulties with his memory and that his intellectual abilities were periodically impaired to the point of his having difficulties at work and in social situations. However, it was only when his wife, Barbara, pointed out some uncharacteristic errors (such as mistakes in the checkbook and forgetting information he was recently told) that he began to truly suspect he may be in the early stages of dementia. His fears were heightened when he became lost driving to work and had to call Barbara to come and get him. Thomas and Barbara then agreed that he must be evaluated. As they began making arrangements for evaluations, Thomas told Barbara that he does not intend to die like his parents and that if he does have Alzheimer's he wants to suicide before he becomes too demented to do it himself. Thomas agreed to Barbara's request that he see a mental health professional to help him deal with stress while awaiting all the test results; however, she does agree with him that if the results do point toward Alzheimer's, and if after he has met with the counselor he still believes that suicide is his best option, she will not stand in his way.

The primary issue that must be determined immediately is whether or not Alzheimer's is the reason for the problems Thomas is experiencing. There are several conditions that can affect the brain and intellectual functioning and although Alzheimer's is the most common and is untreatable, other dementing illnesses have more hopeful prognoses. Alzheimer's can only be diagnosed once all other potential causes for dementia, some of which such as depression and hypoglycemia are reversible, that must be ruled out have been eliminated (Gruetzner, 1988; OTA, 1988). Thomas has some problems that may be indicative of Alzheimer's but without complete physical, mental, and laboratory examinations and monitoring of his behaviors a true diagnosis cannot be given. If Thomas does indeed have Alzheimer's, since the onset was prior to age 60, his illness may progress fairly rapidly, with death in less than five years (Gruetzner, 1988). If other causes are ruled out and it is concluded that Thomas does have Alzheimer's then this could be considered a hopeless condition as defined in criterion 1 (see also Battin, 1994c).

Thomas appears to have the support of his wife in his decision and it is not evident from the information given that he is being pressured by outside forces to suicide. In fact, it appears as if his decision to suicide instead of face dementia appears to have been formulated as a result of his own personal experiences prior to the onset of the disease. Thus, unless something appears upon further examination, the second criterion seems to be met.

It is within the realm of the decision-making process that the potential for an irrational decision appears. Specifically, the question is whether or not Thomas is able to make a sound decision. Gruetzner (1988, pp. 24–36) defines five stages of Alzheimer's. Stage I is called the "Early Confusional Stage" while Stage II is the "Late Confusional Stage." From Gruetzner's descriptions of these stages, Thomas' decision to suicide might be considered rational as long as he had not progressed into Stage III "Early Dementia" because in Stage III decision making is deteriorating markedly and mental status is beginning to be more globally impaired (see also Stanley, 1983). Battin (1994c) asserted that "suicide by the [person with Alzheimer's] is possible only just after diagnosis or in the comparatively early stages of the disease, when he or she is still able to form and act on a plan and is likely to have access to means of suicide" (p. 147). Gruetzner noted that disguised depression often accompanies the early stages of Alzheimer's and that its presence could exacerbate the dementia so this should be considered and treated if present (see also OTA, 1988, pp. 287–288).

The OTA (1988, pp. 272–326) report provided an overview of many structured assessment procedures and instruments. Several mental status exams are listed along with factors that complicate their valid and reliable use with Alzheimer's disease. The key factor in this assessment is the status of the person's decision-making abilities (or "competence"—see chapter 7). Although many people might assume that the presence of Alzheimer's would preclude the possibility of competence, such is not the case. Buchanan and Brock (1989) noted that competence is decision relative:

A person may suffer from cerebral arteriosclerosis, from Alzheimer's disease or other dementias, or from psychosis, and yet still be competent to make some decisions—at least at certain times, in certain environments. To make a judgment that an individual is competent or incompetent is to make a judgment about the adequacy of the person's decision-making capabilities to the task at hand. As such, it cannot be reduced to a medical judgment concerning diagnosis. (p. 281; see also Culver, 1985; OTA, 1988, pp. 170–173; Stanley, 1983)

Therefore, if after testing Thomas is considered to be competent to make decisions regarding his health care, then his decision to suicide may be considered rational. Stanley (1983) describes five ways of assessing for competence and concludes:

for [people] in the early confusional stages of dementia, it is likely that they would be judged competent by all of the standards. However, as the disease progresses into the latter phase of the dementia stage, competence is likely to be achieved only by those standards which employ a minimal amount of assessment. (p. 64)

The second section of this criterion is that the decision be nonimpulsive and the person must have considered alternatives. Although Thomas has apparently thought about the possibility of his developing Alzheimer's for some time, it is not clear that his decision to suicide was nonimpulsive. In other words, he may have concluded suicide was his only option because he saw no way to continue living in a dignified manner and/or he was concerned about the impact on his family. He may not have considered other options such as giving talks about Alzheimer's as a way of providing meaning in his life and getting home health care to help his wife take care of him (see OTA, 1988, pp. 202, 247–262).

Next, there is the examination of how congruent the decision is with the person's values. Although there is not a description of his spiritual beliefs, given Thomas' outspoken support of advance directives and his frequent use of his own ideas about what constitutes a satisfactory quality of life, it appears as if his decision to suicide is consistent with his values.

In regard to the consideration of others, the vignette mentions that Thomas' wife has said that she agrees with his decision. There is no indication that the couple has children or if Thomas has siblings who should be considered. This area would need further examination but if no additional significant others are found then Thomas appears to have satisfied this point.

Finally, significant others and any other relevant professionals should be consulted. As mentioned previously, his wife has been consulted but one may want to make sure that her assent was given voluntarily. It would also be appropriate to see if any additional significant others who had been identified should be consulted. There are numerous additional professionals who could be brought in, including physicians, mental health professionals, and so forth (e.g., see OTA, 1988, pp. 202, 247–262). However, if the above is viewed as valid—that Thomas has made a competent, value-congruent choice that is acceptable to his significant others in the face of a hopeless condition—then no other individuals need be consulted unless Thomas requests their involvement.

In sum, the assessment of rationality in this case rests on two points. First, whether or not Thomas does indeed have Alzheimer's disease and not some treatable form of dementia and, second, if he does have Alzheimer's, at what stage is the illness. If the disease is in the early stages then Thomas can be considered competent to make the decision to suicide, provided he is able to pass the appropriate tests of competence. Given that periods of lucidity may be intermittent, this should be taken into account and the decision he voices during a time of clear competence should be given full weight.

FINAL CONSIDERATIONS

One point that should be evident, but that will be emphasized here, is the majority of people who are now prevented from suiciding would also be screened out by the set of criteria described in this chapter. Those who are psychotic or severely depressed, acting manipulatively or impulsively, have been coerced or deluded, will be detected with these criteria. The criteria also effectively take into account the arguments against rational suicide reviewed in chapter 3. For example, the suicidal person's religious and spiritual beliefs will be taken into account by having the individual consider her or his personal values (criterion 3c). The presence of mental illness or depression that is not allowing a rational consideration of alternatives will be evaluated (criteria 3a, 3b, and 3e). The potentially negative impact on others will be evaluated (criterion 3d and 3e) and the possibility of coercion entering into the suicidal decision is to be considered (criterion 2).

The argument that poses the greatest difficulty for the criteria is the "slippery slope." Recall that the idea is that once allowed for anyone, it will become difficult to restrict suicide to this group. Criterion 1 attempts to take this into account by specifying the person's condition must be "hopeless." However, hopelessness is a relative term, unless it is defined operationally. Many proponents of rational suicide define hopeless as death within a fairly brief time, such as six months or a year (e.g., Oregon Right to Die, 1994). However, the respondents to the surveys conducted thus far did not believe terminal illness was the only condition that could justify a rational suicide.

The view that psychological pain can be as acceptable a reason for suicide as physical pain may be controversial. However, as Maltsberger (1994) noted, "There is a parallel between [the] suffering of the incurable physically ill patient kept alive by artificial means and the suffering of the incurable mentally ill patient being kept alive by prolonged hospitalization and close monitoring" (p. 441). He continued,

> From time to time a patient's treatment response is poor; and suicide continues in his [or her] mind as the best option. The classical example of this difficulty is that of a person only partially recovered from schoizophrenia. It has long been argued that in intracable mental illness where suffering is substantial and recovery unlikely, the prevention of suicide is inhumane (Bleuler, 1950). (Maltsberger, 1994, p. 441)

Many others have noted that the rates of suicide for people with schizophrenia are highest after their symptoms have gone into remission, lending support to the theory that the person is unwilling to face a life with the possibility of periodic psychotic episodes (Battin, 1982; Black & Winokur, 1990; Buda & Tsuang, 1990; Dublin, 1963; Farberow et al., 1976a; Kjervik, 1984; Maltsberger, 1994; Morgan, 1979; Pokorny, 1968; Tanney, 1992; Widiger & Rinaldi, 1983; see also Maguire, 1975; Slater, 1980).

Fletcher (1975) argued for a broader acceptance of times that could be used as justification for hastening death when he said, "*The logic of what I am saying is that we should drop the classical sanctity-of-life ethic and embrace a quality-of-life ethic instead*" (p. 46, emphasis original). However, the issue of quality of life considered unbearable to the person is bound to be contentious. Some may argue that this is too vague and that the threshold for allowing suicide may therefore be set too low. Yet, many authors have emphasized that pain, suffering, and quality of life are subjective states (Barrington, 1980; R. L. Barry, 1994; Battin, 1982; Cappon, 1962; Cassell, 1982; Decker, 1977; Engelhardt & Malloy, 1982; Farberow et al., 1976b; Fox & Lipton, 1983; Heyd & Bloch, 1981; Jacobs & Teicher, 1967; Kjervik, 1984; Leonard, 1967; Maguire, 1975; Maltsberger, 1994; Maris, 1986; Motto, 1981; Nelson, 1984; Peterson, 1985; Quill, 1994; Smith, 1989; Werth, 1992; Widiger & Rinaldi, 1983). Furthermore, courts have held that quality of life and suffering are relevant factors to consider when deciding whether or not to allow the discontinuation of life-sustaining treatment (Peterson, 1985; Sandak, 1978; Smith, 1989).

Cassell (1982) provides an in-depth discussion of suffering and he repeatedly makes the point that suffering is not just a physical experience and that someone may be in great pain but not suffer as much as another person who may have less acute physical pain. He stated that "suffering occurs when an impending destruction of the person is perceived" and said "suffering is ultimately a personal matter" (p. 640). In regard to the latter he discussed the importance of religion, values, and personal meaning. One of the most enlightening and relevant aspects of his article was his "description of the person" (pp. 641–643) in which he pointed out numerous ways in which each person is different and, therefore, numerous factors that will influence the amount of, and one's own personal interpretation and acceptance of, suffering. Cassell offered ideas for the amelioration of suffering but he conceded that some suffering may not be able to be alleviated, and this is when hopelessness (possibly appropriately) occurs.

Therefore, the key to this criterion is the modifier "hopeless." This means that there is an extremely small chance, if any, that the person can expect her or his overall life condition (in Cassell's [1982] terms, the amount of suffering) to improve—regardless of the alternatives implemented (see also Laforet, 1963; Maltsberger, 1994; Mesler, 1995; Schowalter et al., 1973). Granted, some medications may alleviate great pain, but with the side effect of unconsciousness; an operation may prolong life in exchange for limited mental functioning; a procedure may reduce suffering but require losing physical abilities. In these, and other, circumstances, the person whose quality of life is impacted is the best judge of what options are acceptable and which options cost too much. A counselor may have seen a dozen other clients with exactly the same condition as the person currently in front of him or her who decided to choose alternative A and go on to live happily; however, the person in front of the counselor now is unique and just because alternative A was appropriate for those other people does not necessarily mean that it will work for the current individual. What one person may believe is tolerable may be too much for another. Is it appropriate to hold Person X up to Person Z's standards and force her or him to suffer what she or he believes to be unbearable pain just because for one reason or another Person Z can handle more? Does this necessarily make Person X irrational for wanting to suicide? It is in this evaluation of the person's quality of life, from her or his point of view, that the other criteria listed come into play and must be weighed accordingly.

6

Additional Considerations:
Necessary Research, Prejudice, and Values

The purpose of this chapter is threefold. First, to provide some suggestions about further research that is needed on rational suicide. Second, to discuss briefly the potential impact of prejudice and discrimination on the evaluation of rationality. Third, to examine in more depth the impact of values, especially spirituality, on the assessment of rational suicide.

DIRECTIONS FOR FUTURE RESEARCH

The results of the Werth (1994b) study point to several directions for future research. First and foremost, research involving other types of mental health professionals would be important to determine the generalizability of the results. Of special significance would be social workers because their national organization is the only one to set forth new guidelines related to end-of-life decisions (NASW, 1994). In addition, because of the limited representation by non-European American therapists, surveys of ethnic minority professionals might provide important information on the acceptability of suicide and belief in rational suicide within these groups (Backer, 1994). One final group that needs to be surveyed to determine what the acceptable practices of therapists are when working with rationally suicidal clients would be the general public (J. Galassi and R. Pipes, personal communications, February, 1994).

Additional research should begin using conditions other than terminal bone cancer, AIDS, and endogenous depression as precipitating conditions for suicide so that the hypothesized continua of acceptance and action can be more clearly delineated (see also Werth & Liddle, 1994; Werth, 1995). Given that some respondents in both the Werth (1994b) study and the Werth and Cobia (1995a) investigation were for the inclusion of psychologically related conditions (such as schizophrenia and Alzheimer's) while other respondents, especially in the Werth (1994b) study, were opposed vehemently to the inclusion of depression, researchers should consider using persons with these other psychologically related conditions when asking about what circumstances would constitute a rational suicide. However, Werth's (1994b) finding that respondents indicated they would interact less with a man with depression than a man with AIDS warrants further investigation. Also, the presence or absence of pain, even in terminal conditions, may be an important variable that needs further attention (see Martin & Range, 1991).

Another area that needs examination is the impact of the demographic characteristics of the suicidal person. For example, most of the studies investigating acceptability of suicide have used a male ideator; the two studies that compared male and female ideators found that women were viewed more negatively (Deluty, 1989; Lo Presto et al., 1995). This indicates that gender effects need to be looked at more closely. Although the race/ethnicity of the ideator was not specified in Werth's (1994b) vignette, this may be an important characteristic to vary, especially if the respondents are culturally diverse because of both racism and ethnocentrism (see the Racism/Ethnocentrism section later in this chapter) as well as cultural differences regarding the acceptability of suicide (Backer, 1994). In like fashion, the age of the ideator may be crucial. The Werth study and the Werth and Liddle (1994) investigation used middle-aged ideators. An investigation of how respondents feel about younger (e.g., teenagers, people in their mid- to late twenties) and older (e.g., people over the age of 65, people in their eighties or nineties) people suiciding would be helpful. This is especially relevant given the "greying of America" and the possibility that ageism (the discounting of individuals who are older [Schaie, 1993]) could lead respondents to be more accepting of suicide by the elderly. Along these same lines, ideators that differ in terms of disabilities may also offer important data regarding negative views of persons with disabilities (Livneh, 1984). Both age and disability are potentially more relevant stigmatizing factors (in regard to justification for rational suicide) than sexual orientation, so, for example, varying the descriptions of the suicidal ideators in terms of these characteristics may lead to greater levels of acceptance for suicide and less action to prevent suicide for the more disabled and/or older ideators.

Finally, interviews with mental health professionals about their beliefs and experience related to rational suicide would help clarify some of the relevant issues (see Gurrister & Kane, 1978). Such a face-to-face format would allow for distinguishing between the reasons for believing in rational suicide and the professional's personal definition of the concept. In addition, the criteria generated in the Werth (1994b) study and in Werth and Cobia (1995a) could be used to develop a questionnaire or a series of vignettes that differ in their inclusion of the criteria. These instruments could then be used to collect more objective data related specifically to rational suicide.

THE POTENTIAL IMPACT
OF PREJUDICE AND DISCRIMINATION

As mentioned above, additional research is needed to assess the potential impact, if any, of age, gender, ethnicity, and disability on the acceptability of suicide. For example, because Werth (1994b) was concerned that stigma related to homophobia, heterosexism, and "AIDS-phobia" may bias the assessment of rationality, he examined the impact of sexual orientation and type of terminal disease on ratings of acceptability and action. Similar concerns about the fair treatment of suicidality can be raised due to documented incidents of ableism, ageism, racism, and sexism. Since the literature related to discrimination is large, this chapter will not attempt to prove the existence of these conditions. Instead, attention will be given solely to material that specifically relates these types of discrimination to suicide.

Ableism

Gill (1992; see also R. L. Barry, 1994; Battin, 1994d; Clark, 1992; Hendin, 1982) provided an in-depth discussion of suicide and disability. She gave convincing arguments that many suicidal persons with disabilities may not be as rational in their desire to die as nondisabled people may want to believe. She emphasized that individuals with disabilities were devalued by society and that the disadvantages experienced by those with disabilities contributes to depression and, therefore, to suicidality. She alluded to projection on the part of those without disabilities onto those with them as a reason for support of requests to die by persons with disabilities, which leads to an incomplete examination of what she considered to be the real reasons for suicidality and to an incomplete examination of alternatives to death.

Ageism

It is a widely documented fact that older adults suicide more frequently than others, and that there is a higher ratio of completed suicides to attempts among this group. There are undoubtedly numerous reasons for this state of affairs (see Richman, 1992), which are not directly relevant to the present discussion. However, one potential explanation, which is a primary concern of those who are against rational suicide, is that culturally based discrimination against the elderly will lead to an inordinate and inappropriate number of older adults suiciding. This devaluation of the elderly, called ageism, is especially relevant in discussion of rational suicide since some (e.g., Barrington, 1980; Portwood, 1978; Prado, 1990) specifically support the idea of allowing elderly individuals in general to suicide. Numerous authors have mentioned the danger ageism poses to the assessment of rationality of a decision to suicide, especially if economic factors are considered relevant (e.g., R. L. Barry, 1994; Battin, 1982, 1994c, 1994d, 1994e; Clark, 1992; Colt, 1991; Finnerty, 1987; Francis, 1980; Hendin, 1982; Humphry & Wickett, 1990; Maguire, 1975; McIntosh, 1993a; Moore, 1993; "Public Actions," 1992; Richman, 1988, 1992; Ringel, 1980; Siegel, 1982a, 1982b, 1986).

Racism/Ethnocentrism

The opponents of rational suicide have seldom raised the issues of racism or ethnocentrism as a concern; however, they are included here as a logical extension of other fears related to inappropriate application of rational suicide to disenfranchised groups (see "Public Actions," 1992). Some authors have compared statistics and attitudes about suicide among groups in the United States (e.g., Earls, Escobar, & Manson, 1990; McIntosh & Santos, 1984; Reynolds, Kalish, & Farberow, 1975) while others have focused on a specific group (e.g., Early, 1992; Hendin, 1982; Webb & Willard, 1975). In general, these discussions do not address the issues of rational suicide or racism and instead attempt to explain why suicide occurs among these populations and/or what members of these groups believe about suicide (an interesting side note is that Colt [1991] said that 99% of the Hemlock Society's membership is European American). For example, focus is placed on the stresses (e.g., discrimination) members of these disenfranchised groups experience and on the cultural buffers (e.g., family) that may help reduce the overall impact of suicide. Few authors (e.g., Hendin, 1969, 1982; Marzen et al., 1985) specifically mention racism as a reason why young African-American men have such a comparatively high suicide (and homicide) rate.

Sexism

A few authors (e.g., R. L. Barry, 1994, pp. 286–288; Miles & August, 1990) claim that the pattern of court decisions and other incidents related to requests to die shows evidence of sexism and misogyny. For example, Miles and August (1990) concluded that "Gender profoundly affects judicial analysis of right-to-die cases. Judicial reasoning about men stresses the role of personal autonomy in these controversial decisions. Judicial reasoning about women examines the role of caregivers" (p. 91). Barry (1994) argued that this pattern "can be best explained by the influence of sexist bias against" women and the belief that "a man should not be burdened by a woman who cannot fulfill her proper 'feminine' responsibilities. . . ." (p. 288). In contrast to these ideas, Deluty (1989), along with Lo Presto and colleagues (1995), found that in a survey of undergraduates, suicide by a woman was judged more negatively than suicide by a man.

Analysis

The impact of discriminatory attitudes on the evaluation of rational suicide is an important matter. However, the criteria outlined in chapter 5 should provide for adequate checks on the possibility that individual or societal prejudice is entering into the decision about the rationality of a decision to suicide. For example, old age in and of itself is not a hopeless condition; there must be some additional factors present to warrant deeming a life unworthy of living. True, the suicidal elderly person may say that old age by itself is reason enough to suicide; however, exploration of the person's reasoning will probably indicate that there are other operative factors, such as isolation, which could potentially be ameliorated through ideas generated during the consideration of alternatives. Similarly, a person with a disability may say that suicide is the best option but, upon further examination, it may be evident that overwhelmed family members are subtly influencing the individual's decision making.

The possible prejudice in the evaluating therapist could be detected through the use of consultation and collaboration in assessing rationality with a second therapist uninvolved in the case, which is standard practice when working with suicidal clients (see chapter 7). To further examine the possibility of discriminatory attitudes entering into the assessment process, consultation with an expert in a particular area (e.g., family therapy, gerontology, disabilities, diversity, gender issues, chronic/terminal illnesses) may be beneficial.

THE ROLE OF VALUES

Personal values and morals are inextricably intertwined in the issue of rational suicide. Of course, it is inevitable that the counselor's values will play a part in virtually all therapeutic situations (see, e.g., Van Hoose & Kottler, 1985) but, because of the learned emotional response to suicide, the potential conflict between therapist and client is brought into high relief in situations involving suicide (e.g., Beckerman, 1995; deCatanzaro, 1981; Erard, 1994; Heyd & Bloch, 1981; Maltsberger, 1994). On one hand there is the counselor who, by the very nature of his or her work, daily, even hourly, attempts to affirm that change can occur, that life can take a turn for the better, that hope is possible. On the other hand there is the client who, for some possibly rational reason refuses to believe that life is worth living. It is at this basic level that the potential for problems originates.

The notion of a mental health professional forcing her or his values onto a client is unsettling to most practitioners. Although it is widely recognized that counselors cannot be completely value free in sessions, it is also commonly accepted that the client has the right to take actions that appear foolish or are antithetical to the therapist's beliefs or to not act in ways that would meet with the counselor's approval. In most cases it would be viewed as unethical for the professional to force a client to subscribe to her or his values; however, such is not the case with suicide (Werth, 1994a). For it is in the case of suicide, perhaps more than any other, that the counselor may attempt to force her or his values on the client and disregard the client's avowed view. This is not to say that questioning the client's decision is inappropriate but, rather, that dismissing a client's well-reasoned decision to suicide because it conflicts with the therapist's beliefs is improper and shows little respect for the client and her or his personal world view.

Several authors have discussed how the therapist's values impact the counseling process with clients who are suicidal. One of the most common points is that the counselor's belief in the sanctity of life at all costs can lead to lack of consideration of the client's (potentially rational) belief otherwise (e.g., Beckerman, 1995; Diggory, 1968; Hendin, 1982; Kahn, 1990; Maltsberger, 1994; Snipe, 1988; Werth, 1994a). In related fashion, many have noted that suicidal clients in general, and especially clients who may be rational in their suicidality, confront the counselor with existential questions about life's value and meaning (B. Barry, 1984; Snipe, 1988; Szasz, 1986; Widiger & Rinaldi, 1983). Naturally, the easiest way to avoid such an existential crisis is to discard the idea that suicide can be rational or, in reaction to the uneasy feeling, to relentlessly pursue the prevention of all suicides (B. Barry, 1984; Pretzel, 1984; Widiger & Rinaldi, 1983). Similarly, if therapists view a client's suicide as a "failure" then they will be motivated to intervene at all costs (B. Barry, 1984; Beckerman, 1995; Diggory, 1968). In all of these ways one actually learns more about what the counselor needs than what the client needs:

> We suicidologists and physicians have a strong compulsion to meddle with other people's lives, to save their souls, to tell them how to live (and die)—even if it makes them miserable. Suicide prevention often does tell us more about the needs of the helper than about the needs of the suicidal individual. (Maris, 1986, p. 331)

Thus, there is the danger of the therapist believing that her or his values are paramount. Clements, Sider, and Perlmutter (1983) presented the view that the counselor's values are the most important because "with suicide the therapist is working within his [or her] own value system, [therefore] there are no 'right-to-die' issues" (p. 40) and, further, that "the ethical justification for intervention will have to be in terms of the values of the intervener" (p. 32). These authors argued that the client's view is irrelevant and the therapist's is correct (presumably as long as the therapist believes intervention is the best option; see also Motto, 1972; Szasz, 1976).

Mayo pointed out that the approach taken by Clements and her colleagues (1983) rejects "for the most part the relevance of the question 'what is in the best interests of the suicidal person?'"(Mayo, 1983, p. 337). The importance of this question should be clear when rational suicide is considered (B. Barry, 1984). Without considering the best interests of the client, the counselor runs the risk of preventing suicide for the sake of prevention instead of for the sake of the client. On this note, Heyd and Bloch (1981) asserted that with the intrusion of therapist values "there is the danger of an unsympathetic or unduly paternalistic attitude replacing rational evaluation and humane understanding of the [client's] situation" (p. 186; see also Beckerman, 1995; Maltsberger, 1994). This lack of empathy and the belief "that suicide is undesirable may in part derive from a misunderstanding of the personal situations of suicides and a faulty projection of self onto others' circumstances" which may lead to a discounting of the other person's suffering and inability to cope (deCatanzaro, 1981, p. 142; see also Maltsberger, 1994).

Because of the possibility for discounting, misunderstanding, and lacking empathy when counselors impose their values about life and beliefs about suicide on their clients, commentators usually recommend that, "with regard to suicide, therefore, we hold that persons are the best judges of the proper balance of values in their lives" (Lebacqz & Engelhardt, 1977, p. 689; see also Kastenbaum, 1976; Kjervik, 1984). Nelson (1984) put a slightly different emphasis on the point when he asserted that, "Thus in dealing with the potential suicide, the question 'What do I have to live for?,' perhaps should be considered more from the subjective viewpoint of the individual than from the relatively abstract position of social or professional norms" (p. 1330; see also Maltsberger, 1994; Pretzel, 1984).

The concern about how to balance the professional's and the client's perspectives has led Motto (1972, 1981, 1983, 1994a; see also Baelz, 1980; Beckerman, 1995) to note that the therapist is put in a difficult place when faced with a potentially rational client because the counselor must rely on her or his intuitive judgment regarding the rationality of the decision. However, as Battin (1982) has stated, this leaves an "out" for the preventionist because she or he can always claim that intervention was based on intuitive judgment. Still, several professionals (and the courts, see, e.g., Peterson, 1985), even those who advocate for suicide prevention, have stated that as hope for recovery diminishes, the professional's obligation shifts away from intervention (e.g., Clements et al., 1983; Maltsberger, 1994).

The Impact of Spirituality

Spiritual beliefs are one important component of, and influence upon, an individual's values. As a result, the spiritual beliefs of both the client and the counselor are vital components of the rational suicide assessment process. Several authors have noted that the official positions of many religious denominations (and therefore, it is assumed, some cultures) are forcefully against both rational suicide and active euthanasia (e.g., R. L. Barry, 1994; Battin, 1994f; deCatanzaro, 1981; Dublin, 1963; Earls et al., 1990; Early, 1992; Humphry & Wickett, 1990; Maris, 1981; Marzen et al., 1985; Rauscher, 1981). Since entire books have been devoted to explaining and justifying these positions such a discussion will not be repeated here.

Recall that even though self-reported degree of spirituality did not have a significant impact on the ratings of acceptability, action, or stigma in the studies described in chapter 4 (Werth, 1994b; Werth & Liddle, 1994), it was cited (Werth, 1994b) as a reason for objecting to the idea of rational suicide (see chapters 5 and 7). Several studies have investigated the impact of religious denomination on attitudes toward euthanasia and rational suicide and, contrary to expectations, have found equivocal results; however, many have also found that strength of religious beliefs is an important variable among members of the general public (e.g., Blendon, Szalay, & Knox, 1992; Domino & Miller, 1992; Johnson et al., 1980; Lo Presto et al., 1995; Roper Organization of New York City, 1988). Furthermore, it is important to note that such views exist and are particularly strong in some cultures (see, e.g., Earls et al., 1990; Early, 1992).

Although spiritually based arguments should not be used to discard the idea of rational suicide (see chapter 3), it is true that spiritual beliefs do keep some people from suiciding (see, e.g., Courage et al., 1993) and do provide the basis for the interventionist stance of some mental health professionals. The concern here is not for the former but for the latter—when these spiritually based values are forced upon the lives of clients. In other words, it is appropriate and acceptable for a counselor to attempt to discuss the client's spiritual beliefs and values but it is inappropriate and unacceptable for a professional to disregard a clients well-reasoned decision to suicide because it conflicts with the therapist's spiritual beliefs.

The standard approach in mental health work is to refer a client out when therapy is stuck for one reason or another, if one does not have the competence necessary to counsel a particular individual, or if one has professional or personal reasons for not working with a specific person or on a given concern. This should be the case with rational suicide as well (see also Harris, 1994; NASW, 1994). If one cannot, because of one's strongly held religious beliefs or other values, assess for rationality with a suicidal client who is requesting this then the client should be referred to a competent professional who can perform such an assessment (see also Humphry & Wickett, 1990, p. 178). Such an approach is analogous to referring a client for testing or to a therapist who specializes in work with a special issue or population.

CONCLUSION

Clearly, the personal beliefs and values of mental health professionals will impact their attitudes about the acceptability of rational suicide. As a result, it is important for research to survey a broad range of professionals and to manipulate research variables so as to determine if negative beliefs about a particular population are strong enough to lead to bias in assessments of the rationality of a decision to suicide.

In any event, it is crucial that therapists be aware of how their own values may be interfering with the acceptance of a client's rational decision to suicide. Several authors have noted that if a client has genuinely decided she or he wants to die then "one can question whether the therapist is justified in imposing his or her own values rather than permitting the [client] to achieve the result he or she wishes" (Amchin et al., 1990, p. 639; see also Beckerman, 1995; Brandt, 1975; Kjervik, 1984; Werth, 1992). The counselor's values about the necessity of suicide prevention may be based on a spiritual belief system but whether they are or not, therapists have the obligation not to force their values upon clients but to instead refer out those clients they cannot help; or, if one's belief system will allow suicide in some circumstances, then one should attempt to carefully delineate what those conditions would be (see Baelz, 1980, for a discussion of this point in terms of spirituality).

Unfortunately, instead of utilizing an evaluative approach that would consider the client's best interests and take her or his circumstances into account, the ethical and legal standards of care that mental health professionals must follow have been based upon beliefs about the sanctity of life at all costs (see chapter 7). For example, Berman & Cohen-Sandler (1983) noted that "regardless of one's right to suicide, mental health caretakers have a professional responsibility to intervene and are required by law to attempt to prevent opportunity for an anticipated suicidal attempt" (p. 15). Thus, currently, counselors are obligated to force values that they may not even hold upon clients who may also adhere to a different belief system about the sanctity of life, the role of suffering, and the proper way to live and die.

7

Ethical and Legal Implications

Three topics will be covered in this chapter. First, there will be an overview of the currently articulated standards of care when working with clients who are suicidal. Second will be a discussion of the final set of qualitative results from the Werth (1994b) study. Third will be a discussion of the ethical and legal implications of the research described in this book.

CURRENTLY ARTICULATED STANDARDS OF CARE

In order to provide relevant information on the presently accepted standards of care when working with clients who are suicidal, this portion of the text will attend to several different areas. The sections, which will build upon each other, include malpractice, client competence and hospitalization, and recommendations for practice. Technically, there are two ways to be liable for suicide—causing a client to suicide and failing to prevent suicide (e.g., Bednar et al., 1991; Howell, 1978; Knuth, 1979; E. V. Swenson, 1986). The emphasis here will be on failure to prevent a suicide as this is more likely in the case of rational suicide, although the discussion of recommendations will touch upon the causation issue.

Malpractice

There are four elements included in the definition of malpractice: (1) the existence of a duty, (2) a breach of that duty, (3) the client suffers injuries, and (4) there is a causal link between the breach and the injuries. The key component of the definition of malpractice at present is the second condition—whether or not the counselor's actions fell below the accepted standard of practice—read this as "behavior of average, reasonable, practitioner"'—of others in that person's profession (see especially Bongar, 1991; see also Ahia & Martin, 1993; Amchin et al., 1990; Appelbaum & Gutheil, 1991; Austin, Moline, & Williams, 1990; Bednar et al., 1991; Berman & Cohen-Sandler, 1982, 1983; Bongar & Greaney, 1994; Bongar, Maris, Berman, & Litman, 1992; Corey, Corey, & Callanan, 1993; Gutheil, 1992; Gutheil et al., 1983; Harris, 1994; Hoge & Appelbaum, 1989; Knapp & VandeCreek, 1983; Knuth, 1979; Meyer et al., 1988; Robertson, 1988; Slawson, Flinn, & Schwartz, 1974; Stromberg et al., 1988; E. V. Swenson, 1986; L. C. Swenson, 1993; VandeCreek, Knapp, & Herzog, 1987; Van Hoose & Kottler, 1985; Victoroff, 1983; Wood, Marks, & Dilley, 1992). Negligent conduct can be an act or the omission of an act. It should be noted that the fact that a client has suicided does not necessarily mean that the counselor was negligent in the treatment provided; however, courts and juries may still rule in favor of the families of the deceased in an attempt to alleviate suffering (see, e.g., Maltsberger, 1994).

Many authors (e.g., Ahia & Martin, 1993; Amchin et al., 1990; Bednar et al., 1991; Berman & Cohen-Sandler, 1982; Bongar, 1991; Bongar & Greaney, 1994; Bongar et al., 1992; Corey et al., 1993; Howell, 1978; Knapp & VandeCreek, 1983; Knuth, 1979; Stromberg et al., 1988; E. V. Swenson, 1986; Wood et al., 1992) discuss three criteria that could be used to assess for liability when a suicide occurs: (1) foreseeability, (2) reasonableness of judgment in treatment planning, and (3) thoroughness of treatment plan implementation. This formulation may arise out of the court's decision in *Bellah v. Greenson* that "a therapist could be liable for an outpatient's suicide if this conduct could have been reasonably foreseen and the therapist failed to take reasonable preventive measures" (E. V. Swenson, 1986, p. 417). Because foreseeability (recognition) of the suicidal act has been assumed for the purposes of this book, this aspect is not relevant to the discussion here.

In regard to treatment planning, the traditional literature on working with clients who are suicidal clearly defines the required standard of care as action to prevent the suicide, with the only latitude being in terms of the coerciveness of that intervention. Several authors, for example, appear to believe that "certain special relationships, such as that which exists between a therapist and a suicidal client, create the existence of the duty to prevent suicide" (Bednar et al., 1991, p. 94; see also Amchin et al., 1990; Berman & Cohen-Sandler, 1983; Bongar, 1991; Corey et al., 1993; Kjervik, 1984; Knapp & VandeCreek, 1983; Knuth, 1979; Meyer et al., 1988; E. V. Swenson, 1986; Van Hoose & Kottler, 1985; Victoroff, 1983; Wood et al., 1992). Similarly, it is often claimed that "the law requires you to break confidentiality when you assess a client to be of high risk of committing suicide" (Austin, Moline, and Williams, 1990, p. 139; see also Ahia & Martin, 1993; Amchin et al., 1990; Arthur & Swanson, 1993; Corey et al., 1993; L. C. Swenson, 1993; Victoroff, 1983). Finally, others assert that all the major professional organizations of mental health professionals have "taken the position that practitioners must reveal certain information when there is clear and imminent danger to an individual or to society" (Corey et al., 1993, p.109).

Thus, the reasonable precautions typically advocated have as their goal the prevention of any suicide attempt. However, although treatment plans must still be consistent with the standards of care, the idea of what constitutes reasonable precautions has expanded in recent years (Austin et al., 1990; Bongar, 1991; Bongar & Greaney, 1994; Knapp & VandeCreek, 1983; Slawson et al., 1974; L. C. Swenson, 1993; VandeCreek et al., 1987), due in part to the changing opinions of mental health and suicide experts (Berman & Cohen-Sandler, 1982; Bongar, 1991; Knapp

& VandeCreek, 1983). This is important because courts have decided that if there are several acceptable approaches to a problem (e.g., suicide), then the professional can choose among them, even if the chosen action is not the most commonly selected, as long as a "significant" or "respectable" minority of professionals of similar training and experience practice in that manner (Appelbaum & Gutheil, 1991; Bednar et al., 1991; Berman & Cohen-Sandler, 1983; Bongar, 1991, 1993; Knapp & VandeCreek, 1983; Meyer et al., 1988; Robertson, 1988; Stromberg et al., 1988; E. V. Swenson, 1986; Victoroff, 1983; Waltzer, 1980). Consequently, "the respectable minority rule provides that the mere use of a minority approach in treating a [client] is not an automatic breach of the required standard of care" (Robertson, 1988, p. 444).

In the case of suicide prevention, therefore, the suggestions for intervention have broadened in recent years (although conspicuously absent from the literature and, consequently, from the articulated standards of care is the proposal that the counselor assess the rationality of the decision to suicide). Potential ways to try to prevent a client from suiciding include informing significant others (as long as the other individuals will be supportive of the person who is suicidal), contracting, increasing session frequency, referring the client for medication, and hospitalization—voluntary or involuntary (e.g., Bednar et al., 1991; Berman & Cohen-Sandler, 1983; Bongar, 1991; Bongar et al., 1992; Meyer et al., 1988; E. V. Swenson, 1986; Wood et al., 1992).

The determination of whether or not the counselor has practiced up to the standards of care is usually made by expert witnesses (Amchin et al., 1990; Appelbaum & Gutheil, 1991; Bednar et al., 1991; Bongar, 1991; Bongar & Greaney, 1994; Bongar et al., 1992; Knapp & VandeCreek, 1983; Robertson, 1988; Stromberg et al., 1988; VandeCreek et al., 1987; Wood et al., 1992). This has ramifications since, for example, the leadership of the American Association of Suicidology has, for the most part, been staunchly opposed to the idea of rational suicide (Cotton, 1993), even though many of the members of the organization may accept the concept (see the discussion in chapter 5 of Werth & Cobia's [1995b] preliminary results and Kaplan & Adamek [1995]).

However, regarding the applicability of existing standards of care when there is the possibility of rational suicide, Harris (1994), a psychologist–attorney and risk management consultant, said,

> there are, as far as I know, no generally accepted national standards for [mental health professionals] about how to treat [clients] who are considering rational suicide. There are standards which exist for treating [clients] who are considering irrational suicide . . . . But a [mental health professional] is no more expert than any other member of the public in recognizing or preventing "rational" suicide. (p. 2–3; see also Kjervik, 1984)

This also has implications for determining who is qualified to be an expert witness in a case involving a potentially rational suicide since, in order to be considered capable of being an expert witness, one "must demonstrate that he or she has acquired special knowledge of the subject matter about which testimony is to be given" (Berman & Cohen-Sandler, 1983, p. 7.; see also Stromberg et al., 1988).

Competence and Hospitalization

One of the most commonly recommended interventions by experts, although also the most intrusive and paternalistic, when working with a client who is seriously suicidal is to hospitalize the person, involuntarily if necessary. Thus, whether or not a counselor decided to hospitalize an outpatient client may be an important point for courts and expert witnesses when determining liability for a death. In fact, some authors (e.g., Bednar et al., 1991; Robertson, 1988; E. V. Swenson, 1986; Waltzer, 1980) recommend hospitalization for even moderately suicidal clients, overtly for the sake of the client but also as a sign that everything possible was done to prevent death from occurring (see also Greenberg, 1974). However, often missing from discussions of hospitalization is the determination of competence of the client as well as an examination of civil commitment statutes, both of which are extremely relevant in the case of a client who may be rational in her or his suicidality. This section will provide a measure of basic information about competence and will then examine hospitalization, specifically involuntary inpatient commitment, in light of an examination of client competence.

To put the issue of competence in context, it may be helpful to examine first the outline of the "elements of a legally valid decision" which are often discussed in terms of informed consent (e.g., Appelbaum & Grisso, 1995; Culver & Gert, 1982; Grisso, 1986; Maltsberger, 1994; Meisel, Roth, & Lidz, 1977; Tepper & Elwork, 1984). First, the decision must be voluntary or free from coercion. The person must then be provided with information about risks and benefits of available alternatives, including the option of receiving no treatment; the person must be competent; and the person should be able to understand the information provided. Finally, the person needs to make a decision. Of relevance here is the provision that the person be competent—have the capacity to participate in a sound decision-making process.

Because competence is a legal expression and courts often define terms differently from laypeople and mental health professionals, it will help to examine the legal system's definition of competence (Abernathy, 1984; Annas & Densberger, 1984; Appelbaum & Grisso, 1988, 1995; Appelbaum & Gutheil, 1991; Appelbaum & Roth, 1981; Bednar et al., 1991; Brody, 1988; Buchanan & Brock, 1989; Culver, 1985; Culver & Gert, 1982; "Developments," 1974; Freedman, 1981; Grisso, 1986; Halleck, 1980; Roth, Meisel, & Lidz, 1977; Stanley, 1983; Stromberg et al., 1988; Stromberg & Stone, 1983; Tepper & Elwork, 1984; Wood et al., 1992; Yarnell & Battin, 1988). Competence can be equated with decision-making capacity and is therefore directly related to one's abilities/capacities, which means that people can be competent in some areas but not in others. So, in this circumstance, the question is not one of global competence but rather competence to decide about suicide, which is related to the issue of competence to consent to or refuse treatment (see pp. 94–96 and 102 later in this chapter). Furthermore, competence can fluctuate over time. "A competence determination, then, is a determination of a particular person's capacity to perform a particular decision-making task at a particular time and under specified conditions" (Buchanan & Brock, 1989, p. 18). It should also be noted that just because someone is considered mentally ill does not mean the person is incompetent.

General competence is presumed unless there has been a legal determination otherwise (Appelbaum & Gutheil, 1991; Buchanan & Brock, 1989; Halleck, 1980; Stromberg & Stone, 1983; Sullivan, 1980; Szasz, 1986; Tepper & Elwork, 1984; Wood et al., 1992). As a result, individuals' "decisions are to be respected by others in the sense of not being coercively interfered with, even if others view the decisions as being less than optimal, foolish, or not the decisions those others would make in similar circumstances" (Buchanan & Brock, 1989, p. 21). The implication, therefore, is that as long as the person is competent, the decision she or he makes does not have to be the same as that of the evaluator, or even of the "average" person. Some commentators have noted that professionals may ignore this consideration and will automatically question the client's competence if the decision is different from the professional's; however, if the decision is in agreement with the recommendations then the issue of competence may not arise (Abernathy, 1984; Annas & Densberger, 1984; Drane, 1985; Grisso, 1986; Roth et al., 1977; Tepper & Elwork, 1984).

Therefore, because of the possibility of value conflicts between the suicidal person and the evaluator, many have noted that when determining competence one must avoid basing the assessment on the decision that the person has made, since the evaluator's values are bound to cloud judgment (Abernathy, 1984; Annas & Densberger, 1984; Bednar et al., 1991; Brock & Wartman, 1993; Brody, 1988; Buchanan & Brock, 1989; Culver & Gert, 1982; "Developments," 1974; Peterson, 1985; Roth et al., 1977; Sullivan, 1980; Tepper & Elwork, 1984; Yarnell & Battin, 1988; see Watson [1984] for an example of how the evaluator's beliefs could be used to override the client's wishes). Thus, the process of information manipulation is the key, not the outcome of the examination: "If the reasoning process flows logically from its starting premises, though the result might be rejected by most people (e.g., a person refusing potentially lifesaving medical treatment), we cannot say that rational manipulation is impaired" (Appelbaum & Gutheil, 1991, p. 223; see also Bednar et al., 1991; Brody, 1988; Buchanan & Brock, 1989; Stromberg et al., 1988; Stromberg & Stone, 1983).

Since competence is vital to the decision of whether or not to allow someone the autonomy to choose life or death, there must be an acceptable way to assess for competence. Although some (e.g., Erard, 1994; Rogers & Britton, 1994) question the validity of some or all competence assessments, several authors have outlined methods of determining whether or not a given individual is competent to make a specific decision. However, since "objective" tests may not prove useful in such an evaluation (Buchanan & Brock, 1989; see chapter 10 of Grisso, 1986, for an evaluation of forensic instruments used to evaluate competence to consent to treatment), the approaches outlined below rely heavily on the subjective assessment of the evaluator. As was noted above, this could pose problems if the professional allows her or his own values to interfere with the assessment.

However, before moving on, a promising new development deserves mention. Appelbaum, Grisso, and colleagues (Appelbaum & Grisso, 1995; Grisso & Appelbaum, 1995; Grisso, Appelbaum, Mulvey, & Fletcher, 1995) have collaborated in the MacArthur Treatment Competence Study and developed a set of instruments that hold promise for the assessment of competence. Although the authors state that the instruments may not be appropriate for clinical use, they report working on a tool for clinicians (Grisso & Appelbaum, 1995). Yet, for the professional who wants to use more objective measures when assessing the competence of a client who may have made a rational decision to suicide, these instruments may prove useful.

Several authors have outlined areas the professional should evaluate when assessing for competence (e.g., Abernathy, 1984; Annas & Densberger, 1984; Appelbaum & Grisso, 1995; Appelbaum & Gutheil, 1991; Bednar et al., 1991; Brody, 1988; Buchanan & Brock, 1989; Drane, 1985; Grisso, 1986; Gutheil, 1992; Hoge & Appelbaum, 1989; Maltsberger, 1994; Roth et al., 1977; Stromberg et al., 1988; Tepper & Elwork, 1984; Wood et al., 1992) and what follows is an assimilation of recommendations. In order to be viewed as competent, a person should be able to

- Understand and remember the information relevant to the decision that is to be made;
- Appreciate the consequences of the decision;
- Have an underlying set of values that provide some guidance in decision making;
- Use the information to make a decision;
- Communicate the decision and explain the process used.

Although reactive depression and anxiety will complicate assessment, even the diagnosis of a mental illness does not necessarily mean that a person is incompetent to make a given decision (see Grisso & Appelbaum, 1995).

This formulation of competence is consistent with the recommendations of authors who say that the more important the decision, the more stringent the test of competence should be, although the courts have not explicitly adopted this view (e.g. Appelbaum & Grisso, 1988; Buchanan & Brock, 1989; Drane, 1985; Freedman, 1981; Sullivan, 1980; Tepper & Elwork, 1984; see Grisso, 1986 for another view). Given that the decision discussed herein is of a life-or-death nature, it makes sense that the standards for competence should be high. Appelbaum and Roth (1982) stated that "the strictest standard for competency requires that, once understanding has been attained, the rational manipulation of information takes place in the context of the [person's] appreciation of the nature of his [or her] situation" (p. 954; see also Appelbaum & Grisso, 1988; Culver, 1985; Drane, 1985; Freedman, 1981). Note that this standard is based on the individual's personal assessment of the risks and benefits and the ability to draw conclusions that are logically consistent with the premises and her or his values (Appelbaum & Grisso, 1988; Brock & Wartman, 1993; Freedman, 1981). Thus, "assessing the relevant capacities requires examining the [person's] chain of reasoning . . . [the person] should be able to indicate the major factors in [her or his] decisions and the importance assigned to them" (Appelbaum & Grisso, 1988, p. 1636). Annas and Densberger (1984) stated that an approach similar to that advocated above has been used in court decisions of competence "and is probably the most precise concept of competence that we will be able to develop" (p. 572).

As a final point on competence and life-or-death decision making, it is important to emphasize that people who are competent can refuse life-sustaining treatments and can refuse to ask for help that is available to them (Annas & Densberger,

1984; Appelbaum & Gutheil, 1991; Battin, 1994d; Brock & Wartman, 1993; Buchanan & Brock, 1989; Cantor, 1973; Culver, 1985; "Developments," 1974; Engelhardt & Malloy, 1982; Gutheil, 1992; Kjervik, 1984; Peterson, 1985; Quill, 1994; Sandak, 1978; Smith, 1989; Wolhandler, 1984; Wood et al., 1992; Yarnell & Battin, 1988). Buchanan and Brock (1989) argued that "treatment refusal usually does reasonably serve to *trigger* a competence evaluation. On the other hand, a disagreement with the physician's recommendation or refusal of a treatment recommendation is *no basis or evidence whatsoever* for a finding of incompetence" (p. 58, emphasis original). This general medical principle can be extended to suicide as well, for, as Gutheil (in Sadoff & Gutheil, 1990) has noted, "like all competent [clients] in all of medicine, the competent suicidal [client] has the right to reject even life-saving treatment; but, as should be clear, this situation requires careful assessment of this capacity" (p. 338; see also Sandak, 1978). Similarly, Podgers (1980) reported that a former chair of the American Medical Association Ad Hoc Council on Medical Ethics said, "A doctor, after advising a patient fully on his [or her] disease and its treatment must recognize the patient's right to decide the course of treatment and even to choose suicide" (p. 1,500).

Because of court reasoning about the prevention of suicide and the refusal of medical treatment, the discontinuation and refusal of life-saving treatment deserves additional attention at this point. Although the focus in this book is rational suicide and not refusal or removal of medical treatment, the subjects are related because, as it is defined in this book, rational suicide is arguably more similar to the refusal of life-saving treatment than it is to the way suicide is ordinarily conceptualized. For example, Cantor (1973) said that suicide is usually different from refusal of life-saving medical treatment but, when discussing the possibility of a person who refuses medical treatment because of a wish to die, he said,

> If the [person] demonstrates the requisite state of mind, however, and persists in refusal of treatment, that decision should be respected though tantamount to suicide. . . . This position, that the [person] wishing to die should be permitted to decline treatment, has distinct implications for legal approaches to suicide generally. In effect, it means that the "serious suicide," the person whose decision to die is clearly competent, deliberate, and firm, should be permitted to die. The form of self-destruction, refusal of medical treatment versus slashing of wrists or whatever, should not matter. (p. 258; see also Shaffer, 1986; Smith, 1989)

Viewing rational suicide as a variation of refusing treatment instead of a variation of suicide is important because courts have determined that death by suicide should be prevented but death by refusing medical treatment should not necessarily be hindered (e.g., Sandak, 1978). Further, there is a link between some instances of suicide and the refusal of treatment. Sandak (1978) reported that in the New Jersey case of Karen Quinlan, even though the issue in her case was the removal of life-sustaining treatment, "the court suggested the possibility that even if an individual's conduct is subject to classification as attempted suicide under the traditional conception of that term, the existence of extraordinary and compelling circumstances would justify permitting that conduct nonetheless" (p. 304; see also Engelhardt & Malloy, 1982; Smith, 1989).

Similarly, Peterson (1985) discussed the California case of *Bartling v. Superior Court* in which that court held that legally competent adults who are incurably, although not necessarily terminally, ill have "the constitutionally guaranteed right to refuse medical treatment [which] 'must not be abridged'" (pp. 114–115). He said that other courts have declared that "If the life sought to be continued by the compelled treatment will be brief, painful, or extended only by a great degree of bodily intrusion, the state's interest is minimized" (p. 119; see also p. 125). Peterson also noted that in the Bartling case the court showed that, under the circumstances discussed, individual rights were viewed as more important than the state's interest in preventing suicide. Of specific relevance, he said that although the court differentiated removal of life support from suicide, it noted that

> the underlying State interest in this area lies in the prevention of irrational self-destruction. What we consider here is a competent, rational decision to refuse treatment when death is inevitable and the treatment offers no hope of cure or preservation of life. There is no connection between the conduct here in issue and any State concern to prevent suicide. (p. 115; see also Smith, 1989)

However, the decision the court was deliberating, as described in the passage above, could be classified as a rational suicide. Further, Peterson also provided some of a different court's rationale for its decision in the case of Yetter, which, again, would apply equally well for rational suicide as for declining medical treatment:

> In our opinion, the constitutional right to privacy includes the right of a mature competent adult to refuse to accept medical recommendations that may prolong one's life and which, to a third person at least, appear to be in his [or her] best interests; in short, that the right of privacy includes a right to die with which the State should not interfere where there are no minor or unborn children and no clear and present danger to public health, welfare or morals. If the person was competent while being presented with the decision and in making the decision which [he or] she did, the court should not interfere even though [his or] her decision might be considered unwise, foolish, or ridiculous. (p. 134; see also p. 130)

Thus, since rational suicide is related to the refusal of life-saving treatment, courts, physicians, and counselors have no place preventing a rational person from suiciding (see also Appelbaum & Gutheil, 1991; Bloch, 1987; Cantor, 1973; Engelhardt & Malloy, 1982; Gutheil, in Sadoff & Gutheil, 1990; Kjervik, 1984; Shaffer, 1986; Smith, 1989; Wolhandler, 1984). The parallel between the acceptability of a rational refusal of lifesaving medical treatment and a similarly rational refusal of mental health treatment have implications on the appropriateness of certain interventions, such as involuntary commitment.

Therefore, with this discussion of competence and refusal of treatment as a backdrop, involuntary commitment as a potential intervention for clients who may be rational in their decision to suicide may now be examined. Many commentators have declared that a person who is competent should not be involuntarily hospitalized. For example, Meyer and colleagues (1988; see also Lebegue & Clark, 1981) stated that the only way a therapist can treat an involuntarily committed client over her or his objections is with a judicial determination that the client is incompetent. Similarly, Roth (1979) argued that "Absent [client] incompetency to consent or to refuse, no [client] may be committed under the *parens patriae* power because a requisite step in the logic of involuntary medical treatment is missing" (p. 1122; see also Buchanan & Brock, 1989; "Developments," 1974; Smith, 1989; Stromberg & Stone, 1983). Later he said that most people who are a danger to themselves would be treated under the *parens patriae* approach discussed in the article, which included the section just quoted. In the discussion of dangerousness to self he implied that in order for a person to be hospitalized due to a danger to self, the person must be found incompetent due to a mental illness.

Bloch (1987) made a special exception for rational suicide when she was discussing legal duties to prevent suicide. Specifically, after stating that the courts have a legitimate interest in preserving life and, therefore, in preventing suicide, she said that it is important to acknowledge:

> *a small group of suicides who are beyond the reach of current civil commitment statutes and who may not share the ambivalence, reversibility of the desire for death, and the cry for help characteristics. The medical profession is slowly coming to recognize the existence of a small fraction of rational suicides. . . . [When] the suicidal individual is rational and has made a deliberate and determined choice to die, the state parens patriae rationale may not apply. (p. 938)*

Later she stated that "in the rare case of the rational suicide, the state and mental health professionals may have no preventive role to play" (p. 952; see also Engelhardt & Malloy, 1982; Kjervik, 1984). Along these lines, Culver and Gert (1982) insisted that professionals are not justified in hospitalizing a person who is considering suicide if the choice of death is a rational alternative to the choice of continued life. In their example they stated that to involuntarily detain a terminally ill person in order to prevent suicide would be allowing the professional to forcibly substitute forcibly her or his beliefs for the client's, which is unacceptable.

On a separate but related point, Bloom and Faulkner (1987) noted that several commitment statutes include a provision that only individuals who lack "capacity to make an informed decision concerning treatment" (which can be viewed as related to competence) and "as the result of severe mental disorder, the person is a) likely to cause harm to himself [or herself] or to suffer substantial mental or physical deterioration, or b) likely to cause harm to others" can be involuntarily hospitalized (p. 194; see also Lebegue & Clark, 1981; Meyer et al., 1988; Stromberg & Stone, 1983). One way that mental health professionals and courts bypass the fact that many state commitment laws require "the person to be a danger either to self or others by reason of mental illness" (Buchanan & Brock, 1989, p. 351) is by equating suicidality with mental illness (recall the discussion in chapter 3; see also Ahia & Martin, 1993; Amchin et al., 1990; Greenberg, 1974; Harris, 1994; Moskop & Engelhardt, 1979; Victoroff, 1983).

Thus, even though most states' commitment statutes include the provision that the person must be both mentally ill (the definition of which varies from state to state) and a danger to self and/or others (Amchin et al., 1990; Bednar et al., 1991; Bloch, 1987; Bongar, 1991; Colt, 1991; "Developments," 1974; Greenberg, 1974;

Harris, 1994; Hendin & Waldman, 1982; Lebegue & Clark, 1981; Maltsberger, 1994; Meyer et al., 1988; Parry, 1994; Robertson, 1988; Siegel, 1982b; Smith, 1989; Stromberg et al., 1988; VandeCreek et al., 1987; Wood et al., 1992), if the assumption that all people who are suicidal are mentally ill is accepted then suicidality in and of itself is enough for commitment. For example, Harris (1994) stated that all the court cases related to failure to minimize risk and to prevent suicide of which he is aware include the presumption that the person who suicided had a mental illness.

However, if one does not unquestioningly accept the belief that suicidality is always the result of mental illness, then suicidality in and of itself is not a sufficient reason for commitment (see also Greenberg, 1974; Knapp & VandeCreek [1983] stated that this is the case in many state commitment statutes; however, see Meyer et al., 1988, and Stromberg et al., 1988, for another view). Culver and Gert (1982) asserted that people who are suicidal should be involuntarily detained only if there is a high probability that harm will occur, "the person has no adequate reason for suicide," and detention will rapidly lead to a decrease in the chances of self-harm (p. 167). If the evidence of this future harm to self must be "clear and convincing," such data may be difficult to obtain (Amchin et al., 1990; Greenberg, 1974; Hoge & Appelbaum, 1989; Stromberg et al., 1988). Bednar and his coauthors (1991) stated that "in the absence of clear signs of an imminent suicide attempt, it may be difficult to hospitalize clients against their will" (p. 119).

Moskop and Engelhardt (1979) make a concise argument that suicide should not be equated with mental illness and therefore, "if someone actively suicidal does not show indications of mental illness otherwise sufficient for commitment, that person should not be constrained from committing suicide" (p. 56; see also Kjervik, 1984 and chapter 3 of this book). In other words, "the same criteria for mental incompetency should apply to [a suicidal] individual as to anyone else. Thus any suicidal adult whom one could not commit as incompetent could not and should not be restrained from committing suicide" (pp. 56–57). This may already be the case for, "with regard to dangerousness to self, the court [in *Lessard v. Schmidt*] implied that the commitment power should not be invoked even to prevent rational individuals from attempting suicide" ("Developments," 1974, pp. 1212–1213).

Moreover, even if police power commitment of the mentally ill and imminently suicidal is supported by a compelling state interest in preserving life, that justification for commitment is not widely applicable. Most individuals who commit suicide are not mentally ill, and most of the mentally ill do not commit suicide. ("Developments," 1974, pp. 1226–1227)

In summary of this point, Harris (1994) emphasized the fact that since state laws specify that "danger to self must be caused by, or a product of mental illness . . . it would not be legal to commit someone to a hospital who was completely sane and suicidal" (p. 3; see also Robertson, 1988). He also remarked that a living will could be seen as similar to rational suicide and society supports the idea of a living will for competent people. He said that he believed a suit against a therapist who had allowed a terminally ill client to suicide would be unsuccessful.

An additional consideration when deciding about the possibility and appropriateness of hospitalization is that some authors have asserted that commitment may be counterproductive (Appelbaum & Gutheil, 1991; Berman & Cohen-Sandler, 1982; Bongar, 1991; Greenberg, 1974; Hendin & Waldman, 1982; Hoff, 1989; Knuth, 1979; Maltsberger, 1994; Robertson, 1988; Siegel, 1982b; L. C. Swenson, 1993; VandeCreek et al., 1987). Furthermore, since commitment statutes are not mandatory, the counselor should examine other, less restrictive, alternatives before considering commitment (Amchin et al., 1990; Bednar et al., 1991; Bongar, 1991; "Developments," 1974; Hoge & Appelbaum, 1989; Lebegue & Clark, 1981; Meyer et al., 1988; Parry, 1994; Robertson, 1988; Smith, 1989; Stromberg et al., 1988; Stromberg & Stone, 1983; E. V. Swenson, 1986; Wood et al., 1992) although Siegel (1982b) noted that for a number of reasons "a bias toward restrictive actions (confinement or observation) is built into the [professional-client] relationship" (p. 474). Bongar (1991) provided an analysis of when hospitalization might be appropriate and noted that "each management decision is the result of the unique characteristics of the [client] (including his or her social [system]) and the therapist's equally unique capabilities and tolerances for stress and uncertainty" (pp. 104–105; see also Bongar et al., 1992).

One final note regards the intuitive similarities between preventing a client from suiciding and the "duty to protect" requirement growing out of the *Tarasoff* decision. Importantly, courts have expressly not expanded the duty to protect others from harm by the client to include the duty to protect the client from harming self. Specifically, in the case of *Bellah v. Greenson* a judge declared that a therapist was not obligated to notify a client's family of the potential for suicide (Amchin et al., 1990; Austin et al., 1990; Berman & Cohen-Sandler, 1982; Bongar, 1991; Bongar & Greaney, 1994; Bongar et al., 1992; Harris, 1994; Knapp & VandeCreek, 1983; Meyer et al., 1988; Robertson, 1988; E. V. Swenson, 1986; L. C. Swenson, 1993; VandeCreek et al., 1987; Victoroff, 1983). Therefore, although there are some who argue that danger to self provides an exception to confidentiality and that there is a duty to warn (Ahia & Martin, 1993; Arthur & Swanson, 1993; Austin et al., 1990; Bongar, 1991; Corey et al., 1993; L. C. Swenson, 1993), this is not the view of the courts and therefore not required of mental health professionals. Furthermore, as Harris (1994) has noted, the new Code of Conduct and Ethical Principles of Psychologists (APA, 1992) does not specifically mention harm to self as a reason to break confidentiality.

Recommendations for Practice

Any psychologist who agrees and supports the right of his/her [client with AIDS] to commit rational suicide is assuming some measure of risk. In most cases, if one follows the rules that I propose below, I think it is unlikely that one will be found to have been negligent or unethical. (Harris, 1994, p. 5)

The previous discussion of malpractice and negligence as well as of competence and hospitalization points to the possibility of providing some recommendations for practice when working with a client who is potentially rational in her or his suicidal decision. These suggestions, which originate in the literature dealing with clients who are assumed to be irrational in their suicidality, will be augmented with material that makes the ideas more directly applicable to the case of a client who may be rationally suicidal. Note that following these recommendations should serve to demonstrate that one is satisfying both the ethical and legal standards of care.

First and foremost, professionals who may be faced with rationally suicidal clients should examine their own personal and professional limits and perspectives about their role in this situation in advance (Beckerman, 1995; Harris, 1994; Jones & Dilley, 1993; Wood et al., 1992). Harris recommended that the therapist should discuss her or his position early in treatment with relevant clients so that the client can switch therapists if necessary (see also NASW, 1994). He also said that a therapist should not aid and abet, such as by giving advice about, the suicidal act (see also NASW, 1994; "Public Actions," 1992).

Maintaining a solid therapeutic relationship with a client provides protection against a lawsuit, even if there is an unfortunate outcome (Amchin et al., 1990; Appelbaum & Gutheil, 1991; Bednar et al., 1991; Bongar, 1991; Bongar et al., 1992; Gutheil, 1992; Hoge & Appelbaum, 1989). Toward this end, when in doubt, the course of action that is most likely to serve the client's therapeutic interests is the route that should be chosen. A related consideration is abandonment, which is often discussed in terms of terminating a therapeutic relationship when additional treatment is indicated (Ahia & Martin, 1993; Amchin et al., 1990; Appelbaum & Gutheil, 1991; Bednar et al., 1991; Bongar, 1991; Bongar & Greaney, 1994; Knapp & VandeCreek, 1983; Robertson, 1988; Sadoff & Gutheil, 1990; Stromberg et al., 1988). This is of direct relevance in the case of rational suicide since the traditional concept of treatment for suicidal persons presumes continued treatment until the suicidality has become manageable. However, with rational suicide, the treatment may end when the assessment is complete and the counselor has decided that the person is rational.

Abandonment is also a relevant concept with survivors of suicide. Since suits are often borne out of negative feelings, such as guilt, rage, grief, surprise, and psychological desertion, outreach to survivors to help them deal with the loss is not only the appropriate and decent action but it also helps reduce the potential for lawsuits (Appelbaum & Gutheil, 1991; Bongar, 1991; Bongar & Greaney, 1994; Gutheil, 1992; E. V. Swenson, 1986).

Consultation with other mental health professionals and especially with psychiatric colleagues is one of the most commonly suggested ways to reduce the possibility of substandard treatment (Amchin et al., 1990; Appelbaum & Gutheil, 1991; Austin et al., 1990; Bednar et al., 1991; Bongar, 1991, 1993; Bongar & Greaney, 1994; Bongar et al., 1992; Gutheil, 1992; Harris, 1994; Hoge & Appelbaum, 1989; Knapp & VandeCreek, 1983; Maltsberger, 1994; Stromberg et al., 1988; VandeCreek et al., 1987; Victoroff, 1983). Harris specifically urged therapists to consult with knowledgeable peers, and perhaps even an attorney, and noted, "there is no prohibition against trying to determine, in advance, which consultants are most likely to be sympathetic to your position" (p. 6). At least two formal consultations should be undertaken with thorough notes made from each one (Bongar, 1993; Harris, 1994). Among other things, consultation shows that the treatment plan and its implementation were not impulsively decided upon and are in line with the standards of care. Furthermore, as Harris (1994) noted, the new APA ethics code

(1992) recommends consultation when confronted with a difficult ethical situation.

Clear and thorough case notes are also highly recommended (Amchin et al., 1990; Appelbaum & Gutheil, 1991; Austin et al., 1990; Bednar et al., 1991; Berman & Cohen-Sandler, 1983; Bongar, 1991; Bongar & Greaney, 1994; Bongar et al., 1992; Gutheil, 1992; Harris, 1994; Hoge & Appelbaum, 1989; Knapp & VandeCreek, 1983; Maltsberger, 1994; Meyer et al., 1988; Stromberg et al., 1988; L. C. Swenson, 1993; VandeCreek et al., 1987; Victoroff, 1983; Wood et al., 1992). Records should describe, at the outset of treatment and at critical decision points, the client's mental status/competence, what treatment options have been considered and why they were not selected, and all consultations. Some (e.g., Bongar, 1991; Victoroff, 1983) have suggested that the counselor ask the client if she or he wants others to be informed of the suicidality and then get the client to sign a form indicating assent to the notification or denial of the permission to breach confidentiality.

This type of repeated risk/benefit evaluation provides both an acceptable method of clinical decision making and a good deterrent to successful lawsuits or ethics charges. Given that the more the therapist assists in the consideration of suicide as an option, the greater the risk of being second-guessed by others afterward (Harris, 1994), it is important that the counselor keep in mind Appelbaum and Gutheil's (1991) recommendations to prepare for the possibility of future action against the counselor by writing with clarity from the viewpoint of future readers (e.g., ethics committee members, expert witnesses, family members, judges, juries). Another point Appelbaum and Gutheil made is that counselors could use a more narrative approach when taking calculated risks or doing the less conservative intervention. "The justification for this kind of 'thinking out loud' is based on the fact that *not* thinking (or not leaving a record of one's thinking, which may amount to the same thing) may be seen as negligent" (p. 197, emphasis original).

Bednar and his coauthors (1991, p. 99; see also Howell, 1978; Knuth, 1979; E. V. Swenson, 1986) stated that a therapist will not be found negligent if a client's suicide was judged "voluntary." They continue by saying that a suicide is considered involuntary and the therapist viewed as negligent only "if the therapist's negligent act either (1) brings about insanity in the client, which prevents the client from realizing the nature and risk of the act, or (2) causes the client to have an irresistible impulse to suicide." However, E. V. Swenson (1986) remarked:

> *Whether or not there can be a voluntary or rational suicide is relevant to the question of liability for causing suicide, but not for preventing it. This is because in the former, voluntary and rational suicide may be considered a supervening event which breaks the chain of causation. In the latter case, the duty of custodial care is causally related only to the foreseeability of the act. (p. 421)*

On this issue, Bednar and colleagues (1991) stated that courts seemed to be increasingly likely "to recognize a duty by therapists to commit clients who pose a threat of danger to themselves or others" (p. 205). However, they clarified this by saying that "the therapist who chooses not to pursue commitment of an individual who meets the statutory standards for commitment should carefully document the reasons for the decision and, when appropriate, obtain corroborating opinions from other professionals" (p. 205)

Therefore, one possible way to respond to allegations of malpractice, as well as to ethics charges, is to assert "that the [client's] suicidal behavior was competent and volitional" (Amchin et al., 1990, p. 652) because

> *competent [clients] universally can reject or refuse life saving treatment, a suicidal [client] competent to weigh the risks and benefits of giving or withholding information may elect not to call or notify caretakers when suicidal feelings reach the dangerous point—but this is not the clinician's problem. (Appelbaum & Gutheil, 1991, p. 195)*

Furthermore, as noted previously, competent clients should not be hospitalized involuntarily, which should absolve the professional from needing to provide custodial care. As a result, a crucial aspect of case notes when working with clients who are rationally suicidal is the charting of assessments of the client's ability to care for self, competence to refuse treatment and make reasonable decisions, and the rationality of the specific decision to suicide. This is especially effective in countering the claim that the person who suicided needed to be cared for and protected by the therapist; it would also break the causal link from therapist to suicide (Appelbaum & Gutheil, 1991; Bongar, 1991; Gutheil, 1992; Gutheil, Bursztajn, & Brodsky, 1986; Kjervik, 1984; Maltsberger, 1994; Robertson, 1988; L. C. Swenson, 1993). These points can be summed up as follows:

> *For suicide to be truly intentional (or "voluntary"), i.e., for "intention" to have legal meaning, we might argue that the [client] must be competent. Thus, when a tragic outcome is followed by a malpractice claim, the determination of the [client's] previous competence to give informed consent to the treatment actually used may be, in retrospect, a movement of pivotal importance in the clinical history. The therapist's assessment of the [client's] competence may, of course, be challenged; but the stronger the therapist's documented grounds for finding the [client] competent, and thus able to act truly voluntarily, the more remote the prospect of malpractice liability for suicide may be, since it is thus more likely that the [client's] independent and competent action is the proximate cause of the outcome. (Gutheil, Bursztajn, Hamm, & Brodsky, 1983, p. 327. Reprinted with permission of Elsevier Science Ltd.)*

Along these lines, one court (in *Speer v. U.S.*) decided that "in a presumably competent outpatient, the [client's] suicide intent itself, not medical negligence, was deemed to be the causal factor in the suicide; hence, the clinician was not liable" (Gutheil, Bursztajn, & Brodsky, 1986, p. 125). Gutheil and colleagues (1986) proposed that if a client is able to engage in a dialogue with the professional about the risks and benefits of her or his actions, this provides evidence of the client's competence and therefore shifts responsibility for care from the counselor to the client. The editors of *Judicious Practice* ("Public Actions," 1992) provided similar advice for therapists considering assisting in the exploration of suicide as an option:

> *practitioners—using written and videotaped confirmations, and second and third consultations—should document the [client's] request and decision-making process. This material should present the [client's] diagnoses, emotional state, and physical pain, and evidence of his or her competence and studied intent. To date, such documentation has proven vital in defending those assisting others with death. (p. 3)*

In sum, the counselor's case notes should carefully delineate both the process by which the client's competence was determined and, subsequently, the assessment of the other criteria for rational suicide (see also Harris, 1994). An additional way of incorporating the recommendations of suicide preventionists with the approach outlined in this book would be contracting with a client that sessions would be used to evaluate the presence of the criteria for rational suicide. The mental health professional and the client could agree in writing that if the client's decision to suicide does not appear rational then steps (perhaps including hospitalization, if appropriate) will be taken to protect the client but if the evaluation supports the idea that the decision is rational then treatment will be considered complete (see also Harris, 1994). A final point worth considering is that for the rational client, outpatient treatment is arguably the treatment of choice since it is the least restrictive alternative. Thus, such an approach would meet the standard of care and protect against claims of abandonment.

The discussion thus far has centered on the currently articulated standards of practice, with only brief mention of how rational suicide can be conceptualized within this framework. The sections that follow will expand on the discussion to include a final set of data that demonstrate that psychologists (and other mental health professionals) would benefit from revisions to the standards of care for working with clients who are suicidal.

BASES OF BELIEFS ABOUT ACCEPTANCE OF A DECISION TO SUICIDE AND ACTION TAKEN TO PREVENT A SUICIDE

As mentioned in chapter 4, Werth's (1994b) study involving health service providers in psychology had two sections in which participants provided qualitative data. The data and analysis related to definitions and criteria of rational suicide were discussed previously. What follows is a review of the other set of qualitative data, which was analyzed using the procedure discussed in chapter 5.

Recall that the participants, after reading a short vignette, were asked questions related to acceptance, action, and stigma. Of relevance here are the two questions on which the participants were asked to rate on seven-point Likert scales their degree of acceptance of the decision to suicide and the amount of action they would take to prevent the suicide. Immediately after these two questions the participant was asked, "How did you decide what numbers to circle on the scales in questions 2 and 3 on the previous page (i.e., What were the bases for your decisions)?" Responses to this open-ended question provided the data for the analysis that follows.

Examination of the responses to this question revealed three major categories into which the majority of answers could be classified: *Precipitating condition*, *personal reasons*, and *professional reasons*.

Precipitating Condition

The precipitating condition category had two subcategories: terminal illness and depression.

Terminal illness. Several respondents were placed in this subcategory because they specifically mentioned that their decisions were related to terminal conditions. For example, "based on circumstances—terminal, progressive, nature of disease"; "reality that AIDS is a death sentence both currently and in forseeable [*sic*] future"; and "*terminal* cancer is key issue here" (emphasis original).

Depression. Others stated that they advocated for more action and were less accepting of the suicidal decision because of reasons such as, "I assume his decision is the result of his depression," "John's thinking is distorted by his emotional distress," and "there are disturbances in thinking due to depression that can be ameliorated."

Personal Reasons

The personal reasons category had four components: generic personal beliefs, religious/moral beliefs, beliefs in autonomy and individual rights, and personal experience.

Generic personal beliefs. Examples of responses placed in this subcategory include "optimism," "personal judgment," and "personal belief."

Religious/moral beliefs. This subcomponent contained responses such as "social/moral values," "am morally opposed to it," and "personal convictions concerning the purpose of life and morality of suicide."

Beliefs in autonomy and personal rights. This subcategory was the largest in the personal reasons category and one of the largest overall subcategories. Several examples illustrate this area: "It is a personal decision," "belief that people have a right to control their own lives," "[client's] rights to choose quality of life versus death," "I feel John has the right to make his own choices," and "it is his right to have a dignified death."

Personal experiences. Finally, this subcategory included responses such as "personal experience with suicidal persons" and "living with my own 35-year-old daughter prepare [*sic*] to die with ovarian cancer."

Professional Reasons

The largest category was that of professional reasons, which has four subcategories: ethical/legal reasons, professional responsibility/role, additional treatment plans, and professional experience.

Ethical/legal reasons. Although both ethical and legal reasons were mentioned individually by some respondents, "I have legal obligations to prevent suicide—don't want a suit if family changes mind after the fact" and "professional ethics" are examples, most often the two areas were mentioned together. "I have a legal as well as ethical responsibility to try to prevent harm to a [client]," "ethical values of profession; legal imperatives," "ethical and legal considerations for myself and my practice."

Professional responsibility/role. In terms of responsibility/role, several respondents mentioned beliefs similar to the idea that, "My professional role to preserve life and respect it requires me to take action to prevent suicide" or "as a professional it is [my] duty and responsibility to take whatever measures are necessary to save lives" or "because as a psychologist, I have to do what I can to prevent clients from harming themselves." Others mentioned "standards of care" and "choosing in the direction of accepted clinical practice." However, some respondents in this subcategory revealed dissonance between what they perceived to be their role and their personal beliefs: "My personal opinion would be to not intervene as vigorously but I have a professional responsibility to attempt to prevent his death," and "a professional has a duty to help preserve life, but when quality of life has deteriorated said duty becomes qualified," and "personally, I believe anyone should have the right to kill him or herself. Professionally, I am required to intervene."

Additional treatment plans. Professional reasons also included a subcategory composed of additional treatment plans that the respondent felt were necessary such as, "I question how thoroughly his anger and the secondary gain he gets from his symptoms has [*sic*] been explored," "meets criteria of 'danger to self' for involuntary admission," "many intervention strategies, some unconventional, have yet to be tried," "treatments have not been effective, however, other [treatment] modalities need to be done: [for example,] intensive inpatient" and "no evidence that he has gotten appropriate [treatment]: all avenues not explored." Several respondents mentioned consulting with other professionals, such as physicians and ministers.

Professional experience. Typical responses in this area include, "the feelings and experiences of [clients] I have had who have contemplated suicide. Also, the effect of suicide in a family upon the members of that family (also seen in therapy)." "I considered my conduct with [clients] whom I have believed to be suicidal and rated the scales based on my recall of those situations." "Previous experience with terminal [clients]."

Summary

Participants were asked to explain the bases of their decisions about the acceptability of John's decision to suicide and about how much action they would take to prevent the suicide. Some of the participants merely referred to John's condition and basically said that a terminal illness made the decision to suicide acceptable or, for those who received depression scenarios, because of the depression the suicide was unacceptable. These qualitative responses serve to reinforce the quantitative results discussed in chapter 4; that is, a terminal illness is a more acceptable reason to suicide than is depression.

Some of the participants mentioned personal reasons for their answers, such as religious or moral beliefs or, in contrast, beliefs about autonomy and personal rights. These responses were more likely to be related to how the respondent replied to the question about the acceptability of the decision to suicide—it was acceptable because of the respondent's belief in individual rights or it was not acceptable because of the participant's religious values. The largest group of responses was related to professional reasons, which included ethical/legal reasons, beliefs about professional role or responsibility, and additional treatment plans. Logically, these replies were related to the amount of action the psychologist would take to prevent the suicide.

Werth and Liddle (1994) noted a few unsolicited responses that they claimed revealed dissonance on the part of some of the respondents in the terminal bone cancer condition to the Acceptance and Action questions. A more formalized quali-tative investigation (through explicitly asking a question about of the bases of respondents' answers to these questions) in the Werth (1994b) study validated the anecdotal reports Werth and Liddle noted. Specifically, several respondents in the second study acknowledged an internal struggle between their personal beliefs about suicide and what they perceived to be their professional responsibilities. Many cited concerns about potential ethical violations and lawsuits if they did not inter-vene with sufficient intensity to prevent a suicide, such as the respondent who circled "7" on the Action question (she would do *anything/everything including involuntary hospitalization* to prevent John from suiciding) but added "This would be different if I was immune from lawsuits by family/partner" and then circled "2" on the Acceptance question (1 = *completely acceptable*).

These results may explain the somewhat confusing findings of both Gurrister and Kane (1978) and Hammond (1991). These researchers found that many of their respondents said that suicide was acceptable in some cases but then said that they would still do virtually anything in their power to prevent all suicides. It appears as if, at least dating back to 1978, some mental health workers have personally believed that some people should have the right to suicide. However, these same professionals would intervene even in these cases because of their perceptions of their professional responsibilities or out of fear of legal or ethical charges if they did not actively attempt to prevent a suicide (see also Werth & Liddle, 1994).

IMPLICATIONS OF RESEARCH ON ATTITUDES ABOUT RATIONAL SUICIDE

Both the significant and nonsignificant results of the research discussed above and in chapters 4 and 5 have important implications for mental health profession-als, especially when viewed in conjunction with the results of the analysis of the demographic variables. However, because of the limitations outlined in chapter 6, these results are in need of replication. Nonetheless, it is encouraging that Werth's (1994b) combination of results indicated that psychologists, regardless of age, gender, or other demographic qualities, may not differentiate among terminal ill-ness conditions in regard to how accepting they are of a suicide that may be rational. Further, the amount of acceptance respondents demonstrated for a deci-sion to suicide by a possibly rational client with a terminal illness may not be a function of how stigmatized the illness is by society. Thus, even though persons with AIDS, in general, are stigmatized more than persons with terminal cancer, in general, this stigma may not be an important factor when assessing the acceptabil-ity of a decision to suicide or when attributing stigma to the suicidal person.

Additional evidence for this conclusion is provided by the lack of significant differences between the two terminal illness conditions on the three measures of stigma. This lack of significant differences occurred even though there were dif-ferences between the terminal illness conditions and the depression condition on the professional and/or social contact scales, revealing that some suicidal individu-als are stigmatized more than others. Finally, the finding that individuals who believed in rational suicide were significantly more accepting and would take significantly less action but did not attach more or less stigma to the suicidal ideators than those who did not believe in this concept appears to substantiate the interpretation that stigma may not be a crucial variable when considering whether or not a suicide may be rational.

Rogers and Britton (1994), in a reaction article, expressed concern with Werth's (1992) call for an acceptance of rational suicide for some persons with AIDS. In their conclusion they appear to imply that Werth's views and the opinions of those advocating for rational suicide for some persons with AIDS were the result of "society's phobic reaction to this devastating and stigmatized illness" (pp. 176–177). As noted above, the Werth (1994b) study, although not designed with this intent, provided results that should help alleviate the concerns of those like Rogers and Britton who believe that acceptance of suicide by some persons with AIDS is a result of the general stigma associated with the disease. The finding that reactions to men with AIDS did not differ significantly from men with terminal bone cancer on any of the six dependent variables and that men with AIDS were not stigmatized more than men with endogenous depression indicate that it is not the specific disease but, rather, a general terminal diagnosis that is the operative variable when looking at the acceptance of a potential suicide.

The idea that terminal illness in a generic sense is important when considering rational suicide is further substantiated by the criteria for rational suicide generated in the Werth (1994b) study, which essentially replicated those set forth by Werth and Cobia (1995a). Both sets of criteria (see Table 5.1) listed terminal illness as a reason for considering suicide; neither study had respondents distinguishing between nor among different terminal illnesses.

Both the Werth and Liddle (1994) survey and the Werth (1994b) study provide empirical support for Werth's (1992, 1995; see also Jackson, 1957) hypothesis that suicidal ideators can be placed along a continuum of intervention (see Table 7.1). This continuum can range from conditions that warrant a great deal of action

Table 7.1 Suicide Intervention Continuum

Acceptance: Action:	Low Much		High Little
	<-->		
(Werth, 1992)	Psychosis	Physical pain	AIDS
(Werth, 1995)	Asymptomatic HIV disease	Symptomatic HIV disease	AIDS
(Werth & Liddle, 1994)	Bankruptcy	Psychological or physical pain	Terminal cancer
(Werth, 1994b)	Endogenous depression		AIDS or terminal cancer

Note. Adapted from Werth (1995, p. 74).

(e.g., bankruptcy) to those that require less intervention (terminal illness). In the latter case, this intervention should include an assessment of rationality, such as is advocated for in chapter 5.

Similar to the results of the Werth and Liddle (1994) and the Werth and Cobia (1995a) studies, the Werth (1994b) investigation makes a strong case that the current ethical and legal standards of care need to be reexamined in regard to the acceptable course of action with some suicidal clients. First, both the Werth and Liddle study and the Werth investigation found that more than 80% of the respondents to the question about belief in rational suicide stated that they believed in the concept (Jones & Dilley [1993] reported that 64% of their sample of people with HIV disease supported rational suicide with only 3% [one person] opposed). This percentage is higher than Pope, Tabachnick, and Keith-Spiegel (1987, 1988) found in a survey of psychologists belonging to the Division of Psychotherapy of the APA (the same Division surveyed by Werth & Liddle). Pope and his colleagues reported that nearly half of their respondents believed that "accepting a client's decision to commit suicide" was always poor (48%) and unethical (45.2%). It is possible that the seven or more years that elapsed between the Pope study and the Werth investigation could account for this difference in level of acceptance and/or that the different context or dissimilar phrasing of the questions contributed to the discrepancy.

Another important finding in the Werth (1994b) study was that 20% of the respondents indicated that they had seen at least one rationally suicidal person. This percentage is similar to one reported from the survey of psychotherapists conducted by Pope and his colleagues (1987); these authors stated that "about one in five of the respondents has accepted either rarely (16.4%) or more frequently (4.1%), a client's decision to kill himself or herself" (p. 1,003). Jones and Dilley (1993) stated that 18% of their sample of people infected with HIV reported knowing someone who had rationally suicided. These results should counter arguments by critics who say that rational suicide is too rare to be worthy of concern (e.g., Hendin, 1982; Siegel, 1986) or that it is nonexistent (e.g., Litman, 1965; Shneidman, 1981, 1992b).

Further evidence for the need to reevaluate the currently articulated standards of care comes from an examination of both the unsolicited responses in the Werth and Liddle (1994) study and the solicited responses in the Werth (1994b) investigation concerning what the bases for respondents' answers to the Acceptance and Action questions were. These replies illustrate that many psychologists may be acting differently from what they personally believe is appropriate because they are concerned about the potential repercussions of allowing a client, even one who is rational, to suicide. One example from the Werth (1994b) study sums up this position well:

> *I would take all steps necessary to keep a [client] from committing suicide even though I support rational suicide because his/her family could successfully put me out of practice and sue me, since by our state's law as well as the current ethics of our profession, we cannot exercise discretionary judgement about this. If the law were different, my actions might very well be different. (p. 84)*

It may also be the case that, if the results from the Pope (Pope et al., 1987, 1988) study are viewed in combination with the results from this study, approximately

20% of psychologists are already violating the acknowledged standards of care by knowingly allowing some of their clients to suicide. These compassionate professionals may adhere to beliefs similar to the 77% of the responding ethicists surveyed by Pope and Bajt (1988, p. 828) who "believed 'that formal legal and ethical standards should never be violated on the basis of [client] welfare or other deeper values.'"

Furthermore, on a separate but related point, the discrepancy between what it takes for a suicide to be considered rational (e.g., consultation with others, including mental health professionals) and what psychologists (and perhaps other mental health professionals) perceive to be their responsibility when working with a person who is suicidal (e.g., intervene or possibly face a malpractice suit), leaves the client in a no-win situation. In other words, if she or he does not confer with others then the suicide was irrational but if he or she does consult a mental health professional he or she will be prevented from following through with what may be a rational choice (Werth, 1994a). It would therefore again appear as if the standards of care related to acceptable interventions with clients who are suicidal should be reexamined.

Werth and Liddle (1994) concluded that, based on their results, "perhaps it is time to re-examine the profession's stance that a psychotherapist is ethically obligated to intervene with every actively suicidal client" (p. 447). They then called for additional research on the idea that there is a continuum of acceptance that can be superimposed on the intensity of suicide intervention continuum noted previously. They also asked a series of questions that needed to be answered, including how rational suicide should be defined, how one can assess for rationality, and what psychotherapists' responsibilities are when working with rational suicidal clients. The Werth (1994b) study provides provisional responses to each of these questions.

As is evident from an examination of the results on both the SSDS and the Acceptance question (see chapter 4), there appears to be a continuum of acceptability that parallels the continuum of action discussed previously; however, perhaps because of the fear about lawsuits noted above, the respondents might take more action than is consistent with the amount of acceptance they have for the suicide in those circumstances.

Both the Werth (1994b) investigation and the Werth and Cobia (1995a) qualitative analysis answer the question of how rational suicide can be defined and address assessment of the condition. In regard to the duties of the psychotherapist, the qualitative data in the Werth and the Werth and Cobia studies address both the current standards and perceived expectations. These data also provide some direction about what the therapist's responsibilities would be if the standards of care were altered to allow suicide in a limited number of cases (i.e., a counselor would be expected to assess suicidal clients using the criteria for rational suicide listed in chapter 5).

CONCLUSION

Although some authors (e.g., Ahia & Martin, 1993; "Public Actions," 1992) warn that professionals should not attempt to differentiate rational from irrational suicides, it is apparent that "[a] shift is under way in societal thinking [about rational suicide], the *zeitgeist* is changing" (Cotton, 1993, p. 797). Similarly, Wood, Marks, and Dilley (1992) stated that "ethical standards regarding suicide are changing and some practitioners and physicians consider it ethical to assist in a [client's] 'rational suicide' when doing so will mitigate the [client's] pain and suffering" (p. 71).

This shift has important implications for the standard of care with clients who are suicidal. Given the data described in this book, it is evident that mental health practitioners *should* attempt to assess for rationality in clients who are suicidal. The standards of care should be changed so as to acknowledge the assessment of rationality as an appropriate and acceptable approach. It should no longer be the case that compassionate therapists are forced to choose between their personal beliefs and perceived professional standards when working with clients who appear to have made a rational decision to suicide.

The discussion provided in this chapter should demonstrate that rational suicide can be accommodated by the current system and, in fact, would not entail dramatic revisions. The standards of care could be easily modified to accept an assessment of rationality, which would free professionals to be less concerned with restrictive and coercive interventions and more focused on the client as a unique suffering individual.

8

Conclusions and Predictions

This final chapter provides a synthesis of the material presented in the previous chapters and provides some predictions for the future. This discussion covers implications for mental health professionals and their clients who are suicidal. The framework used is an examination of how the professional's role should change when working with clients who are suicidal, with emphasis placed on the evaluation of rationality.

A REVISED APPROACH

The world is changing. Medicine and technology have advanced to the point that people can be kept alive for years beyond the point at which their life has meaning for them or their loved ones. The courts, legislatures, and public are moving forward with changes to return autonomy, dignity, and respect back to those affected most by medical progress—the infirm elderly, the terminally ill, and the hopelessly suffering. However, mental health professionals have not played a part in the changes taking placing around them. Mayo (1993) noted this and recommended that mental health professionals become proactive in debates about rational suicide and the establishment of criteria, in the creation and implementation of physician aid-in-dying programs (such as took place in New Mexico, where psychologists were asked to help draft legislation; Larson, 1995), and in the assessment of individuals who state that they want to die. In addition, the editors of *Judicious Practice* ("Public Actions," 1992) asserted that people involved in the care of individuals who are suffering should meet to discuss the emotional and practical (and ethical and legal) difficulties associated with rational suicide.

Participation in such discussions cannot and will not take place unless and until modifications are made to the present paternalistic view of death and dying, especially regarding suicide, articulated in the standards of care. Without recognition that some individuals may be rational in their suicidality, counselors will be ill-prepared for the future. The biggest change necessary is a shift from the traditional mandatory preventionist stance to a more contextual approach that takes into account the reasoning behind the decision to suicide (Werth, 1995). The new approach should

> *(1) save, through methods entailing minimal unpleasantness, the lives of as many as possible of those who do not wish to die; (2) interfere as little as possible with those who after some chance for consideration persist in wanting to die; and (3) afford maximum protection against interference with the liberty of those who pose no threat of suicide. (Greenberg, 1974, pp. 242–243)*

The method outlined in this book meets these goals. When properly implemented, the assessment of rationality provides maximum protection for the client's rights and personal values. However, it is true that, as with any choice, the decision to not intervene actively and coercively with a client who may or may not be rational in her or his suicidality entails some risk for the client and the counselor. Heyd and Bloch (1981) provide a good illustration of the issues that must be balanced when determining whether or not to intervene (p. 199; see Table 8.1). They created this table to illustrate that "the ethical dilemma of whether to intervene in a suicidal act is intensified by the fact that whatever we do, a price must be paid" (p. 198).

This dilemma is actually one that has not been faced, for the most part, by counselors. As was discussed earlier, the traditional approach and the assumed

Table 8.1 Intervention versus Nonintervention with Clients who are Suicidal

Intervention	Nonintervention
Taking the *patient's* decision as irrational, impulsive, distorted by mental illness.	Taking the *person's* decision as authentic, deliberate, clear-headed, and rational.
On the assumption that his decision is reversible, certain steps, which are also reversible are taken to prolong his life.	On the assumption that his decision is irreversible, no steps are taken, thus irreversibly letting him commit suicide.
Paternalism: forcing the patient to act rationally as an expression of care for his real interests.	Respect for the person's autonomy and liberty to kill himself as to [make] any other decision, even if it seems irrational to us.
Care for the patient's family who usually ask for intervention.	Taking the person's side rather than that of his family. Priority of his freedom over the family's interests.
The price: forcing him to act against his will, prolongation of his mental and physical misery, serious loss of liberty.	*The price*: missed opportunities, the infinite loss involved in death, possibility of the most "tragic mistake."
Underlying assumption: the instinctive drive to save other people's lives plus the professional duty and practice of doctors to do so.	*Underlying assumption*: "nothing in life is as much under the direct jurisdiction of each individual as are his own person and life" (Schopenhauer).

Note. From Heyd & Bloch (1981, p. 199). Reprinted with permission.

proper practice has been to prevent any client from suiciding. Therefore, revisions to the currently accepted system, such as those advocated for in this book, would entail significant changes in the way mental health professionals practice when working with clients who are suicidal. Instead of automatically assuming the thoughts about, and/or the decision to, suicide are irrational and therefore moving immediately into a preventionist stance, counselors would need to determine if the person has made a rational decision (e.g., Amchin et al., 1990; Battin, 1994b; Decker, 1977; Mayo, 1993; Werth, 1995; Werth & Cobia, 1995a; Yarnell & Battin, 1988). Thus, the focus would shift from immediate intervention to assessment. Werth (1995) noted that this altered focus would create a need for additional knowledge and skill, which might then lead to a greater acceptance of a contextual approach to suicide prevention (Inman, Bascue, Kahn, & Shaw, 1984). This new way of thinking may also open up brand new areas within existing disciplines. For example, Kastenbaum (1976) noted that if suicide could be seen in some instances as the "preferred mode of death" then:

> *suicidology would have two distinct aspects—a continuation of the present effort to understand, predict, and prevent self-destructive behavior, and a sensitive new approach designed to help people in certain circumstances attain the particular form of death recommended to them both by cultural idealizations and their own promptings. (p. 440)*

The idea of a preferred or "appropriate death" was introduced by Weisman and Hackett (1961). These authors state that "a death that is appropriate for one person may be quite out of character for another" and that "the physician is also committed to help his [or her] patient achieve an appropriate emotional world in which to die" (p. 248). In a later piece Weisman (1966) said, "In short, an appropriate death is one which a person might choose for himself [or herself], had he [or she] an option" (p. 191) but he also stated that suicide could not be an appropriate death (see also Weisman & Hackett, 1961). Lester (1969) noted that, given Weisman's description, suicide could be an appropriate death. He then provided responses to counter Weisman's reasons that suicide differed from appropriate death (see Lester, 1970 for another view of an appropriate death). He asserted that the decision of whether or not the person's quality of life warrants continued life should be up to the person who is suffering:

> *The notion of an appropriate death is a crucial one for counselors, therapists, and doctors. It is perhaps one of our responsibilities to ensure that a person dies an appropriate death. To do this, we must first be aware of the alternative concepts and then we must seek the concept that makes sense for the person we are counseling. If death for him [or her] is more appropriate in one way than another, then perhaps it is our duty to allow him [or her] to die in that way. (Lester, 1977, p. 196)*

WHAT IS THE PROFESSIONAL'S APPROPRIATE ROLE?

Given the views previously espoused about the inappropriateness of intervention at times and the notion that suicide can be, in certain circumstances, an appropriate death, questions about the proper role of mental health professionals when working with a client who may be rationally suicidal naturally arise. For example, Pretzel (1984) wondered about the lengths a counselor should go to in order to prevent a person from suiciding:

> *Is the proper role one of respecting the wishes of such a [client] or one of attempting to persuade or even coerce a [client] to accept the frustration or hope of continued exist-ence? (p. 254)*

He then answered by stating:

> *Suicide is a highly personal act and although it does affect the culture in general and certain specific related individuals in a special way, I think we have often gone too far in trying to protect individuals from their own wishes about their own death. (pp. 254–255)*

Similarly, when discussing psychologists' responsibilities when working with clients with AIDS who are considering suicide, Harris (1994) asked the following questions:

> *Does the psychologist have a responsibility to society to intervene in order to prevent the suicide from occurring. Does the psychologist have a duty to the [client] to assist him/her in making the most sound personal decision about his/her own condition. Can the psychologist make recommendations of suicide or attend or participate in the sui-cide itself. (p. 1; see also Beckerman, 1995)*

Later Harris stated, "I think one can persuasively argue that a good therapist ought to empathically listen to the [client's] struggle to make his/her own decision on this extraordinarily difficult personal decision" (p. 7).

Harris' (1994) and Pretzel's (1984) comments reflect the ideas set forth by the National Association of Social Workers (NASW) in their policy statement on "Client Self-Determination in End-of-Life Decisions." Significantly, the statement urged that social workers should be free to examine all options available to their clients, including "assisted suicide" (which is one form of rational suicide), and if the social worker is unable to participate fully in this discussion of options the social worker should refer the client to another professional who can address end-of-life issues within the client's value system instead of solely within the social worker's. Finally, the statement even declared that social workers could be present during an "assisted suicide."

The editors of *Judicious Practice* ("NASW Approves," 1993) said that the NASW guidelines provided for an important change in the involvement of social workers in the lives of clients with long-term illnesses. "Counselors often develop close professional relationships with clients, and their support may be particularly im-portant in easing the transition from life to death" (p. 2). They concluded:

> *In the end, bringing suicide out of the closet and into therapy, even up to the moment of death, enables mental health professionals to protect against poorly considered sui-cides or shadowy attempts to influence dying clients.*

But the most important aspect of all of this is that people who choose to die should not have to do so alone. If counseling is about transitions, counselors . . . belong with clients making the ultimate transition. (p. 3)

The points raised by the NASW statement and the *Judicious Practice* editors are central to the discussion of the mental health professional's role in decisions about suicide. This book is not the first (nor hopefully the last) to call for a revision in the approach of mental health professionals when working with clients who are suicidal. For example, in a succinct summation, Kjervik (1984) stated that "psychotherapists should be expected to work with suicidal persons in order to understand suicidal thoughts and attempts and to determine whether a rational basis for the suicide exists" (p. 208). Cotton (1993) added that one of his interviewees said, "society should 'bring [suicide] out of the closet' so the doctor, patient, and family can talk about it without facing legal action or forced psychiatric care" (p. 797; see also Battin, 1992; Werth, 1994a, 1994b). In what may be a more controversial statement, Wood and colleagues (1992) argued: "there is a growing body of law and public opinion that supports the argument that [clients] in unbearable pain or facing death have the right to commit suicide, and that the humane practitioner may actually facilitate this right" (pp. 58–59).

In order to attempt to understand fully the reasoning of the client and to help her or him make the most rational decision, the counselor must assess whether or not the decision to suicide is a considered one. Thus, one of the professional's roles may be to help in the exploration of alternatives and determine if suicide truly is a reasonable and rational option (Beckerman, 1995; Brandt, 1975; Clements et al., 1983; Green & Irish, 1971; Mackenzie & Popkin, 1990; Mayo, 1983, 1993; Nelson, 1984; Quill, 1994). Indeed, some (e.g., Brandt, 1975; Wood, 1980) argue that in order to make sure the decision to suicide is rational the person should discuss it with another person, preferably a mental health professional. Based on concerns such as these, others (e.g., Cotton, 1993; Portwood, 1978; Werth, 1994b; Werth & Cobia, 1995a) state that counseling should be a part of the decision-making process.

The involvement of a professional during this decision-making process will also give the suicidal person someone to turn to in case she or he decides that suicide is not the best option but fears she or he may still kill herself or himself (Choron, 1972; Portwood, 1978) and will help screen out those who are not truly rational (Battin, 1982; Nelson, 1984). For, as Szasz (1976) said, "counseling, psychotherapy, or any other *voluntary measure*, especially for persons troubled by their own suicidal inclinations and seeking such help, [are] unobjectionable, and indeed generally desirable interventions" (p. 168, emphasis original). However, as Bongar and colleagues (1992) noted, "we must not rule out the possibility that proper care may help individuals see more clearly and rationally that their future is relatively hopeless and devoid of sufficient quality of life to be reasonably continued" (p. 458). Or, as Jones and Dilley (1993) so eloquently highlighted the issue:

it is likely that people will continue to consider self-deliverance as an alternative to continued pain and suffering. The challenge to clinicians and therapists will be to manage their feelings of counter-transference, remain non-judgmental, and to help provide an environment that will encourage their clients' exploration of choices. It is crucial for therapists to understand their clients' circumstances and to consider a situation in which dying with dignity is more important than prolonging life. (p. 6)

BALANCING VALUES

As discussed in chapter 6 and mentioned briefly previously in this chapter, the values of the counselor are an important aspect of the work with clients who are suicidal. The beliefs the counselor holds about suicide can, obviously, interfere with her or his ability to work appropriately with clients, especially those who are rational and who are suicidal. Along these lines, McKegney and Lange (1971) and Maltsberger (1994) said that gaps in communication and beliefs between the professional and the client may lead to clients not using therapy. Similarly, Roy (1988) said that "professionals have to learn that decisions about dying are meant to be *shared* decisions. The dying person is meant to be *master* of his or her own dying, not the professional" (p. 138, emphasis original). McKegney and Lange (1971) summarized this point well:

> *psychotherapy may be essential in the process of a [client] deciding that life is worth living. However, if the psychotherapist assumes . . . that it would be preferable for the [client] to live [for example,] on dialysis rather than to withdraw and die, therapy is probably doomed from the outset. (pp. 52–53; see also Battin, 1994b; Beckerman, 1995; Maltsberger, 1994; Siegel, 1982b)*

When discussing this point, Battin (1994h) declared that the traditional interventionist stance is appropriate with many people but it is not the correct approach for those with terminal illnesses and may therefore be useless for those with hopeless conditions. She said that in these cases counselors should not presume that prevention is required but rather help the client to decide "whether it is the 'right' or 'best' or 'rational' choice *for this person*" (p. 174, emphasis original). Furthermore,

> *[W]hat is needed is counseling designed to help a [client] think through the issues in "rational suicide," including requests for assistance or for physician-performed euthanasia. Such suicide-neutral counseling takes the request at face value and seeks to help the [client] be sure she or he has considered all consequences, acknowledged his or her own emotions, and recognized all conflicts or affirmations of value such a choice might involve. (p. 175; see also Battin, 1994b; Maltsberger, 1994)*

A FINAL NOTE

The opinions provided in this chapter support the idea that the proper role for mental health professionals is to help clients achieve an appropriate death; a death that is based on the client's own value system and well-reasoned decisions. However, the only way this will happen is if professionals—counselors, marriage and family therapists, psychologists, psychiatrists, social workers, suicidologists—work to change the standards of care. What type of work is necessary? Presentations, publications, and discussions; research, case studies, personal viewpoints; any effort to demonstrate that at least a respectable minority of professionals who work with clients who are suicidal believe that under certain circumstances a decision to suicide can be rational and the professional's obligation is to assess but not necessarily to intervene. Clients who are suicidal will then receive the respectful care they deserve.

Appendix

SUICIDE IN OLD AGE

This case example will allow you to compare your analysis of the criteria for rational suicide to the author's. Although you may emphasize slightly different points in your approach, if you have a solid grasp of the criteria, as they have been conceptualized and presented, then you should come to the same conclusions about whether or not the case satisfies each individual criterion, meets the entire set of criteria, and what you could do next.

The case of the woman with the physical disability presented in chapter 5 was slightly adapted from Brody (1988). The following case is also taken from this source. Although both of these cases do not provide the amount and type of information necessary to examine all the criteria in detail, this does have its advantages. First, this state of affairs will provide you with the opportunity to examine what additional information you would need in order to fully assess the rationality of the decision to suicide. Second, this may provide a more realistic picture of what you would be facing when someone presents in your office, a colleague asks you to consult about a case, or you are a mental health consultant in a state (such as Oregon) where physician aid-in-dying is legal.

After you have read the case and answered the seven questions, compare your analysis of the case with the author's and Brody's (1988).

Mrs. Gordon is an 83-year-old woman who has suffered from circulation problems in her lower extremities for the past twenty years and who became bedridden and institutionalized in a nursing home seven years ago. Two years ago, she became incontinent; she also began to report that she suffers from constant body pain, the etiology of which is unclear. Recently, she was found in her room in the nursing home having difficulties breathing and was brought to the emergency room. There, her $PaCO_2$ was 70, so she underwent emergency intubation and was admitted to the ICU. It is difficult to communicate with her, and Psychiatry is not prepared to make a formal assessment of her *competency, but she is alert and oriented and writes in response to questions that she is suffering from so many diseases that she just wants to be allowed to die. The trouble is that the etiology of her current problems is unclear. Is her retention of CO_2 caused by drugs? Does it indicate significant obstructive pulmonary disease? No clear answer has emerged, the team is not at all convinced that she is suffering from a terminal illness, and she has no family to consult.*

1. Does Mrs. Gordon have a "hopeless condition" as defined in criterion 1?
2. Is Mrs. Gordon being pressured by outside forces to decide to die?
3. Is Mrs. Gordon competent?
4. Has Mrs. Gordon nonimpulsively considered all alternative to death?
5. Has Mrs. Gordon considered her values in making her decision?
6 Has Mrs. Gordon considered the impact on other people if she was to die?
7. Have appropriate professionals and significant others been consulted regarding her decision?

Both Brody (1988) and the author view this as a quality-of-life issue. She may have a terminal illness, she apparently does have an unknown physical pain, and there are other factors that appear to be, in her eyes, reducing the quality of her life so much that it does not seem worthwhile to continue living. If these negative influences could be alleviated or relieved in some way then her desire to die may fade; however, her social, physical, and perhaps emotional state may not improve in the foreseeable future (see also Courage et al., 1993). On this issue, Brody (1988) stated that some people may argue that "we have no way of assessing her quality of life" but he said that "*her* assessment of these factors" is crucial. He continued by stressing that her personal review "leads her to want not to be treated" and "leads her to the conclusion that her continued existence is a loss rather than a gain" (p. 124, emphasis original).

From the information provided there is no evidence of overt coercion by others. However, this point needs to be evaluated further. Some might say that her suicidality is the result of nonexistent interpersonal relationships. This may be true and in and of itself it is not coercion but rather both a quality of life issue and something to be explored in the search for alternatives. A relevant issue is the potential that Mrs. Gordon feels pressured by the nursing home workers, hospital personnel, or by societal attitudes, which subtly tell her that she is costing too much compared to her value to society. Brody (1988) discussed this concern and said that there may be prejudice against elderly individuals so therefore one should not allow her to die in order to fight this prejudice; yet, he also said that imposing choices on the elderly who may have made competent decisions for themselves is another form of prejudice. The author's personal view is that a skillful counselor will be able to determine the degree to which outside pressure is influencing her decision making.

In regard to competence, Brody (1988) argues that Mrs. Gordon, although she might have a reactive depression, is competent. Without the benefit of actual contact with her, more thorough assessment of her competence would be required before affirming this view. Brody and the author do agree that, since there is no evidence of her thinking around death and dying, it appears as if her decision to die is a relatively recent one. Furthermore, she may not have considered fully alternatives to death and disconfirming this would be a major task of the counselor. Although there is a hint about her beliefs regarding quality of life, there should be additional exploration of her values in this area as well as of her spiritual beliefs. Since, as presented in the case, there are no significant others to consider and consult with, these aspects of the final two criteria are moot. However, consultation with professionals such as clergy, medical specialists, and the nursing home personnel may be helpful.

In sum, further exploration is needed around Mrs. Gordon's quality of life concerns, the possibility of subtle pressure pushing her toward death, and the completeness of her decision-making process. After these tasks are accomplished it may be apparent that her decision to die is rational. However, with the information presented, the author must disagree with Brody (1988) and say that Mrs. Gordon's decision to die cannot be considered rational, yet.

OVERVIEWS OF ADDITIONAL CASES

As was mentioned in chapter 5, many discussions of suicide present cases to illustrate the points presented in the article or book. However, for the most part, these cases are of clients whose suicidal ideation is clearly irrational. You may want to peruse some of this material to verify for yourself the claim that the criteria outlined in this book will effectively screen out the clients who are not rationally suicidal. There are a few cases in the literature that would allow for a more thorough use of the criteria. See Table A.1 for the reference and then a checklist of whether or not the author believes the person in the case has met each of the criteria for rational suicide.

QUESTIONS AND ACTIVITIES FOR DISCUSSION

In order to assist you in further examining your personal beliefs about rational suicide, next you will find some suggested activities and questions that may be helpful for you individually or may provide interesting group discussion (see Corey et al., 1993; Werth & Carney, 1994). If this discussion takes place in a group setting (such as a class) the goal should not necessarily be to come up with *the* right answer. Instead, a more appropriate goal might be to have the participants begin exploring this issue and hear the process undertaken by others to help each person clarify her or his own personal point of view (Werth & Carney, 1994).

1. Have a discussion about a case presented in this book or from a different setting. Have a debate about how the following questions could be answered—perhaps with one side arguing the interventionist view and the other for the evaluative and/or acceptance view.
2. Review the idea of a continuum of acceptance of suicide and action to prevent suicide. Where would you place different conditions on such continua? Where is the line that separates a condition that is an acceptable reason for rational suicide and an unacceptable reason (i.e., what constitutes a hopeless condition)?

Table A.1 Additional Cases

Case	Criterion						
	1	2	3a	3b	3c	3d	3e
Ackerman & Strong #1.8	Y?	Y	Y?	N?	N?	N	N
Brody #1	N	N	Y?	N	N	N	N
Brody #2	Y	N	Y?	N	N	N	N
Brody #37	Y	Y	Y?	Y?	N	Y?	N
Hatton & Valente #20	Y?	Y?	N?	N?	N?	Y?	N?
Hatton & Valente #21	Y?	Y?	N?	N?	N	N?	N?
Heyd & Bloch A	Y	?	Y?	Y?	Y?	N?	N?
Heyd & Bloch B	N	Y?	N?	N	N?	N	N
Jellinek et al.	N?	Y?	Y?	N	Y?	N	N
Quill (1991)[a]	Y	Y	Y	Y	Y	Y	Y
Saunders et al. (1993)	Y	Y	Y	Y	Y?	Y	Y?
Vinogradov et al.	Y	N?	Y	N?	?	Y?	Y?
White & Engelhardt[b]	Y?	Y	Y	Y?	Y	Y?	Y?

[a] See also Quill (1994), p. 318

[b] See also Culver & Gert, pp. 152–154; Annas & Densberger, p. 574.

Note. Y = my impression from the information is that the criterion was met; N = my impression from the information is that the criterion was not met; ? = not enough information was provided to judge either way; Y? = criterion may be met; N? = criterion may not be met.

3. What is the impact of the mental health professional's values on treatment decisions and interventions? Should a counselor refer out a client who may have made a rational decision to suicide if the counselor is against such an act?
4. Analyze relevant codes of ethics and recent publications to determine your view of the presently accepted standard of care when working with clients considering suicide. Do counselors have the ethical and/or legal responsibility (and/or right) to prevent clients from suiciding? How important is respect for the client's autonomy? How should the counselor's decision be implemented? What are the potential ramifications of the decision? What factors impact the counselor's decision-making process? How much weight should be given to the beliefs of significant others? How would you justify your position to a peer review panel?
5. What do you think of the criteria for rational suicide outlined in the book? What would you add? What would you delete? Why?
6. How would you respond, professionally and emotionally, to a suicide which might be rational based on the criteria in this book?
7. If you decide to assess for rationality in a suicidal client, how should the information be documented?
8. Should the client provide a written or taped absolution of blame for the counselor? Would such a statement mean anything to a court or to the client's significant others?

Of course these questions are just a few of the innumerable points that could be considered, debated, and researched. The goal here is merely to help you begin to address this issue and provide you with some ideas for how to generate discussions on this topic regardless of your setting (e.g., courses, staff meetings, informal conversations) and, hopefully, to induce you to carry out your own research on this topic, to submit ideas for presentations at conferences, and to write articles on your own beliefs and or experiences.

References

Abernathy, V. (1984). Compassion, control, and decisions about competency. *American Journal of Psychiatry, 141*, 53–58.

Ackerman, T. F., & Strong, C. (1989). Paternalism in the therapeutic relationship. In *A casebook of medical ethics* (pp. 3–44). New York: Oxford University Press.

Adam, K. S. (1990). Environmental, psychosocial, and psychoanalytic aspects of suicidal behavior. In S. J. Blumenthal & D. J. Kupfer (Eds.), *Suicide over the life cycle: Risk factors, assessment, and treatment of suicidal patients* (pp. 39–96). Washington, DC: American Psychiatric Press.

Ahia, C. E., & Martin, D. (1993). *"The danger-to-self-or-others exception to confidentiality."* Alexandria, VA: American Counseling Association.

Alexander, L. (1949). Medical science under dictatorship. *New England Journal of Medicine, 241*, 39–47.

Allen, N. (1977). History and background of suicidology. In C. L. Hatton, S. M. Valente, & A. Rink (Eds.), *Suicide: Assessment and intervention* (pp. 1–19). New York: Appleton-Century-Crofts.

Alvarez, A. (1971). *The savage god.* London: Weidenfield and Nicolson.

Amchin, J., Wettstein, R. M., & Roth, L. H. (1990). Suicide, ethics, and the law. In S. J. Blumenthal & D. J. Kupfer (Eds.), *Suicide over the life cycle: Risk factors, assessment, and treatment of suicidal patients* (pp. 637–663). Washington, DC: American Psychiatric Press.

American Counseling Association. (1988). *Ethical standards of the American Counseling Association* (3rd rev. ed.). Alexandria, VA: Author.

American Psychiatric Association. (1994). *Diagnostic and statistical manual of the mental disorders* (4th ed.). Washington, DC: American Psychiatric Association.

American Psychological Association. (1992). Ethical principles of psychologists and code of conduct. *American Psychologist, 47*, 1597–1611.

American Psychological Association Committee on Lesbian and Gay Concerns.

(1991). *Bias in psychotherapy with lesbians and gay men.* Washington, DC: American Psychological Association.

American Psychological Association Committee on Psychology and AIDS. (1994, March). *Ethics project.* Committee on Psychology and AIDS Agenda Book, 30–31. Washington, DC: APA Office on AIDS.

Angell, M. (1982). The quality of mercy. *New England Journal of Medicine, 306,* 98–99.

Annas, G. J., & Densberger, J. E. (1984). Competence to refuse medical treatment: Autonomy vs. paternalism. *University of Toledo Law Review, 15,* 561–596.

Appelbaum, P. S., & Grisso, T. (1988). Assessing patients' capacities to consent to treatment. *New England Journal of Medicine, 319,* 1635–1638.

Appelbaum, P. S., & Grisso, T. (1995). The MacArthur Treatment Competence Study, I: Mental illness and competence to consent to treatment. *Law and Human Behavior, 19,* 105–126.

Appelbaum, P. S., & Gutheil, T. G. (1991). *Clinical handbook of psychiatry and the law* (2nd ed.). Baltimore, MD: Williams & Wilkins.

Appelbaum, P. S., & Roth, L. H. (1981). Clinical issues in the assessment of competency. *American Journal of Psychiatry, 138,* 1462–1467.

Appelbaum, P. S., & Roth, L. H. (1982). Competency to consent to research. *Archives of General Psychiatry, 39,* 951–958.

Arthur, G. L., & Swanson, C. D. (1993). *"Confidentiality and privileged communication."* Alexandria, VA: American Counseling Association.

Austin, K. M., Moline, M. E., & Williams, G. T. (1990). *Confronting malpractice: Legal and ethical dilemmas in psychotherapy.* Newbury Park, CA: Sage.

Backer, T. (1994, August). AIDS and suicide in the Hispanic communities. In B. Bongar & J. L. Werth, Jr. (Cochairs), *Modern psychotherapists, HIV seropositivity, and rational suicide.* Symposium conducted at the annual convention of the American Psychological Association, Los Angeles, CA.

Baelz, P. R. (1980). Suicide: Some theological reflections. In M. P. Battin & D. J. Mayo (Eds.), *Suicide: The philosophical issues* (pp. 71–83). New York: St. Martin's Press.

Barret, B. (Chair). (1993, August). *Confidentiality in clinical services for HIV-infected clients.* Symposium conducted at the annual convention of the American Psychological Convention, Toronto, Ontario, Canada.

Barrington, M. R. (1980). Apologia for suicide. In M. P. Battin & D. J. Mayo (Eds.), *Suicide: The philosophical issues* (pp. 90–103). New York: St. Martin's Press.

Barry, B. (1984). Perceptions of suicide. *Death Education, 8*(Suppl.), 17–25.

Barry, B. (1989). Suicide: The ultimate escape. *Death Studies, 13,* 185–190.

Barry, R. L. (1994). *Breaking the thread of life: On rational suicide.* New Brunswick, NJ: Transaction Publishers.

Battin, M. P. (1982). *Ethical issues in suicide.* Englewood Cliffs, NJ: Prentice-Hall.

Battin, M. P. (1988). Why the slippery slope isn't slippery: A reply to Walter M. Weber on the right to die. *Suicide and Life-Threatening Behavior, 18,* 189–193.

Battin, M. P. (1992). [Review of the book *Final Exit*]. *Suicide and Life-Threatening Behavior, 22,* 518–520.

Battin, M. P. (1994a). A dozen caveats concerning the discussion of euthanasia in the Netherlands. In *The least worst death* (pp. 130–144). New York: Oxford.

Battin, M. P. (1994b). Assisting in suicide: Seventeen questions physicians and mental-health professionals should ask. In *The least worst death* (pp. 271–276). New York: Oxford.

Battin, M. P. (1994c). Fiction as forecast: Euthanasia in Alzheimer's disease? In *The least worst death* (pp. 145–162). New York: Oxford.

Battin, M. P. (1994d). Introduction: The politics of dying. In *The least worst death* (pp. 3–29). New York: Oxford.

Battin, M. P. (1994e). Manipulated suicide. In *The least worst death* (pp. 195–204). New York: Oxford.

Battin, M. P. (1994f). Prohibition and invitation: The paradox of religious views about suicide. In *The least worst death* (pp. 205–253). New York: Oxford.

Battin, M. P. (1994g). Suicide: The basic issues. In *The least worst death* (pp. 185–194). New York: Oxford.

Battin, M. P. (1994h). Voluntary euthanasia and the risks of abuse. In *The least worst death* (pp. 163–181). New York: Oxford.

Battin, M. P., & Mayo, D. J. (Eds.). (1980). *Suicide: The philosophical issues.* New York: St. Martin's.

Beauchamp, T. L., & Perlin, S. (Eds.). (1978). *Ethical issues in death and dying.* Englewood Cliffs, NJ: Prentice-Hall.

Beckerman, N. L. (1995). Suicide in relation to AIDS. *Death Studies, 19,* 223–243.

Bednar, R. L., Bednar, S. C., Lambert, M. J., & Waite, D. R. (1991). *Psychotherapy with high-risk clients: Legal and professional standards.* Pacific Grove, CA: Brooks/Cole.

Berman, A. I., & Cohen-Sandler, R. (1982). Suicide and the standard of care: Optimal vs. acceptable. *Suicide and Life-Threatening Behavior, 12,* 114–122.

Berman, A. I., & Cohen-Sandler, R. (1983). Suicide and malpractice: Expert testimony and the standard of care. *Professional Psychology: Research and Practice, 14,* 6–19.

Black, D. W., & Winokur, G. (1990). Suicide and psychiatric diagnosis. In S. J. Blumenthal & D. J. Kupfer (Eds.), *Suicide over the life cycle: Risk factors, assessment, and treatment of suicidal patients* (pp. 135–153). Washington, DC: American Psychiatric Press.

Blendon, R. J., Szalay, U. S., & Knox, R. A. (1992). Should physicians aid their patients in dying? The public perspective. *Journal of the American Medical Association, 267,* 2658–2662.

Bleuler, E. (1950). *Dementia praecox or the group of schizophrenias.* New York: International Universities Press.

Bloch, K. E. (1987). The role of law in suicide prevention: Beyond civil commitment—A bystander duty to report suicide threats. *Stanford Law Review, 39,* 929–953.

Bloom, J. D., & Faulkner, L. R. (1987). Competency determinations in civil commitment. *American Journal of Psychiatry, 144,* 193–196.

Blumenthal, S. J. (1990). An overview and synopsis of risk factors, assessment, and treatment of suicidal patients over the life-cycle. In S. J. Blumenthal & D. J. Kupfer (Eds.), *Suicide over the life cycle: Risk factors, assessment, and treatment of suicidal patients* (pp. 685–733). Washington, DC: American Psychiatric Press.

Blumenthal, S. J., & Kupfer, D. J. (1986). Generalizable treatment strategies for suicidal behavior. *Annals of New York Academy of Sciences, 487*, 327–340.

Bogdan, R. C., & Biklen, S. K. (1982). *Qualitative research for education: An introduction to theory and methods.* Boston: Allyn & Bacon.

Bongar, B. (1991). *The suicidal patient: Clinical and legal standards of care.* Washington, DC: American Psychological Association.

Bongar, B. (1993). Consultation and the suicidal patient. *Suicide and Life-Threatening Behavior, 23*, 299–306.

Bongar, B., & Greaney, S. A. (1994). Essential clinical and legal issues when working with the suicidal patient. *Death Studies, 18*, 529–548.

Bongar, B., & Harmatz, M. (1989). Graduate training in clinical psychology and the study of suicide. *Professional Psychology: Research and Practice, 20*, 209–213.

Bongar, B., Maris, R. W., Berman, A. L., & Litman, R. E. (1992). Outpatient standards of care and the suicidal patient. *Suicide and Life-Threatening Behavior, 22*, 453–478.

Bongar, B., & Werth, J. L., Jr. (Cochairs). (1993, August). *Rational suicide: A possibility?* Symposium conducted at the annual convention of the American Psychological Association, Toronto, Ontario, Canada.

Bongar, B., & Werth, J. L., Jr. (Cochairs). (1994, August). *Modern psychotherapists, HIV seropositivity, and rational suicide.* Symposium conducted at the annual convention of the American Psychological Association, Los Angeles, CA.

Brandt, R. B. (1975). The morality and rationality of suicide. In S. Perlin (Ed.), *A handbook for the study of suicide* (pp. 61–76). New York: Oxford University Press.

Brock, D. W., & Wartman, S. A. (1993). When competent patients make irrational choices. In D. W. Brock, *Life and death: Philosophical essays in biomedical ethics* (pp. 80–92). Cambridge, England: Cambridge University Press.

Brody, B. A. (1988). *Life and death decision making.* New York: Oxford University Press.

Bromberg, S., & Cassel, C. K. (1983). Suicide in the elderly: The limits of paternalism. *Journal of the American Geriatrics Society, 31*, 698–703.

Brown, H. N. (1987). The impact of suicides on therapists in training. *Comprehensive Psychiatry, 28*, 101–112.

Brown, J. H., Henteleff, P., Barakat, S., & Rowe, C. J. (1986). Is it normal for terminally ill patients to desire death? *American Journal of Psychiatry, 143*, 208–211.

Buchanan, A. E., & Brock, D. W. (1989). *Deciding for others: The ethics of surrogate decision making.* Cambridge: Cambridge University Press.

Buda, M., & Tsuang, M. T. (1990). The epidemiology of suicide: Implications for clinical practice. In S. J. Blumenthal & D. J. Kupfer (Eds.), *Suicide over the life cycle: Risk factors, assessment, and treatment of suicidal patients* (pp. 17–37). Washington, DC: American Psychiatric Press.

Callahan, J. (1994). The ethics of assisted suicide. *Health and Social Work, 19,* 237–244

Cantor, J., & Pilkington, N. (1992, August). *Homophobia in psychology programs: A survey of graduate students.* Paper presented at the annual convention of the American Psychological Association, Washington, DC.

Cantor, N. L. (1973). A patient's decision to decline life-saving medical treatment: Bodily integrity versus the preservation of life. *Rutgers Law Review, 26,* 228–264.

Cappon, D. (1962). Attitudes of and towards the dying. *Canadian Medical Association Journal, 87,* 693–700.

Cassel, C. K., & Goldstein, M. K. (1988). Ethical considerations. In L. F. Jarvik, & C. H. Winograd (Eds.), *Treatments for the Alzheimer patient: The long haul* (pp. 80–95). New York: Springer Publishing Company.

Cassell, E. J. (1982). The nature of suffering and the goals of medicine. *New England Journal of Medicine, 306,* 639–645.

Cavan, R. S. (1928). *Suicide.* New York: Russell & Russell.

Chapman Dick, L. (1991, March/April). To die or not to die—That was the question: Euthanasia survey results. *The Forum, 16,* 4–6.

Chemtob, C. M., Bauer, G. B., Hamada, R. S., Pelowski, S. R., & Muraoka, M. Y. (1989). Patient suicide: Occupational hazard for psychologists and psychiatrists. *Professional Psychology: Research and Practice, 20,* 294–300.

Choron, J. (1972). *Suicide.* New York: Charles Scribner's Sons.

Clark, D. C. (1992). "Rational" suicide and people with terminal conditions or disabilities. *Issues in Law and Medicine, 8,* 147–166.

Clark, D. C., & Horton-Deutsch, S. L. (1992). Assessment *in absentia*: The value of the psychological autopsy method for studying antecedents of suicide and predicting future suicides. In R. W. Maris, A. L. Berman, J. T. Maltsberger, & R. I. Yufit (Eds.), *Assessment and prediction of suicide* (pp. 144–182). New York: The Guilford Press.

Clements, C. D., Sider, R. C., & Perlmutter, R. (1983). Suicide: Bad act or good intervention. *Suicide and Life-Threatening Behavior, 13,* 28–41.

Clum, G. A. (1987). Abandon the suicidal? A reply to Szasz. *American Psychologist, 42,* 883–885.

Colt, G. H. (1991). *The enigma of suicide.* New York: Summit Books.

Conwell, Y., & Caine, E. D. (1991). Rational suicide and the right to die. *New England Journal of Medicine, 325,* 1100–1103.

Corey, G., Corey, M. S., & Callanan, P. (1993). *Issues & ethics in the helping professions* (4th ed.). Monterey, CA: Brooks/Cole.

Cotton, P. (1993). Rational suicide: No longer 'crazy'? *Journal of the American Medical Association, 270,* 797.

Courage, M. M., Godbey, K. L., Ingram, D. A., Schramm, L. L., & Hale, W. E. (1993). Suicide in the elderly: Staying in control. *Journal of Psychosocial Nursing and Mental Health Services, 31*(7), 26–31.

Crawford, I., Humfleet, G., Ribordy, S. C., Ho, F. C., & Vickers, V. L. (1991). Stigmatization of AIDS patients by mental health professionals. *Professional Psychology: Research and Practice, 22,* 357–361.

Crocker, J., & Major, B. (1989). Social stigma and self-esteem: The self-protective properties of stigma. *Psychological Review, 96,* 608–630.

Culver, C. M. (1985). The clinical determination of competence. In M. B. Kapp, H. E. Pies, & A. E. Doudera (Eds.), *Legal and ethical aspects of health care for the elderly* (pp. 276–285). Ann Arbor, MI: Health Administration Press.

Culver, C. M., & Gert, B. (1982). *Philosophy in medicine: Conceptual and ethical issues in medicine and psychiatry.* New York: Oxford University Press.

deCatanzaro, D. (1981). Ethics and suicide. In *Suicide and self-damaging behavior: A sociobiological perspective* (pp. 139–146). New York: Academic Press.

Decker, N. (1977). The wish to die: Pathological depression or rational decision. In W. E. Fann, I. Karacan, A. D. Pokorny, & R. L. Williams (Eds.), *Phenomenology and treatment of depression* (pp. 187–195). New York: Spectrum Publications.

Deluty, R. (1988). Physical illness, psychiatric illness, and the acceptability of suicide. *Omega, 19,* 79–91.

Deluty, R. (1989). Factors affecting the acceptability of suicide. *Omega, 19,* 315–326.

Developments in the law: Civil commitment of the mentally ill. (1974). *Harvard Law Review, 87,* 1190–1406.

Diekstra, R. F. W. (1986). The significance of Nico Speijer's suicide: How and when should suicide be prevented? *Suicide and Life-Threatening Behavior, 16,* 13–15.

Diggory, J. C. (1968). Suicide and value. In H. L. P. Resnik (Ed.), *Suicidal behaviors: Diagnosis and management* (pp. 3–18). Boston: Little Brown and Co.

Domino, G., Gibson, L., Poling, S., & Westlake, L. (1980). Students' attitudes toward suicide. *Social Psychiatry, 15,* 127–130.

Domino, G., & Miller, K. (1992). Religiosity and attitudes toward suicide. *Omega, 25,* 271–282.

Domino, G., & Swain, B. J. (1986). Recognition of suicide lethality and attitudes toward suicide in mental health professionals. *Omega, 16,* 301–308.

Dorpat, T. L., Anderson, W. F., & Ripley, H. S. (1968). The relationship of physical illness to suicide. In H. L. P. Resnik (Ed.), *Suicidal behaviors: Diagnosis and management* (pp. 209–219). Boston: Little Brown and Co.

Drane, J. F. (1985). The many faces of competency. *Hastings Center Report, 15*(2), 17–21.

Drinan, R. F. (1977). Should there be a legal right to die. In R. F. Weir (Ed.), *Ethical issues in death and dying* (pp. 297–307). New York: Columbia University Press.

Droogas, A., Siiter, R., & O'Connell, A. N. (1982). Effects of personal and situational factors on attitudes toward suicide. *Omega, 13,* 127–144.

Dublin, L. I. (1963). *Suicide: A sociological and statistical study.* New York: Ronald Press.

Dunshee, S. J. (1994, April). Compassion in dying. *Focus: A Guide to AIDS Research and Counseling, 9*(5), 5–6.

Dyck, A. J. (1977). An alternative to the ethic of euthanasia. In R. F. Weir (Ed.), *Ethical issues in death and dying* (pp. 281–296). New York: Columbia University Press.

Earls, F., Escobar, J. I., & Manson, S. M. (1990). Suicide in minority groups: Epidemiologic and cultural perspectives. In S. J. Blumenthal & D. J. Kupfer (Eds.), *Suicide over the life cycle: Risk factors, assessment, and treatment of suicidal patients* (pp. 571–598). Washington, DC: American Psychiatric Press.

Early, K. E. (1992). *Religion and suicide in the African-American community.* Westport, CT: Greenwood Press.

Engelhardt, H. T., Jr. (1989). Death by free choice: Modern variations on an antique theme. In B. A. Brody (Ed.), *Suicide and euthanasia: Historical and contemporary themes* (pp. 251–280). Boston: Kluwer Academic Publishers.

Engelhardt, H. T., Jr., & Malloy, M. (1982). Suicide and assisting suicide: A critique of legal sanctions. *Southwestern Law Journal, 36,* 1003–1037.

Ennis, B. J., & Litwack, T. R. (1974). Psychiatry and the presumption of expertise: Flipping coins in the courtroom. *California Law Review, 62,* 693–752.

Erard, R. E. (1994, August). Assessing competence to choose death—Dilemmas for treating and consulting psychologists under proposed assisted suicide legislation. In L. T. Pantano (Chair) *Assisted suicide—Mercy or murder? Michigan's experience.* Symposium conducted at the annual convention of the American Psychological Association, Los Angeles, CA.

Farberow, N. L. (Ed.). (1975). *Suicide in different cultures.* Baltimore, MD: University Park Press.

Farberow, N. L., & Shneidman, E. S. (Eds.). (1961). *The cry for help.* New York: McGraw-Hill.

Farberow, N. L., Shneidman, E. S., & Leonard, C. V. (1976a). Suicidal risk among schizophrenic patients. In E. S. Shneidman, N. L. Farberow, & R. E. Litman (Eds.), *The psychology of suicide* (pp. 307–324). New York: Jason Aronson, Inc.

Farberow, N. L., Shneidman, E. S., & Leonard, C. V. (1976b). Suicide among patients with malignant neoplasms. In E. S. Shneidman, N. L. Farberow, & R. E. Litman (Eds.), *The psychology of suicide* (pp. 325–344). New York: Jason Aronson, Inc.

Fedden, H. R. (1938). *Suicide: A social and historical study.* London: Peter Davies Limited.

Finnerty, J. L. (1987). Ethics in rational suicide. *Critical Care Nursing Quarterly, 10,* 86–90.

Flavin, D. K., Franklin, J. E., Jr., & Frances, R. J. (1990). Substance abuse and suicidal behavior. In S. J. Blumenthal & D. J. Kupfer (Eds.), *Suicide over the life cycle: Risk factors, assessment, and treatment of suicidal patients* (pp. 177–204). Washington, DC: American Psychiatric Press.

Fletcher, J. (1975). The "right" to live and the "right" to die. In M. Kohl (Ed.), *Beneficent euthanasia* (pp. 44–53). Buffalo, NY: Promethus Books.

Fletcher, J. (1977). Ethics and euthanasia. In R. F. Weir (Ed.), *Ethical issues in death and dying* (pp. 348–359). New York: Columbia University Press.

Fliszar, G. M. (1993). *Attitudes toward persons with AIDS among psychologists in training.* Unpublished doctoral dissertation, Texas Tech University, Lubbock, TX.

Fox, M., & Lipton, H. L. (1983). The decision to perform cardiopulmonary resuscitation. *New England Journal of Medicine, 309,* 607–608.

Francis, L. P (1980). Assisting suicide: A problem for the clinical law. In M. P. Battin & D. J. Mayo (Eds.), *Suicide: The philosophical issues* (pp. 254–266). New York: St. Martin's Press.

Freedman, B. (1981). Competence, marginal and otherwise: Concepts and ethics. *International Journal of Law and Psychiatry, 4*, 53–72.

Garmezy, N. (1982). Forward. In E. E. Werner & R. S. Smith, *Vulnerable but invincible* (pp. xiii–xix). New York: McGraw-Hill.

Gill, C. J. (1992). Suicide intervention for people with disabilities: A lesson in inequality. *Issues in Law and Medicine, 8*, 37–53.

Goldfarb, A. I. (1983). The need for predetermined guidelines. In Group for the Advancement of Psychiatry (Ed.), *The right to die: Decision and decision makers*, (pp. 76–77). New York: Jason Aronson.

Goldsmith, S. J., Fyer, M., & Frances, A. (1990). Personality and suicide. In S. J. Blumenthal & D. J. Kupfer (Eds.), *Suicide over the life cycle: Risk factors, assessment, and treatment of suicidal patients* (pp. 155–176). Washington, DC: American Psychiatric Press.

Govin, M. E. (1989). *Effects of client sexual orientation and presence of HIV infection on counselor perceptions and willingness to counsel.* Unpublished master's thesis, Central State University, Edmond, OK.

Graham, D. L. R., Rawlings, E. I., Halpern, H. S., & Hermes, J. (1984). Therapists' needs for training in counseling lesbians and gay men. *Professional Psychology: Research and Practice, 15*, 482–496.

Green, B. R., & Irish, D. P. (1971). *Death education: Preparation for living* (pp. 119–122). Cambridge, MA: Schenkman Publishing Co.

Greenberg, D. F. (1974). Involuntary psychiatric commitments to prevent suicide. *New York University Law Review, 49*, 227–269.

Griesinger, W. (1867). *Mental pathology and therapeutics* (C.L. Robertson & J. Rutherford, Trans.). London: The New Syndenham Society.

Grisso, T. (1986). *Evaluating competencies: Forensic assessments and instruments.* New York: Plenum Press.

Grisso, T., & Appelbaum, P. S. (1995). The MacArthur Treatment Competence Study, III: Abilities of patients to consent to psychiatric and medical treatments. *Law and Human Behavior, 19,*149–174.

Grisso, T., Appelbaum, P. S., Mulvey, E. P., & Fletcher, K. (1995). The MacArthur Treatment Competence Study, II: Measures of abilities related to competence to consent to treatment. *Law and Human Behavior, 19,* 127–148.

Gruetzner, H. (1988). *Alzheimer's: A caregiver's guide and sourcebook.* New York: John Wiley & Sons, Inc.

Gurrister, L., & Kane, R. A. (1978). How therapists perceive and treat suicidal clients. *Community Mental Health Journal, 14,* 3–13.

Gutheil, T. G. (1992). Suicide and suit: Liability after self-destruction. In D. Jacobs (Ed.), *Suicide and clinical practice* (pp. 147–167). Washington, DC: American Psychiatric Press.

Gutheil, T. G., Bursztajn, H., & Brodsky, A. (1986). The multidimensional assessment of dangerousness: Competence assessment in patient care and liability prevention. *Bulletin of the American Academy of Psychiatry and the Law, 14,* 123–129.

Gutheil, T. G., Bursztajn, H., Hamm, R. M., & Brodsky, A. (1983). Subjective data and suicide assessment in the light of recent legal developments. *International Journal of Law and Psychiatry, 6*, 317–329.

Halleck, S. L. (1980). Miscellaneous expert witness roles in the civil courts. In S. L. Halleck, *Law in the practice of psychiatry: A handbook for clinicians* (pp. 267–279). New York: Plenum Medical Book Company.

Hammond, L. K. (1991). *Attitudes of clinical psychologists, psychiatrists, and oncologists toward suicide.* Unpublished doctoral dissertation, University of Maryland Baltimore County, Catonsville, MD.

Harris, E. A. (1994, August). Legal aspects of rational suicide for persons with AIDS. In B. Bongar & J. L. Werth, Jr. (Cochairs), *Modern psychotherapists, HIV seropositivity, and rational suicide.* Symposium conducted at the annual convention of the American Psychological Association, Los Angeles, CA.

Hatton, C. L., & Valente, S. M. (1984). Eight clinical examples. In C. L. Hatton & S. M. Valente (Eds.), *Suicide: Assessment and intervention* (2nd ed.) (pp. 239–247). Norwalk, CT: Appleton-Century-Crofts.

Hauerwas, S. (1981). Rational suicide and reasons for living. In M. D. Basson (Ed.), *Rights and responsibilities in modern medicine: The second volume in a series on ethics, humanism, and medicine* (pp. 185–199). New York: Alan R. Liss, Inc.

Hayes, J. A., & Gelso, C. J. (1993). Male counselors' discomfort with gay and HIV-infected clients. *Journal of Counseling Psychology, 40*, 86–93.

Heifetz, M. D. (1975). Suicide: A right? In *The right to die: A neurosurgeon speaks of death with candor* (pp. 73–98). New York: G. P. Putnam's Sons.

Hendin, H. (1969). *Black suicide.* New York: Basic Books.

Hendin, H. (1982). *Suicide in America.* New York: W.W. Norton.

Hendin, H., & Waldman, L. (1982). Involuntary commitment. In H. Hendin, *Suicide in America* (pp. 188–208). New York: W.W. Norton.

Herek, G. M. (1990). Illness, stigma, and AIDS. In P. T. Costa, Jr. & G. R. VandenBos (Eds.), *Psychological aspects of serious illness: Chronic conditions, fatal diseases, and clinical care* (pp. 107–149). Washington, DC: American Psychological Association.

Herek, G. M., & Glunt, E. K. (1988). An epidemic of stigma: Public reactions to AIDS. *American Psychologist, 43*, 886–891.

Heyd, D., & Bloch, S. (1981). The ethics of suicide. In S. Bloch & P. Chodoff (Eds.), *Psychiatric ethics* (pp. 185–202). Oxford: Oxford University Press.

Hoff, L. A. (1989). *People in crisis: Understanding and helping* (3rd ed.). Redwood City, CA: Addison-Wesley.

Hoffman, M. A. (Chair). (1992, August). *Ethical and legal issues related to HIV.* Symposium conducted at the annual convention of the American Psychological Association, Washington, DC.

Hoge, S. K., & Appelbaum, P. S. (1989). Legal issues in outpatient psychiatry. In A. Lazare (Ed.), *Outpatient psychiatry: Diagnosis and treatment* (2nd ed.) (pp. 605–621). Baltimore, MD: Williams & Wilkins.

Holmes, C. B. (1987). Comment on Szasz's view of suicide prevention. *American Psychologist, 42*, 881–882.

Hook, S. (1927). The ethics of suicide. *International Journal of Ethics, 37*, 173–188.

Howell, J. A. (1978). Civil liability for suicide: An analysis of the causation issue. *Arizona State Law Journal, 573*–615.

Huber, R., Cox, V. M., & Edelen, W. B. (1992). Right-to-die responses from a random sample of 200. *The Hospice Journal, 8*(3), 1–19.

Humphry, D. (1987). The case for rational suicide. *Suicide and Life-Threatening Behavior, 17*, 335–338.

Humphry, D. (1991). *Final exit: The practicalities of self-deliverance and assisted suicide for the dying.* Eugene, OR: The Hemlock Society.

Humphry, D., & Wickett, A. (1990). *The right to die: Understanding euthanasia.* Eugene, OR: The Hemlock Society.

Huyse, F. J., & van Tilburg, W. (1993). Euthanasia policy in the Netherlands: The role of consultation-liaison psychiatrists. *Hospital and Community Psychiatry, 44*, 733–738.

Iga, M., & Tatai, K. (1975). Characteristics of suicides and attitudes toward suicide in Japan. In N. L. Farberow (Ed.), *Suicide in different cultures* (pp. 255–280). Baltimore, MD: University Park Press.

Inman, D. J., Bascue, L. O., Kahn, W. J., & Shaw, P. A. (1984). The relationship between suicide knowledge and suicide interviewing skill. *Death Education, 8*, 179–184.

Jackson, D. D. (1957). Theories of suicide. In E. S. Shneidman & N. L. Farberow (Eds.), *Clues to suicide* (11–21). New York: McGraw-Hill.

Jackson, D. L., & Younger, S. (1979). Patient autonomy and "death with dignity." *New England Journal of Medicine, 301*, 404–408.

Jacobs, J., & Teicher, J. D. (1967). Broken homes and social isolation in attempted suicides of adolescents. *International Journal of Social Psychiatry, 13*, 139–149.

Jellinek, M., Brandt, R. B., & Litman, R. E. (1979). A suicide attempt and emergency room ethics. *Hastings Center Report, 9*(4), 12–13.

Johnson, D., Fitch, S. D., Alston, J. P., & McIntosh, W. A. (1980). Acceptance of conditional suicide and euthanasia among adult Americans. *Suicide and Life-Threatening Behavior, 10*, 157–166.

Jones, J. R., & Dilley, J. W. (1993, July). Rational suicide and HIV disease. *Focus: A Guide to AIDS Research and Counseling, 8*(8), 5–6.

Jonsen, A. R., Lo, B., Luce, J., Yarnell, S. K., & Younger, S. J. (1987, April). *AIDS and rational suicide: Euthanasia.* Symposium conducted at the annual meeting of the American Association of Suicidology, San Francisco, CA.

Judd, S. (1995, January-February). Oregon's Measure 16 blocked. *TimeLines, 60*(1), 4–5.

Kahn, A. (1990). Principles of psychotherapy with suicidal patients. In S. J. Blumenthal & D. J. Kupfer (Eds.), *Suicide over the life cycle: Risk factors, assessment, and treatment of suicidal patients* (pp. 441–467). Washington, DC: American Psychiatric Press.

Kaplan, M., & Adamek, M. (1995, March). *Managing elderly suicide: Preliminary results of a national survey.* Paper presented at the Annual Meeting of the American Society on Aging, Atlanta, GA.

Kastenbaum, R. (1976). Suicide as the preferred way of death. In E. S. Shneidman

(Ed.), *Suicidology: Contemporary developments* (pp. 421–441). New York: Grune and Stratton.

Kelly, J. A., St. Lawrence, J. S., Smith, S., Hood, H. V., & Cook, D. J. (1987). Stigmatization of AIDS patients by physicians. *American Journal of Public Health, 77*, 789–791.

Kelly, J. A., St. Lawrence, J. S., Smith, S., Hood, H. V., & Cook, D. J. (1988). Nurses' attitudes toward AIDS. *Journal of Continuing Education in Nursing, 19*, 78–83.

Kitchener, K. S. (1984). Intuition, critical evaluation and ethical principles: The foundation for ethical decisions in counseling psychology. *The Counseling Psychologist, 12*, 43–55.

Kjervik, D. K. (1984). The psychotherapist's duty to act reasonably to prevent suicide: A proposal to allow rational suicide. *Behavioral Sciences and the Law, 2*, 207–218.

Kleespies, P. M. (1993). The stress of patient suicidal behavior: Implications for interns and training programs in psychology. *Professional Psychology: Research and Practice, 24*, 477–482.

Kleespies, P. M., Penk, W. E., & Forsyth, J. P. (1993). The stress of patient suicidal behavior during clinical training: Incidence, impact, and recovery. *Professional Psychology: Research and Practice, 24*, 293–303.

Kleespies, P. M., Smith, M. R., & Becker, B. R. (1990). Psychology interns as patient suicide survivors: Incidence, impact, and recovery. *Professional Psychology: Research and Practice, 21*, 257–263.

Klopfer, F. J., & Price, W. F. (1978). Euthanasia acceptance as related to after-life belief and other attitudes. *Omega, 9*, 245–253.

Knapp, S., & VandeCreek, L. (1983). Malpractice risks with suicidal patients. *Psychotherapy: Theory, Research and Practice, 20*, 274–280.

Knox, M. D., Dow, M. G., & Cotton, D. A. (1989) Mental health care providers: The need for AIDS education. *AIDS Education and Prevention, 1*, 285–290.

Knuth, M. O. (1979). Civil liability for causing or failing to prevent suicide. *Loyola of Los Angeles Law Review, 12*, 967–999.

Kobler, A. L., & Stotland, E. (1964). *The end of hope.* London: The Free Press of Glencoe.

Kohl, M. (1975). Voluntary beneficent euthanasia. In M. Kohl (Ed.), *Beneficent euthanasia* (pp. 130–141). Buffalo, NY: Promethus Books.

Kushner, H. I. (1989). *Self-destruction in the promised land: A psychocultural biology of American suicide.* New Brunswick, NJ: Rutgers University Press.

Laforet, E. G. (1963). The "hopeless case." *Archives of Internal Medicine, 112*, 314–326.

Larson, K. (1995, March-April). Legislation! *TimeLines, 61*(1), 4–5.

Lebacqz, K., & Engelhardt, H. T., Jr. (1977). Suicide. In D. J. Horan & D. Mall (Eds.), *Death, dying, and euthanasia* (pp. 669–705). Washington, DC: University Publications of America.

Lebegue, B., & Clark, L. D. (1981). Incompetence to refuse treatment: A necessary condition for civil commitment. *American Journal of Psychiatry, 138*, 1075–1077.

Lecky, W. E. H. (1898). *History of European morals from Augustus to Charlemagne. Vol. I* (3rd ed.). New York: D. Appleton and Co.

Leenaars, A. A. (1992). Suicide notes of the older adult. *Suicide and Life-Threatening Behavior, 22,* 62–79.

Leo, J. (1994, May 16). Assisted suicide's slippery slope. *U.S. News & World Report, 116*(19), 22.

Leonard, C. V. (1967). *Understanding and preventing suicide.* Springfield, IL: Charles C. Thomas.

Lester, D. (1969). Suicide as a positive act. *Psychology, 6*(3), 43–48.

Lester, D. (1970). The concept of an appropriate death. *Psychology, 7*(4), 61–66.

Lester, D. (1977). Bereavement and suicide: A positive perspective. In B. L. Danto & A. H. Kutscher (Eds.), *Suicide and bereavement* (pp. 194–198). New York: MSS Information Corporation.

Lester, D. (1992). Alcoholism and drug abuse. In R. W. Maris, A. L. Berman, J. T. Maltsberger, & R. I. Yufit (Eds.), *Assessment and prediction of suicide* (pp. 321–336). New York: The Guilford Press.

Levy, M. (1995, January-February). Appeals court review Rothstein decision. *TimeLines, 60*(3).

Litman, R. E. (1965). When patients commit suicide. *American Journal of Psychotherapy, 19,* 570–576.

Litman, R. E. (1976). Sigmund Freud on suicide. In E. S. Shneidman, N. L. Farberow, & R. E. Litman (Eds.), *The psychology of suicide* (pp. 565–586). New York: Jason Aronson, Inc.

Livneh, H. (1984). On the origins of negative attitudes toward people with disabilities. In R. P. Marnelli & A. E. Dell Orto (Eds.), *The psychological and social impact of physical disability* (pp. 167–184). New York: Springer.

Lo Presto, C. T., Sherman, M. F., & DiCarlo, M. A. (1995). Factors affecting the unacceptability of suicide and the effects of evaluator depression and religiosity. *Omega, 30,* 205–221.

Lowenthal, U. (1976). Suicide—The other side. *Archives of General Psychiatry, 33,* 838–842.

Mackenzie, T. B., & Popkin, M. K. (1990). Medical illness and suicide. In S. J. Blumenthal & D. J. Kupfer (Eds.), *Suicide over the life cycle: Risk factors, assessment, and treatment of suicidal patients* (pp. 205–232). Washington, DC: American Psychiatric Press.

Maguire, D. C. (1975). *Death by choice.* New York: Shocken Books.

Mair, A. W. (1922). Suicide (Greek and Roman). In J. Hastings (Ed.), *Encyclopaedia of religion and ethics, Vol. XII* (pp. 26–33). New York: Charles Scribner's Sons.

Malcolm, A. H. (1990, June 1). Giving death a hand: Rending issue. *New York Times,* A6.

Maltsberger, J.T. (1994). Calculated risk taking in the treatment of suicidal patients: Ethical and legal problems. *Death Sudies, 18,* 439–452.

Maris, R. (1982). Rational suicide: An impoverished self-transformation. *Suicide and Life-Threatening Behavior, 12,* 4–16.

Maris, R. W. (1981). *Pathways to suicide: A survey of self-destructive behaviors.* Baltimore, MD: Johns Hopkins University Press.

Maris, R. W. (1983). Suicide: Rights and rationality. *Suicide and Life-Threatening Behavior, 13*, 223–230.

Maris, R. W. (1986). Basic issues in suicide prevention: Resolutions of liberty and love (The Dublin Lecture). *Suicide and Life-Threatening Behavior, 16*, 326–334.

Maris, R. W. (1992a). How are suicides different. In R. W. Maris, A. L. Berman, J. T. Maltsberger, & R. I. Yufit (Eds.), *Assessment and prediction of suicide* (pp. 65–87). New York: The Guilford Press.

Maris, R. W. (1992b). Overview of the study of suicide assessment and prediction. In R. W. Maris, A. L. Berman, J. T. Maltsberger, & R. I. Yufit (Eds.), *Assessment and prediction of suicide* (pp. 3–22). New York: The Guilford Press.

Maris, R. W., Berman, A. L., & Maltsberger, J. T. (1992). Summary and conclusions: What have we learned about suicide assessment and prediction. In R. W. Maris, A. L. Berman, J. T. Maltsberger, & R. I. Yufit (Eds.), *Assessment and prediction of suicide* (pp. 640–672). New York: The Guilford Press.

Maris, R. W. Berman, A. L. Maltsberger, J. T. & Yufit, R. I. (Eds.). (1992). *Assessment and prediction of suicide*. New York: The Guilford Press.

Marshall, J. R., Burnett, W., & Brasure, J. (1983). On precipitating factors: Cancer as a cause of suicide. *Suicide and Life-Threatening Behavior, 13*, 15–27.

Martin, R. M. (1980). Suicide and false desires. In M. P. Battin & D. J. Mayo (Eds.), *Suicide: The philosophical issues* (pp. 144–150). New York: St. Martin's Press.

Martin, S. K., & Range, L. M. (1991). Extenuating circumstances in perceptions of suicide: Disease diagnosis (AIDS, cancer), pain level, and life expectancy. *Omega, 22*, 187–197.

Marzen, T. J., O'Dowd, M. K., Crone, D., & Balch, T. J. (1985). Suicide: A constitutional right? *Duquesne Law Review, 24*, 1–242.

Marzuk, P. M. (1994). Suicide and terminal illness. *Death Studies, 18*, 497–512.

Mather, D. B. (1987). The case against preventing suicide prevention: Comments on Szasz. *American Psychologist, 42*, 882–883.

Mayo, D. (1993, August). The case for rational suicide. In B. Bongar & J. L. Werth, Jr. (Cochairs), *Rational suicide: A possibility?* Symposium conducted at the annual convention of the American Psychological Association, Toronto, Ontario, Canada.

Mayo, D. J. (1983). Contemporary philosophical literature on suicide: A review. *Suicide and Life-Threatening Behavior, 13*, 313–345.

Mayo, D. J. (1986). The concept of rational suicide. *Journal of Medicine and Philosophy, 11*, 143–155.

Mayo, D. J., & Werth, J. L., Jr. (Cochairs). (1994, April). *Rational suicide defined: A panel discussion*. Symposium conducted at the annual conference of the American Association of Suicidology, New York, NY.

McCartney, J. R. (1978). Suicide vs. right to refuse treatment in the chronically ill. *Psychosomatics, 19*, 548–551.

McIntosh, J. L. (1985). Ethics of suicide: Moral, philosophical, religious, and legal aspects. In *Research on suicide: A bibliography* (pp. 220–244). Westport, CT: Greenwood Press.

McIntosh, J. L. (1993a, August). Arguments against rational and assisted suicide.

In B. Bongar & J. L. Werth, Jr. (Cochairs), *Rational suicide: A possibility?* Symposium conducted at the annual convention of the American Psychological Association, Toronto, Ontario, Canada.

McIntosh, J. L. (1993b). Assisted and rational suicide: The issues will not disappear. *Newslink, 19*(4), 3–4.

McIntosh, J. L., & Santos, J. F. (1984). Suicide counseling and intervention with racial/ethnic minorities. In C. L. Hatton & S. M. Valente (Eds.), *Suicide: Assessment and intervention* (2nd ed.) (pp. 175–194). Norwalk, CT: Appleton-Century-Crofts.

McKegney, F. P., & Lange, P. (1971). The decision to no longer live on chronic hemodialysis. *American Journal of Psychiatry, 128,* 267–273.

McKinney, G. (1987). Suicide and AIDS testing. *Newslink, 13*(3), 3.

Meerloo, J. A. M. (1962). The multifarious motivations for suicide. In *Suicide and mass suicide* (pp. 18–29). New York: Grune & Stratton, Inc.

Meisel, A., Roth, L. H., & Lidz, C. W. (1977). Toward a model of the legal doctrine of informed consent. *American Journal of Psychiatry, 134,* 285–289.

Mesler, M.A. (1995). The philosophy and practice of patient control in hospice: The dynamics of autonomy versus paternalism. *Omega, 30,* 173–189.

Meyer, R. G., Landis, E. R., & Hays, J. R. (1988). *Law for the psychotherapist.* New York: Norton.

Miles, S. H., & August, A. (1990). Courts, gender and "the right to die". *Law, Medicine & Health Care, 18,* 85–95.

Minear, J. D., & Brush, L. R. (1981). The correlations of attitudes toward suicide with death anxiety, religiosity, and personal closeness to suicide. *Omega, 11,* 317–324.

Moore, S. L. (1993). Rational suicide among older adults: A cause for concern? *Archives of Psychiatric Nursing, 7,* 106–110.

Morgan, H. G. (1979). *Death wishes? The understanding and management of deliberate self-harm.* New York: John Wiley & Sons Limited.

Moskop, J., & Engelhardt, H. T., Jr. (1979). The ethics of suicide: A secular view. In L. D. Hankoff & B. Einsidler (Eds.), *Suicide: Theory and clinical aspects.* Littleton, MA: PSG Publishing Group.

Motto, J. A. (1972). The right to suicide: A psychiatrist's view. *Life-Threatening Behavior, 2,* 183–188.

Motto, J. A. (1981). Rational suicide and medical ethics. In M. D. Basson (Ed.), *Rights and responsibilities in modern medicine: The second volume in a series on ethics, humanism, and medicine* (pp. 201–209). New York: Alan R. Liss, Inc.

Motto, J. A. (1983). Clinical implications of moral theory regarding suicide. *Suicide and Life-Threatening Behavior, 13,* 304–312.

Motto, J. A. (1994a, April). Rational suicide: Then and now, when and how. *Focus: A Guide to AIDS Research and Counseling, 9*(5), 1–4.

Motto, J. A. (1994b, April). Response to an empirically based definition of rational suicide. In D. J. Mayo & J. L. Werth, Jr. (Cochairs), *Rational suicide defined: A panel discussion.* Symposium conducted at the annual conference of the American Association of Suicidology, New York, NY.

Murphy, G. E. (1973). Suicide and the right to die. *American Journal of Psychiatry, 130,* 472–473.

Murphy, G. E., & Robins, E. (1968). The communication of suicidal ideas. In H. L. P. Resnik (Ed.), *Suicidal behaviors: Diagnosis and management* (pp. 163–170). Boston: Little Brown and Co.

NASW approves new guidelines for attending client suicides. (1993). *Judicious Practice, 5,* 1–3.

National Association of Social Workers (1994). Client self-determination in end-of-life decisions. *Social Work Speaks* (3rd ed.) (pp. 58–61). Washington, DC: NASW Press.

Nelson, F. L. (1984). Suicide: Issues of prevention, intervention, and facilitation. *Journal of Clinical Psychology, 40,* 1328–1333.

Ness, D. E., & Pfeffer, C. R. (1990). Sequelae of bereavement resulting from suicide. *American Journal of Psychiatry, 147,* 279–285.

Neu, S., & Kjellstrand, C. M. (1986). Stopping long-term dialysis: An empirical study of withdrawal of life-supporting treatment. *New England Journal of Medicine, 314,* 14–20.

Nisbett, R. E., & Ross, L. D. (1980). *Human inference: Strategies and shortcomings of social judgment.* Englewood Cliffs, NJ: Prentice-Hall.

Office of Technology Assessment Task Force (1988). *Confronting Alzheimer's disease and other dementias.* Philadelphia, PA: Science Information Resource Center.

Oregon Right to Die. (1994). *Oregon death with dignity act.* Portland, OR: Author.

Pantano, L. T. (Chair). (1994, August). *Assisted suicide—Mercy or murder? Michigan's experience.* Symposium conducted at the annual convention of the American Psychological Association, Los Angeles, CA.

Parry, J. (1994). Involuntary civil commitment in the 90s: A constitutional perspective. *Mental and Physical Disability Law Reporter, 18,* 320–336.

Patel, N. S. (1973). Pathology of suicide. *Medicine, Science, and the Law, 13,* 103–109.

Peterson, G. W. (1985). Balancing the right to die with competing interests: A socio-legal enigma. *Pepperdine Law Review, 13,* 109–155.

Podgers, J. (1980). 'Rational suicide' raises patient rights issues. *American Bar Association Journal, 66,* 1499–1501.

Pohlmeier, H. (1985). Suicide and euthanasia—Special types of partner relationships. *Suicide and Life-Threatening Behavior, 15,* 117–123.

Pokorny, A. D. (1968). Myths about suicide. In H. L. P. Resnik (Ed.), *Suicidal behaviors: Diagnosis and management* (pp. 57–72). Boston: Little Brown and Co.

Pope, K. S., & Bajt, T. R. (1988). When laws and values conflict: A dilemma for psychologists. *American Psychologist, 43,* 828–829.

Pope, K. S., Tabachnick, B. G., & Keith-Spiegel, P. (1987). Ethics of practice: The beliefs and behaviors of psychologists as therapists. *American Psychologist, 42,* 993–1006.

Pope, K. S., Tabachnick, B. G., & Keith-Spiegel, P. (1988). Good and poor practices in psychotherapy: National survey of beliefs of psychologists. *Professional Psychology: Research and Practice, 19,* 547–552.

Portwood, D. (1978). *Common sense suicide.* Los Angeles: National Hemlock Society.

Powell, C. J. (1984). Ethical principles and issues of competence in counseling adolescents. *The Counseling Psychologist, 12,* 57–68.

Prado, C. G. (1990) *The last choice: Preemptive suicide in advanced age.* Westport, CT: Greenwood Press.

Pretzel, P.W. (1977). Philosophical and ethical considerations of suicide prevention. In R. F. Weir (Ed.), *Ethical issues in death and dying* (pp. 387–400). New York: Columbia University Press.

Pretzel, P. W. (1984). A personal statement. In C. L. Hatton & S. M. Valente (Eds.), *Suicide: Assessment and intervention* (2nd ed.) (pp. 249–256). Norwalk, CT: Appleton-Century-Crofts.

Public actions clarifying the right to die. (1992). *Judicious Practice, 4,* 1–3.

Quill, T. E. (1991). Death and dignity: A case of individualized decision making. *New England Journal of Medicine, 324,* 691–694.

Quill, T. E. (1994). Physician-assisted death: Progress or peril? *Suicide and Life-Threatening Behavior, 24,* 315–325.

Quill, T. E., Cassel, C. K., & Meier, D. E. (1992). Proposed clinical criteria for physician-assisted suicide. *New England Journal of Medicine, 327,* 1380–1384.

Range, L.M. & Alliston, J.R. (1995). Reacting to AIDS-related sucide: Does time since diagnosis matter? *Death Studies, 19,* 277–282.

Range, L. M. & Martin, S. K. (1990). How knowledge of extenuating circumstances influences community reactions toward suicide victims and their bereaved families. *Omega, 21,* 191–198.

Rangell, L. (1988). The decision to terminate one's life: Psychoanalytic thoughts on suicide. *Suicide and Life-Threatening Behavior, 18,* 28–46.

Rao, A. V. (1975). Suicide in India. In. N. L. Farberow (Ed.), *Suicide in different cultures* (pp. 231–238). Baltimore, MD: University Park Press.

Rauscher, W. V. (1981). *The case against suicide.* New York: St. Martin's Press.

Redlich, F., & Mollica, R. F. (1976). Overview: Ethical issues in contemporary psychiatry. *American Journal of Psychiatry, 133,* 125–136.

Rees, W. D. (1972). The distress of dying. *British Medical Journal, 3,* 105–107.

Reynolds, D. K., Kalish, R. A., & Farberow, N. L. (1975). A cross-ethnic study of suicide attitudes and expectations in the United States. In N. L. Farberow (Ed.), *Suicide in different cultures* (pp. 35–50). Baltimore, MD: University Park Press.

Richman, J. (1988). The case against rational suicide. *Suicide and Life-Threatening Behavior, 18,* 285–289.

Richman, J. (1992). A rational approach to rational suicide. *Suicide and Life-Threatening Behavior, 22,* 130–141.

Ringel, E. (1980). Suicide prevention and the value of human life. In M. P. Battin & D. J. Mayo (Eds.), *Suicide: The philosophical issues* (pp. 205–211). New York: St. Martin's Press.

Robertson, J. D. (1988). *Psychiatric malpractice: Liability of mental health professionals.* New York: John Wiley & Sons.

Rogers, J. R., & Britton, P. J. (1994). AIDS and rational suicide: A counseling psychology perspective or a slide on the slippery slope. *The Counseling Psychologist, 22,* 171–178.

Roper Organization of New York City. (1988). *The 1988 Roper Poll on attitudes toward active voluntary euthanasia.* Los Angeles: National Hemlock Society.

Rosen, G. (1975). History. In S. Perlin (Ed.), *A handbook for the study of suicide* (pp. 3–29). New York: Oxford University Press.

Roth, L. H. (1979). A commitment law for patients, doctors, and lawyers. *American Journal of Psychiatry, 136*, 1121–1127.

Roth, L. H., Meisel, A., & Lidz, C. W. (1977). Tests of competency to consent to treatment. *American Journal of Psychiatry, 134*, 279–284.

Roy, D. J. (1988). Is dying a matter of ethics? *Death Studies, 12*, 137–145.

Rudolph, J. (1988). Counselors' attitudes toward homosexuality: A selective review of the literature. *Journal of Counseling and Development, 67*, 165–168.

Rudolph, J. (1989). The impact of contemporary idealogy and AIDS on the counseling of gay clients. *Counseling and Values, 33*, 96–108.

Sadoff, R. L., & Gutheil, T. G. (1990). Expert opinion: Death in hindsight. In R. I. Simon (Ed.), *American Psychiatric Press review of clinical psychiatry and the law, Vol. 1* (pp. 329–339). Washington, DC: American Psychiatric Press.

Sandak, L. R. (1978). Suicide and the compulsion of lifesaving medical procedures: An analysis of the refusal of treatment cases. *Brooklyn Law Review, 44*, 285–316.

Saunders, J. M., & Bunchingham, S. (1987, April). *AIDS and suicide: Conceptual considerations.* Paper presented at the annual meeting of the American Association of Suicidology, San Francisco, CA.

Saunders, J. M., & Valente, S. M. (1988). Cancer and suicide. *Oncology Nursing Forum, 15*, 575–581.

Saunders, J. M., Valente, S. M., & Berman, A. L. (1993). Nicole: Suicide and terminal illness. *Suicide and Life-Threatening Behavior, 23*, 76–82.

Schaie, K. W. (1993). Ageist language in psychological research. *American Psychologist, 48*, 49–51.

Schowalter, J. E., Ferholt, J. B., & Mann, N. M. (1973). The adolescent patient's decision to die. *Pediatrics, 51*, 97–103.

Shaffer, C. D. (1986). Criminal liability for assisting suicide. *Columbia Law Review, 86*, 348–376.

Shanfield, S. B., Benjamin, A. H., & Swain, B. J. (1984). Parents' reactions to the death of an adult child from cancer. *American Journal of Psychiatry, 141*, 1092–1094.

Shapiro, J. P. (1994, May 16). A "Roe V. Wade" on suicide? *U.S. News and World Report, 116*(19), 20.

Shepherd, D., & Barraclough, B. M. (1974). The aftermath of suicide. *British Medical Journal, 2*, 600–603.

Shneidman, E. S. (1981). Psychotherapy with suicidal patients. *Suicide and Life-Threatening Behavior, 11*, 341–348.

Shneidman, E. S. (1987). A psychological approach to suicide. In G. R. VandenBos & B. K. Bryant (Eds.), *Cataclysms, crises, and catastrophes: Psychology in action* (pp. 147–183). Washington, DC: American Psychological Association.

Shneidman, E. S. (1992a). A conspectus of the suicidal scenario. In R. W. Maris, A. L. Berman, J. T. Maltsberger, & R. I. Yufit (Eds.), *Assessment and prediction of suicide* (pp. 50–64). New York: The Guilford Press.

Shneidman, E. S. (1992b). Rational suicide and psychiatric disorders. *New England Journal of Medicine, 326*, 889–890.

Shneidman, E. S. (1993). Suicide as psychache. *Journal of Nervous and Mental Disease, 181*, 147–149.

Shneidman, E. S., & Farberow, N. L. (1976). The logic of suicide. In E. S. Shneidman, N. L. Farberow, & R. E. Litman (Eds.), *The psychology of suicide* (pp. 63–71). New York: Jason Aronson, Inc.

Shneidman, E. S., Farberow, N. L., & Litman, R. E. (1961). The suicide prevention center. In N. L. Farberow & E. S. Shneidman (Eds.), *The cry for help* (pp. 6–18). New York: McGraw-Hill.

Siegel, K. (1982a). Rational suicide: Considerations for the clinician. *Psychiatric Quarterly, 54*, 77–84.

Siegel, K. (1982b). Society, suicide, and social policy. *Journal of Psychiatric Treatment and Evaluation, 4*, 473–482.

Siegel, K. (1986). Psychosocial aspects of rational suicide. *American Journal of Psychotherapy, 40*, 405–418.

Siegel, K., & Tuckel, P. (1984). Rational suicide and the terminally ill cancer patient. *Omega, 15*, 263–269.

Silverman, E., Range, L., & Overholser, J. (1994). Bereavement from suicide as compared to other forms of bereavement. *Omega, 30*, 41–51.

Singh, B. K., Williams, J. S., & Ryther, B. J. (1986). Public approval of suicide: A situational analysis. *Suicide and Life-Threatening Behavior, 16*, 409–418.

Slater, E. (1976). Assisted suicide: Some ethical considerations. *International Journal of Health Services, 6*, 321–330.

Slater, E. (1980). Choosing the time to die. In M. P. Battin & D. J. Mayo (Eds.), *Suicide: The philosophical issues* (pp. 199–204). New York: St. Martin's Press.

Slawson, P. F., Flinn, D. E., & Schwartz, D. A. (1974). Legal responsibility for suicide. *The Psychiatric Quarterly, 48*, 50–64.

Smith, G. P., II. (1989). All's well that ends well: Toward a policy of assisted rational suicide or merely enlightened self-determination? *University of California, Davis Law Review, 22*, 275–419.

Snipe, R. M. (1988). Ethical issues in the assessment and treatment of a rational suicidal client. *The Counseling Psychologist, 16*, 128–138.

Soll, I. (1979). Commentary on Joyce Carol Oates "The art of suicide." In *The reevaluation of existing values and the search for absolute values* (pp. 191–193). Vol. I of the *Proceedings of the Seventh International Conference on the Unity of the Sciences*. New York: The International Cultural Foundation Press.

Stanley, B. (1983). Senile dementia and informed consent. *Behavioral Sciences and the Law, 1*, 57–71.

St. Lawrence, J. S., Kelly, J. A., Owen, A. D., Hogan, I. G., & Wilson, R. A. (1990). Psychologists' attitudes toward AIDS. *Psychology and Health, 4*, 357–365.

Stillion, J., M., & McDowell, E. E. (1991). Examining suicide from a life-span perspective. *Death Studies, 15*, 327–354.

Stromberg, C. D., Haggarty, D. J., Leibenluft, R. F., McMillian, M. H., Mishkin, B., Rubin, B. L., & Trilling, H. R. (1988). *The psychologist's legal handbook*. Washington, DC: The Council for the National Register of Health Service Providers in Psychology.

Stromberg, C. D., & Stone, A. A. (1983). A model state law on civil commitment of the mentally ill. *Harvard Journal on Legislation, 20*, 275–396.

Sullivan, A. (1980). A constitutional right to suicide. In M. P. Battin & D. J.

Mayo (Eds.), *Suicide: The philosophical issues* (pp. 229–253). New York: St. Martin's Press.

Swain, B. J., & Domino, G. (1985). Attitudes toward suicide among mental health professionals. *Death Studies, 9,* 455–468.

Swenson, E. V. (1986). Legal liability for a patient's suicide. *Journal of Psychiatry & Law, 14,* 409–434.

Swenson, L. C. (1993). *Psychology and law for the helping professions.* Pacific Grove, CA: Brooks/Cole Publishing Company.

Szasz, T. S. (1976). The ethics of suicide. In B. B. Wolman (Ed.), *Between survival and suicide* (pp. 163–185). New York: Gardner Press.

Szasz, T. (1986). The case against suicide prevention. *American Psychologist, 41,* 806–812.

Tanney, B. L. (1992). Mental disorders, psychiatric patients, and suicide. In R. W. Maris, A. L. Berman, J. T. Maltsberger, & R. I. Yufit (Eds.), *Assessment and prediction of suicide* (pp. 277–320). New York: The Guilford Press.

Temoche, A., Pugh, T. F., & MacMahon, B. (1964). Suicide rates among current and former mental institution patients. *Journal of Nervous and Mental Disease, 138,* 124–130.

Tepper, A. M., & Elwork, A. (1984). Competence to consent to treatment as a psycholegal construct. *Law and Human Behavior, 8,* 205–223.

Tuckman, J., Kleiner, R. J., & Lavell, M. (1959). Emotional content of suicide notes. *American Journal of Psychiatry, 116,* 59–63.

Vaillant, G. E., & Blumenthal, S. J. (1990). Introduction—Suicide over the life cycle: Risk factors and life-span development. In S. J. Blumenthal & D. J. Kupfer (Eds.), *Suicide over the life cycle: Risk factors, assessment, and treatment of suicidal patients* (pp. 1–14). Washington, DC: American Psychiatric Press.

Valente, M. (1984). The history of suicide. In C. L. Hatton & S. M. Valente (Eds.), *Suicide: Assessment and intervention* (2nd ed.) (pp. 1–15). Norwalk, CT: Appleton-Century-Crofts.

VandeCreek, L., Knapp, S., & Herzog, C. (1987). Malpractice risks in the treatment of dangerous patients. *Psychotherapy, 24,* 145–153.

Van Hoose, W. H., & Kottler, J. A. (1985). *Ethical and legal issues in counseling and psychotherapy* (2nd ed.). San Francisco: Jossey-Bass.

Victoroff, V. M. (1983). *The suicidal patient: Recognition, intervention, management.* Oradell, NJ: Medical Economics Books.

Vinogradov, S., Thornton, J. E., Levinson, A-J., R., & Callen, M. L. (1984). "If I have AIDS, then let me die now!" *Hastings Center Report, 14,* 24–26.

Waltzer, H. (1980). Malpractice liability in a patient's suicide. *American Journal of Psychotherapy, 34,* 89–98.

Wanzer, S. H., Federman, D. D., Adelstein, S. J., Cassel, C. K., Cassem, E. H., Cranford, R. E., Hook, E. W., Lo, B., Moertel, C. G., Safar, P., Stone, A., & van Eys, J. (1989). The physician's responsibility toward hopelessly ill patients. *New England Journal of Medicine, 320,* 844–849.

Watson, A. S. (1984). Comment [on Abernathy, 1984]. *American Journal of Psychiatry, 141,* 58–60.

Webb, J. P., & Willard, W. (1975). Six American Indian patterns of suicide. In

N. L. Farberow (Ed.), *Suicide in different cultures* (pp. 17–33). Baltimore, MD: University Park Press.

Weber, W. M. (1988). What right to die? *Suicide and Life-Threatening Behavior, 18,* 181–188.

Weishaar, M. E., & Beck, A. T. (1990). Cognitive approaches to understanding and treating suicidal behavior. In S. J. Blumenthal & D. J. Kupfer (Eds.), *Suicide over the life cycle: Risk factors, assessment, and treatment of suicidal patients* (pp. 469–498). Washington, DC: American Psychiatric Press.

Weishaar, M. E., & Beck, A. T. (1992). Clinical and cognitive predictors of suicide. In R. W. Maris, A. L. Berman, J. T. Maltsberger, & R. I. Yufit (Eds.), *Assessment and prediction of suicide* (pp. 467–483). New York: The Guilford Press.

Weisman, A. D. (1966). Discussion [of E. S. Shneidman, "Orientations toward death: A vital aspect of the study of lives"]. *International Journal of Psychiatry, 2,* 190–193.

Weisman, A. D., & Hackett, T. P. (1961). Predilection to death: Death and dying as a psychiatric problem. *Psychosomatic Medicine, 23,* 232–256.

Weiss, R. S. (1994). *Learning from strangers: The art and method of qualitative interview studies.* New York: The Free Press.

Werth, J. L., Jr. (1992). Rational suicide and AIDS: Considerations for the psychotherapist. *The Counseling Psychologist, 20,* 645–659.

Werth, J. L., Jr. (1994a). Can a person with AIDS make a rational decision to commit suicide? *Psychology & AIDS Exchange, 14,* 3, 10.

Werth, J. L., Jr. (1994b). *The effects of precipitating circumstances, stigma, and social support on psychologists' perceptions of suicidal ideators.* Unpublished doctoral dissertation, Auburn University, AL.

Werth, J. L., Jr. (1995). Rational suicide reconsidered: AIDS as an impetus for change. *Death Studies, 19,* 65–80.

Werth, J. L., Jr., & Carney, J. (1994). Incorporating HIV-related issues into graduate student training. *Professional Psychology: Research and Practice, 25,* 458–465.

Werth, J. L., Jr., & Cobia, D. C. (1995a). Empirically-based criteria for rational suicide: A survey of psychotherapists. *Suicide and Life-Threatening Behavior, 25,* 231–240.

Werth, J. L., Jr., & Cobia, D. C. (1995b). [Expert opinions on the assessment of rational suicide]. Unpublished raw data.

Werth, J. L., Jr., & Liddle, B. J. (1994). Psychotherapists' attitudes toward suicide. *Psychotherapy: Theory, Research and Practice, 31,* 440–448.

White, R. B., & Engelhardt, H. T., Jr. (1975). A demand to die. *Hastings Center Report, 5*(3), 9–10, 47.

Whitlock, F. A. (1986). Suicide and physical illness. In A. Roy (Ed.), *Suicide* (pp. 151–170). Baltimore, MD: Williams & Wilkins.

Widiger, T. A., & Rinaldi, M. (1983). An acceptance of suicide. *Psychotherapy: Theory, Research and Practice, 20,* 263–273.

Williams, G. (1968). The prohibition of suicide. In *The sanctity of life and the criminal law* (p. 248–310). New York: Alfred A. Knopf.

Winokur, G., & Black, D. W. (1992). Suicide—what can be done? *New England Journal of Medicine, 327,* 490–491.

Winslow, F. (1840). *The anatomy of suicide.* London: Henry Renshaw.

Wolhandler, S. J. (1984). Voluntary active euthanasia for the terminally ill and the Constitutional right to privacy. *Cornell Law Review, 69*, 363–383.

Wood, D. (1980). Suicide as instrument and expression. In M. P. Battin & D. J. Mayo (Eds.), *Suicide: The philosophical issues* (pp. 151–160). New York: St. Martin's Press.

Wood, G. J., Marks, R., & Dilley, J. W. (1992). *AIDS law for mental health professionals* (updated version). San Francisco: AIDS Health Project.

Wortman, C. B., & Silver, R. C. (1989). The myths of coping with loss. *Journal of Consulting and Clinical Psychology, 57*, 349–357.

Yarnell, S. K., & Battin, M. P. (1988). AIDS, psychiatry, and euthanasia. *Psychiatric Annals, 18*, 598–603.

Zinner, E. S. (1984). Twenty-first century law: Supreme Court ruling supports right to suicide. *Death Education, 8*(Suppl.), 137–151.

NOTES

1. The material from *The Enigma of Suicide* by George H. Colt are reprinted by permission of Simon & Schuster Inc. and International Creative Management.
2. The material from "The ethics of suicide" by D. Heyd and S. Bloch in *Psychiatric Ethics* is reprinted by permission of Oxford University Press.
3. The material from "Balancing the right to die with competing interests: A socio-legal enigma" by Glenn W. Peterson in the *Pepperdine Law Review* is reprinted by permission. Copyright © 1985 by the Pepperdine University School of Law.
4. The material from "Ethical principles and issues of competence in counseling adolescents" by C. J. Powell in *The Counseling Psychologist* is reprinted by permission of Sage Publications, Inc.
5. The material from *Suicide: A Sociological and Statistical Study* by Louis I. Dublin is reprinted by permission of John Wiley & Sons, Inc.
6. The material from *Self-Destruction in the Promised Land: A Psychocultural Biology of American Suicide* by Howard I. Kushner is reprinted by permission. Copyright © 1989 Rutgers, The State University.
7. The material from *Suicide* by Ruth S. Cavan is reprinted with permission of Scribner. Copyright © 1928 by Charles Scribner's Sons.
8. The material from *The Right to Die* by Derek Humphry and Ann Wickett is reprinted with permission of The Hemlock Society.
9. The material from "Client self-determination in end-of-life decisions" in *Social Work Speaks* is reprinted with permission. Copyright © 1994, National Association of Social Workers, Inc.
10. The material from *Deciding for Others: The Ethics of Surrogate Decision Making* by A. E. Buchanan and D. W. Brock is reprinted with the permission of Cambridge University Press.
11. The material from "Legal aspects of rational suicide for persons with AIDS" by Eric A. Harris is reprinted by permission of the author.
12. The material from *Life and Death Decision Making* by Baruch A. Brody is reprinted by permission. Copyright © 1988 by Oxford University Press, Inc.

Index